T0190741

THROUGH
THE VALLEY
OF GRIEF

THROUGH THE VALLEY OF GRIEF

*A 365-Day Devotional of Spiritual
Practices for Hope in Suffering*

Mattie Jackson

WaterBrook

Published in the United States by WaterBrook, an imprint of Random House, a division of Penguin Random House LLC.

WaterBrook and colophon are registered trademarks of Penguin Random House LLC.

Library of Congress Cataloging-in-Publication Data

Names: Jackson, Mattie, author.
Title: Through the valley of grief : a 365-day devotional of spiritual practices for hope in suffering / Mattie Jackson.
Description: First edition. | Colorado Springs : WaterBrook, 2024. | Includes bibliographical references.
Identifiers: LCCN 2024000561 | ISBN 9780593601235 (hardcover) | ISBN 9780593601242 (ebook)
Subjects: LCSH: Hope—Religious aspects—Christianity. | Grief—Religious aspects—Christianity. | Devotional exercises.
Classification: LCC BV4638 .J34 2024 | DDC 234/.25—dc23/eng/20240214
LC record available at https://lccn.loc.gov/2024000561

Printed in the United States of America on acid-free paper

waterbrookmultnomah.com

9 8 7 6 5 4 3 2 1

First Edition

Book design by Diane Hobbing

Most WaterBrook books are available at special quantity discounts for bulk purchase for premiums, fundraising, and corporate and educational needs by organizations, churches, and businesses. Special books or book excerpts also can be created to fit specific needs. For details, contact specialmarketscms@penguinrandomhouse.com.

To Mom. You have cried for me, walked with me, and relentlessly fought for me in prayer through my worst valley. More than that, your life has modeled for me what faithful disappointment, waiting, and trust look like. You have suffered your own dear losses with resilience and endured seasons of heartbreak and sickness without knowing what God's answers to your "heal us" and "heal me" prayers would look like. On the other side, your love for the Lord shines all the brighter to everyone who knows you. You are an obedient warrior and radiant survivor. Thank you for showing me what it means to fight with hope.

Introduction

Three weeks before my first wedding anniversary at age twenty-eight, I clung to my young husband's body as doctors and nurses took him off life support. One week later, I sat beside our family and friends and buried him. My life went from newlywed bliss to unforeseen widowhood in an instant. I had no idea how to survive, much less if my faith would.

Ben's death seemingly gave me every reason to walk away from God. How could He permit this to happen if He loved me? Only by His daily, endless, supernatural grace have I found new streams in this desert. By wrestling with, questioning, and clinging to the truth of who Jesus is—my actual Living Hope—I've steadily come to know Him and love Him more deeply than I ever imagined possible.

This book is the one I longed for in the first year after Ben's death. I needed grounding practices to keep me connected to the God I felt so hurt by. I needed something Scripture-rich, brief, and easy to process because my mind was so clouded with grief. I needed daily reminders from the Word of God that the heart of God could be trusted—that His mercies and power were accessible to me and new to me every morning.

Throughout this 365-day devotional, four spiritual practices will lead you from a broken, resentful daughter or son back to restored relationship with and trust in your heavenly Father.

These practices help you navigate the clinical stages of grief—denial and isolation, anger, bargaining, depression, and acceptance.[1] These rhythms saved my life. They ignited my faith and enriched my relationship with the Lord beyond description. They taught me how to be fully broken, while remaining radically hopeful in the Lord. They carried me through the valley.

- **Wail:** These pages are a safe place for you to express your pain. God invites you to mourn what you've lost and the new realities you're facing. In the practice of lament, I pray you can grieve fully and honestly with God.

  With *lament,* you overcome denial.

- **Connect:** Connection is a vital part of your spiritual and mental well-being as you grieve. You certainly need intentional periods of rest and solitude. But you also need healthy relationships to defend against the desire to withdraw too much.

  When you *connect*—with others, God, yourself, and nature—you resist the temptation to isolate.

- **Worship:** This part didn't come easily to me. It felt forced at best and dishonest at worst to praise the God I felt had let me down in such a tragic way. But worshipping God anyway—even when you feel reluctant—works miracles in your heart that words can't sufficiently explain.

  When you *worship,* you soften anger and distrust toward God.

- **Hope:** Hope is an anchor of peace for you and a light to guide you as you traverse the darkness you're in. And may you never forget: "Even though I walk through the valley of the shadow of death, I will fear no evil, *for you are with me*" (Psalm 23:4, emphasis added).

  When you *hope,* you drive back depression and move toward acceptance.

These practices aren't a perfect solution; healing is a process. But like they did for me, they will equip you to live in the tension between your fragile humanity and God's perfect control and loving presence, which is ever with you in the valley.

How to Use This Book

Each entry includes a Scripture passage and a brief devotional drawn from one of the four spiritual practices. Simple prompts follow each devotional to call you one step further into these rhythms.

I encourage you to keep a journal or write in the margins of this book to make it your own, cataloging your responses throughout the year. You'll be amazed at the record of God's faithfulness you'll accrue there.

As you learn these spiritual practices, you are renewing your mind and training yourself to trust Jesus, your Living Hope, even as you grieve and ultimately move toward peaceful acceptance.

You won't be in this valley forever. You will heal. One day at a time.

> For this reason I bow my knees before the Father, from whom every family in heaven and on earth is named, that according to the riches of his glory he may grant you to be strengthened with power through his Spirit in your inner being, so that Christ may dwell in your hearts through faith . . . that you may be filled with all the fullness of God.
>
> Now to him who is able to do far more abundantly than all that we ask or think, according to the power at work within us, to him be glory in the church and in Christ Jesus throughout all generations, forever and ever. Amen.
>
> —EPHESIANS 3:14–17, 19–21

THROUGH
THE VALLEY
OF GRIEF

Day 1

Seek the LORD and his strength;
  seek his presence continually!
Remember the wondrous works that he has done,
  his miracles and the judgments he uttered.

—I CHRONICLES 16:11–12

My friend, I am sorry you are so weary. I have been too. I have fought for hope and lost. Chased peace and found no rest. It seemed like every day, with what little strength remained, I merely endured from one moment to the next. What else could I possibly do?

The answer is so much simpler than we expect—and far more powerful than we can imagine. Call on the Lord! As Jesus walked on this earth in human flesh, He faced exhaustion, persecution, and despair. He called out to His Father in His darkest hours. He knew the power of putting human sorrow into the hands of divine strength.

God *never* expects you to carry life's burdens on your own. Seek His heart in Scripture, His tender presence in prayer, every moment you feel weary. And His supernatural strength will surely be given to you. If this feels hard to believe, look back on the countless ways the Lord has carried you when you were weak, scared, or unsure in earlier seasons of your life. Ask friends to share how they've seen God work for your good (and their own) in the past. Let me be the first to remind you: He is with you yesterday, today, and tomorrow. He is still your rock and your redeemer.

Look back over the past weeks or months. What is one moment of peace, strength, joy, or rest you can hold on to for today?

> O Lord, all my longing is before you;
>   my sighing is not hidden from you.

—PSALM 38:9

The Lord loved you and chose you before the foundation of the world (Ephesians 1:4). And because He knows every corner of your hurting heart, you can bring your whole self before Him—your spirit, your heart, your mind, and all the details of your life. In your suffering, you can draw nearer to God than ever before. He is your creator, your Father, and your beloved groom (John 3:29).

Perhaps some have misled you, saying, "Don't question God about the pain you're suffering. Everything happens for a reason." Please hear me! You have every right to grieve the affliction that's befallen you. Like any good father, God is brokenhearted when you suffer. Though He may not always remove your pain, miracles happen when you courageously offer Him the hurts and hopes of your heart. The Holy Spirit works in you to bring tiny moments of lightness in the midst of such heaviness.

When you bring every fear, desire, and uncertainty to your Savior, you are singing a song of complete trust—a song that resounds sweetly in His ears. He hears you, beloved. He is with you.

What question, doubt, or frustration have you been withholding from God? Shout it out in prayer to Him! Lay it brokenly and honestly at His feet, and rest in His tender love for you.

Day 3

> No one comprehends the thoughts of God except the
> Spirit of God. Now we have received not the spirit of the
> world, but the Spirit who is from God, that we might
> understand the things freely given us by God.
>
> —1 CORINTHIANS 2:11–12

Grief brings constant inner turmoil. Especially in times of trial, we crave explanation, vindication, and retribution. We long for answers to all the whys and the how-longs of this uncontrollable situation. Like me, you may want an apology from God for allowing this to happen. We wish we had a timeline from Him to help us understand what's happening. But remember, the Lord is outside time. His ways are higher than our ways (Isaiah 55:9), and His plan is infinitely larger than we can comprehend.

That said, God hasn't left you alone. The moment you accepted Christ, He gave you the Holy Spirit, who dwells in you and will never leave you. He may not give you the answers you desire, but He *will* give you "love, joy, peace, patience, kindness, goodness, faithfulness, gentleness, self-control," and countless other gifts (Galatians 5:22–23). You have access to all of this through Christ! Rest in this promise, even as your mind reels with questions. The fruit of His Spirit is free to you. Call out to God and receive it.

Lord, thank You for providing every gift I need in order to survive today. Please produce the fruit of Your Spirit in me. For Your glory, amen.

"Go out and stand on the mount before the LORD." And behold, the LORD passed by, and a great and strong wind tore the mountains and broke in pieces the rocks before the LORD, but the LORD was not in the wind. And after the wind an earthquake, but the LORD was not in the earthquake. And after the earthquake a fire, but the LORD was not in the fire. And after the fire the sound of a low whisper.

—I KINGS 19:11–12

God wants to meet with you personally, just as His Spirit did with Elijah. He hears your every cry. His heart swells with love for you when you call on His power and hope in His promises. Jesus lived and died because He wants to meet you right in the middle of your struggles and sorrows.

Some days you will feel the Holy Spirit almost palpably. Thank God for those. But you will also have days when the Spirit's presence won't be obvious in grand impressions or poignant moments. Many days He will speak in a whisper, not through an earthquake or fire. For me, it was a specific whisper of wind. After a long, tearful walk with my dog, Ryman, I stood atop a small hill in Ben's and my neighborhood. I felt the most arrestingly gentle breeze, and I remembered this story. I remembered that God is always in the tender whispers. Hold tight to those hushed moments of intimacy with Him. Know that He is with you. Continue to ask Him for what your weary soul needs, and wait expectantly with open eyes and ears. Ask God to show you daily signs of His presence.

Take five minutes to silently listen to and observe the world around you today, and ask the Lord for a sweet whisper from the Spirit.

Day 5

> See what kind of love the Father has given to us, that
> we should be called children of God; and so we are.
>
> — I JOHN 3:1

When I felt hurt or scared as a child, I would *sprint* down the long upstairs hallway toward my parents' room, often in the middle of the night. Even if they couldn't fix what was broken or make my nightmares go away, with them was still the only place I felt safe. In your most painful moments, God desires to be near you to comfort you. You are His child. Whether you feel like it or not, He wants you to sprint to Him.

The Lord chose you, specifically, to be His child—a daughter or son of the King of the universe and a co-heir with the risen Christ. Your heavenly Father's arms are always open to you, His beloved child. He *can* fix what is broken. No matter what you're facing, He is a safe lap to climb into, a strong hand to cling to, and a loving Father to run to in the dark. God can calm your fear and comfort you in your pain infinitely more than earthly parents can. Fall into His arms. Wail to Him. Rest with Him. He is always a safe place.

What are you most afraid of today? Speak it aloud to your loving Father, and pray for His supernatural comfort.

> What is sown is perishable; what is raised is imperishable.
> It is sown in dishonor; it is raised in glory. It is sown in
> weakness; it is raised in power. It is sown a natural body;
> it is raised a spiritual body.
>
> —1 CORINTHIANS 15:42–44

The kingdom of God is a kingdom defined by sacrifice—physical and spiritual deaths. We know this and acknowledge it every spring when we celebrate Christ's ultimate sacrifice on the cross. Yet what we celebrate in the life of Jesus, we fear and avoid at all costs in our own lives. We long for glory but distrust God when He allows the pain that often comes first. We so easily pray, "Father, take this cup from me," but struggle to say, "Not as I will, but as You will" (Luke 22:42).

Hear this loud and clear: God doesn't like to see you suffer. He is always good and loving and fighting for the flourishing of His kids. I believe He hurts for us when we face difficulties. But even when He allows them, He never wastes them. Though it doesn't feel like it now, there is valuable treasure for you to find in this trial. He can do abundantly more than you can ask or imagine with your suffering (Ephesians 3:20). As you endure faithfully, laying down the person or things you've lost, God's work to raise you back up and refine you never stops. He is a restorer. "The sufferings of this present time are not worth comparing with the glory that is to be revealed to [you]" (Romans 8:18). He is making you glorious.

> *Lord, I hate the pain I'm in right now. Remind me today that grieving honestly and hopefully with You is worth it because of the goodness, growth, and glory You're working in me.*

Day 7

Thus says the Lord GOD: Behold, I, I myself will search
for my sheep and will seek them out.

—EZEKIEL 34:11

Sometimes pain feels so overwhelming, so smothering, you become blind to God's presence. Sometimes fear is so great, it's hard to hear His voice. Even in nights of desperation, calling out for a word or a dream to comfort me, I didn't always get answers. Many times the Father's reply was simply "Wait." He is going to feel absent at times in your grief, but I assure you, He is always near. The volume of all that's happening in your life is so loud, the mixed messages and emotions swirling around you so unclear, it's no wonder God's gentle voice can be hard to hear.

God isn't playing spiritual hide-and-seek with you. You already have what you need through the Holy Spirit. He is your Good Shepherd who seeks you every time you're lost. You're never beyond His protective gaze. Jesus is always pursuing you, so put yourself in an expectant posture, ready and eager to hear His voice. Quiet the other voices, turn down the noise, and find a still place where you have the capacity to receive Him.

What is distracting you from hearing God's voice? What do you need to turn off, hit pause on, or say no to?

Day 8

> You were straying like sheep, but have now returned to
> the Shepherd and Overseer of your souls.
>
> —I PETER 2:25

In seasons of contentment, it can be difficult to recognize our harmful patterns and sinful tendencies. When life is good, we forget how desperately we need God's direction, His overseeing of our souls. We are quite content to do our own thing. This is why even unjust suffering and trials are beautiful in God's kingdom. When loss or uncertainty strips you of the illusion of control, you have a renewed chance to release the reins of your life and hand them repentantly back to the Lord.

As you grieve and endure, you'll have moments when your ugliest flaws come surging to the surface. Are you impulsively lashing out at loved ones? Relying on unhealthy habits to numb the pain? Seeking comfort with unsafe people? Don't hang your head in shame when you react sinfully to this suffering that's pressing in on you. You only need to surrender your sins and race back into the arms of Christ, the Shepherd and Overseer of your soul. He'll receive you with a greeting of grace.

What sinful action or reaction can you release to Jesus today? Confess it, thank Him for His incredible grace, and leave the shame behind.

No temptation has overtaken you that is not common to man. God is faithful, and he will not let you be tempted beyond your ability, but with the temptation he will also provide the way of escape, that you may be able to endure it.

— I CORINTHIANS 10:13

Verses like this one are quoted sometimes as trite, though well-meaning, comfort. All God's Word is trustworthy and true, so the apostle Paul's words of encouragement to the Corinthians are true. No temptation will overcome you, if you call out to Jesus for help. In a similar way, no degree of grief can destroy you, in Jesus' name. He sympathizes with *every single* human weakness. He gets it!

Still, this verse isn't saying we will never be overwhelmed. Don't let a condemning voice—either your own or someone else's—shame you for feeling helpless or overwhelmed by the dreadful sufferings you're facing. Many things in this life are too broken, evil, and devastating to overcome on our own. We need God's power, His Spirit! The promise here is that Christ has *already* overcome all of it for us in His mighty name! This is your hope. You won't have the strength to handle every loss, but you don't have to. The cross and resurrection of Jesus ensure that He, as your Risen Lord, carries every possible burden you could bear.

What is something that makes you feel like you're drowning? What are you trying to handle in your own strength that you need to surrender to the Lord?

Day 10

> By this we know that we abide in him and he in us,
> because he has given us of his Spirit.
>
> —1 JOHN 4:13

Kind people have likely asked you what you need in this difficult time. Embrace their help, and thank God for those He sends to walk this tough road with you. You need countless things right now in order to survive, to heal, to believe in real hope for your situation again. But don't forget that what you need most is the Spirit of God.

The Holy Spirit is called the Helper (John 14:26), given to God's children that they may have access to His wisdom and power. He is what enabled Shadrach, Meshach, and Abednego to stand up to the evil Nebuchadnezzar, even in the face of a brutal death threat. He is what emboldened Paul to continually risk his life for the sake of sharing the gospel. He is what empowered Jesus to resist the devil's temptation in the desert and, ultimately, to overcome the grave. Embrace all the help you get from generous people in your life, but remember, your greatest asset is already dwelling inside you. Call on the Holy Spirit to lead you and provide all that you need.

Reflect on the truth that your ultimate source of hope and healing power is already in your full possession. Ask the Holy Spirit for the help you need today.

Day 11

Blessed be the God and Father of our Lord Jesus Christ!
According to his great mercy, he has caused us to be born
again to a living hope through the resurrection of Jesus
Christ from the dead.

—1 PETER 1:3

I remember thinking a lot about heaven after Ben died. About him reveling in the grandest mountains, most luscious forests, and bluest seas—a beauty I can't fathom until I'm home with the Lord too. I'd remind myself that our relationships on earth only scratch the surface of the love we'll bask in forever in Jesus' full, unhindered, adoring presence. And honestly, sometimes these promises felt more like fairy tales than truths. But they are truths for those who believe! They're truths that kept steering me toward hope.

The world hopes by wishing for something that, by chance or luck, might come true. That kind of hope is a gamble. Through Jesus, we have a better hope that is active and certain, accessible and unchanging. This kind of hope is a guarantee. Jesus, our Living Hope, offers us peace in knowing that all our pain will be redeemed. Holy hoping may not change your situation, but it always changes your perspective. Even while you remain here in the valley of this broken world, walking closely with Christ enables you to keep your eyes fixed on the glory of what's to come.

Can you imagine a moment of beauty, restoration, even peace,
a month from now? A year from now? Share it with the God
of Living Hope today, and ask Him to ignite that hope in you.

> The devil prowls around like a roaring lion, seeking someone to devour. Resist him, firm in your faith, knowing that the same kinds of suffering are being experienced by your brotherhood throughout the world.
>
> —I PETER 5:8–9

The day you committed your life to Christ, you became a target of the Evil One. His goal is simple: to turn your focus and trust away from the God who saved you and loves you. Don't fear; the devil's schemes are no match for the power of Christ that is in you. At the same time, be watchful.

Believers in pain are the Enemy's top priority to prey on and try to deceive. You are understandably weak right now, and he knows you are the most vulnerable when in pain and isolation. Just as animals are safer in herds, you are safer in a community of strong believers. We need safe, trusted people praying for us, checking in on us, *helping* us. I remember feeling like such a burden to my loved ones until I realized that if the tables were turned, I'd give anything to be able to help them. We aren't designed to endure hardship or fight evil alone. Avoid isolation. Create an inner circle of faithful people to build you up and help you fend off the Enemy's attacks. Though it's natural to withdraw, cling to your community. It will help protect you from the attacks of the prowling Enemy.

Who is a safe, trusted person you can ask to join you in prayer as you walk through this season?

Day 13

My beloved brothers, be steadfast, immovable, always abounding in the work of the Lord, knowing that in the Lord your labor is not in vain.

—1 CORINTHIANS 15:58

When life hurts, it's tempting to fix it through busyness—by doing things for God. At least I did. I was running a women's organization serving widows when I was a new widow in need of rest and service myself! Please hear me: All the ways you honor the Lord, obey Him, and worship Him in your suffering are beautiful in His eyes and bring glory to His name. But the call to be obedient isn't always about action. Often the more important thing is to be still and let God fight for you (Exodus 14:14).

Sometimes the most courageous way to obey the Lord is to surrender your circumstances to Him. To stop doing and simply be with God. To make margin for true rest, so He can reenergize you and restore you. The most productive thing you can do is to give your struggle up to Him daily. Patient trust is worship. Waiting on the Lord *is* obedient work, and God honors this sacrificial worship and sows His supernatural peace deeper and deeper in your soul. You may not see earthly resolutions as quickly as you'd like, but rest assured, as His beloved child, the labor of faithfully entrusting your pain to Jesus will never be in vain.

What is one thing on your calendar you can reschedule or adjust to create some quiet time of rest and surrender with the Lord?

He is before all things, and in him all things hold together.

—COLOSSIANS 1:17

As your world spins out of order and the tides of change disorient you, you may think, *Has God missed something here? Why would He let this happen? How is He going to make anything about this right?* But remember, He is the same, forever unchanging (Hebrews 13:8), which means, if you trusted Him when life was going smoothly, you can trust Him now when you feel it's falling apart. God and His promises haven't changed just because your circumstances have.

Ever since He spoke the first molecules of creation into being, the Lord has been holding everything in the universe together. Stars, oceans, ecosystems, men and women—all of it He holds intentionally and diligently in His hands. That's impossible for us to understand fully, but even when disaster strikes or the Enemy afflicts God's children, we remain safely in the palm of His hands. You don't have the strength to hold yourself or your family or your situation together, and that's okay. Stay rooted in Jesus. Cling to Him because in Him all things *will* hold together.

Close your eyes, and repeat today's verse three times. Take a deep breath, and thank God that this is true.

Day 15

He satisfies the longing soul,
  and the hungry soul he fills with good things.

—PSALM 107:9

Longing and hunger certainly aren't comfortable feelings. Our culture prioritizes comfort, convenience, and instant gratification; we discredit the value of being in want. Scripture says those who hunger and thirst for righteousness are blessed (Matthew 5:6). So, these feelings of discomfort and lack may not be how we'd choose to feel, but they're the posture that will bring us to healing. Because they're the posture that brings us to the feet of Jesus.

Be wary, though, because when you grieve, it's easy to run to hollow substitutes to fill your spiritual and emotional lack. Lest you think I handled this perfectly, there were days I tried to fill emptiness with escape, wine, and the wrong people. I learned you can't fill this hole on your own. You need supernatural sustenance. And all God needs to heal you is your need. Acknowledge your extreme lack today, your lifesaving neediness, and run to the Lord, who alone can and will fill you up. Your longing is your greatest asset when it drives you to God. The emptier you are, the more room you leave for His presence and His Word to fill you up.

Lord, I feel so empty, so helpless. Remind me that all this loss and lack I'm facing is making more room to experience You. Fill me up today.

Behold, I stand at the door and knock. If anyone hears my voice and opens the door, I will come in to him and eat with him, and he with me.

—REVELATION 3:20

The search for God and His presence is far simpler than many expect it to be. It's really less of a search and more of a conscious decision to pay attention to the truth that God is with you already. Certainly, we can always find Him in His Word, in worship, and in prayer. But access to the Lord doesn't require following any strict steps or protocol. Jesus is already standing at the door. You know you need Him. All you have to do is open the door.

And when you do pursue Christ with an honest and humbled heart, not only will He throw His arms around you and wash you completely clean, He will also feast with you. He knocks because He wants to share space with you. The home is where family gathers. It's where grievances are heard, where needs are abundant, and where we navigate one another's messes. It's where we all are nourished and refreshed. Welcome Jesus in, and don't worry about cleaning up. After all, you are family.

Jesus, thank You that You want to be with me, especially in my hurt.

Day 17

Encourage one another and build one another up, just as
you are doing.

—I THESSALONIANS 5:11

Are you depleted? In survival mode? Does the thought of serving
others feel impossible? I remember thinking often, *How can I be there
to encourage, celebrate, or listen to this person when I can hardly show up
for myself?* But "what is impossible with man is possible with God"
(Luke 18:27). Remember, His kingdom is a mysterious paradox,
intended in every way to point us back to His sovereign goodness
and renew our trust in Him, even when what He asks of us doesn't
seem to make sense.

Consider Jesus in His last days. Exhausted, beaten, accused,
rejected, tortured. Yet in His weakest and most depleted moment,
He carried out the most powerful act of all human history, and He
did it for *us*. I can imagine that as a man, He would have preferred to
bypass the divine plan for His death, but He put us first and went
obediently to the cross. He built us up, for eternity, even as His body
and soul were being torn down and destroyed. I know it feels impossible, but in your seasons of despair and weakness, take time to
encourage and pray for someone else. Take your eyes off your pain
for a moment, and offer compassion for another's. "It is more blessed
to give than to receive" (Acts 20:35). Not only do these small, simple
acts of compassion toward others make us more generous, empa-
thetic friends, but God also uses our choice to love others to advance
our own healing.

In what simple way can you encourage someone today?

Day **18**

If anyone is in Christ, he is a new creation. The old has passed away; behold, the new has come.

—2 CORINTHIANS 5:17

The moment you surrendered your heart and life to Christ as Savior, you were washed by His perfect, sacrificial blood. Your past, present, and future were wiped clean and made new by Christ. In that moment, you were justified in full and adopted permanently into His family. You are, through and through, a new creation.

I'm humbled and overwhelmingly thankful every day that my continual sinning will never be held against me. But I'm quick to forget that Jesus died and rose to free me not just from sin but also from the sufferings, patterns, and traumas of my past. When we face tragedy or hardship of any kind, it can often dredge up old wounds, fears, and insecurities we thought we had moved past. This is normal! When you have moments of old pain resurfacing, I encourage you to talk it through with a trusted friend or counselor. And then remind yourself that Christ has made you a new creation, free not just from sin but from your past sufferings as well.

What past and present hurts or fears do you need to talk through and entrust to the Lord today?

Brothers, stand firm and hold to the traditions that you were taught by us, either by our spoken word or by our letter.

Now may our Lord Jesus Christ himself, and God our Father . . . comfort your hearts and establish them in every good work and word.

—2 THESSALONIANS 2:15–17

Though chaos, uncertainty, and risk surround you, the most powerful defense you have in this battle is to stand firm in God's Word and in His mighty presence. This doesn't mean you should deny your pain. Rather, remind yourself, as often as your worried mind needs, that everything you see spinning out of control is still under God's control. That doesn't mean He will change your circumstances in the way or time frame you prefer, but it *does* mean He will comfort your heart, mind, and soul in ways only His Holy Spirit can.

His comfort isn't a spiritual Band-Aid, a denial of reality, or a temporary fix. Because of Jesus' finished work on the cross, God's comfort is your complete sustenance—your daily bread—in the face of darkness. His peace is yours (John 14:27), not just at the end of your life but in every moment. Immanuel is with you. As you stand firm, He will give you everything you need in order to endure. I am begging you—stand firm.

The next time you feel overwhelmed or out of control, stand firm in God's name—Immanuel, which means "God with us."

Day 20

I am sure of this, that he who began a good work in you will bring it to completion at the day of Jesus Christ.

—PHILIPPIANS 1:6

As you face tribulation, I know it can feel like all eyes are on you. How will you handle this? How will you endure? What choices will you make? Will you share your pain with others or withdraw and shut down? Will you stay stuck and despairing or move forward too quickly? I also imagine, like me, in your heart of hearts, you long for this pain to yield purpose—for this trial not to be wasted. So, trust this truth: In God's hands, nothing is wasted.

But don't force purpose. Let God work in you, twenty-four hours at a time. His grace isn't dependent on your ability to grieve well, find the silver lining, or make sense of this loss. You can't perform your way into His blessing or into faster healing. If, like me, you long to see good from your pain, continue to ask God for it. He will surely do it! But remember, His timeline is often much slower than we'd like. Good fruit always takes time and toil. Redemption stories don't unfold quickly. Absolutely take your space to grieve how painfully slow the process can be, but keep praying for purpose and patience as you navigate this hardship with Him.

Meditate on this today: *I don't need to force a specific result from my sorrow. God is at work.*

Day 21

Remember the wondrous works that he has done,
his miracles, and the judgments he uttered.

—PSALM 105:5

As much as you strain to see what's next, the most powerful thing you can do is look back. Look at God's faithful works in your rearview when you can't see the road ahead! Remember how He's shown up for you in the past. Have you ever gotten a text with the exact words you needed to hear? Ever had a door open when it seemed impossible? Ever seen a rainbow on a drive home after receiving awful news? Remember your prayers God has answered in powerful ways. Remember that the power that raised Jesus from the grave also lives in you (Romans 8:11).

I know your heart is anxious about what's ahead. But if the Lord revealed all that's to come to you, you'd be at risk of relying more on what He can do for you than on who He is to you. He is I AM. He is Immanuel, God with us. Remind yourself of His power and faithfulness. As you look back, rest assured He holds your future.

Recall a time when God's goodness and comfort showed up in a powerful way.

I lift up my eyes to the hills.
    From where does my help come?
My help comes from the LORD,
    who made heaven and earth.

—PSALM 121:1–2

Patience is one of the most arduous virtues to learn as we follow Christ. Living with patience as we wait for God's plan to unfold means trusting without answers, waiting without a timeline, and enduring without explanation. Though so unnatural for our fearful, impatient human nature, waiting on the Lord is how we build unshakable trust in Him. There is purpose in every season—good or bad—just as there is unique purpose in each of the four seasons in nature.

You could watch trees for days and never see measurable evidence of their growth. Yet, over long periods of time, they grow taller. So also the Lord is working in you, His beloved creation. Slowly and meticulously, He is using every season—sunny or snowy—to make you more beautiful. Let creation be your reminder to be patient. Though you often can't see it, God is always working in you. You are precious to Him. In every season, His redeeming hands are shaping you.

Take time to consider how God faithfully tends to the world—from the smallest flower to the largest tree. Praise Him for the patient ways He tends to you.

Day 23

He raises the poor from the dust
    and lifts the needy from the ash heap,
to make them sit with princes,
    with the princes of his people.

—PSALM 113:7–8

Though you are the grandest treasure of all God's creation, made intentionally in His image, sometimes you can't help but feel like dust. It may feel impossible to imagine a life filled with joy again. When tragedy strikes and the world breaks your heart, Satan is relentless in his attempts to make you forget who you are in Christ—to convince you that you are nothing more than dust. I've certainly felt that way. But guess what? Dust is God's favorite raw material for making beautiful things.

The more broken you are, the more God can shape your heart and spirit. No broken person or circumstance is beyond His redemptive power. His desire isn't simply for you to survive this, limping across the finish line. No! He wants to renew your strength, hope, and God-given beauty as He sanctifies you through this. You aren't just a survivor; you are royalty in the everlasting kingdom of God. You are made of dust but bound for glory.

In what ways do you feel like dust right now—are you feeling inadequate, weak, doubtful? Aloud or in your journal, speak honestly to God about it.

The eternal God is your dwelling place,
and underneath are the everlasting arms.

—DEUTERONOMY 33:27

The Creator of the universe is your dwelling place. Really think about that. It means there is nothing you do, experience, or face that He isn't a part of. It means He is in every step you take and choice you make. Think about a physical place that you go to for safety. Maybe you retreat there to think through a decision. Maybe you run there to escape from conflict. Maybe you go there because it feels like the only place in the world you can rest. Then know that the Lord is infinitely more peaceful and safe than that place.

It's important to have personal places of solace, especially as you work through trials or grief. Find a place—or make a place—where you know you can slow down, listen for God's voice, and recharge your heart, mind, and body. But remember even there, God created this physical world to always point you back to Himself. He is your ultimate, constant dwelling place. So, when you retreat to your safe place, remember that there and everywhere the Lord is with you.

Take ten minutes to rest in a safe place this week. Specifically pray to feel God's miraculous presence and the ultimate safety that comes from drawing near to Him.

When Jesus heard it, he said to them, "Those who are
well have no need of a physician, but those who are sick.
I came not to call the righteous, but sinners."

—MARK 2:17

Besides occasional well checks, doctor's visits are always prompted
by symptoms of sickness, discomfort, or injury. You don't have the
ability to diagnose and heal what is broken, so you turn with hope,
as well as maybe a little fear, to the professional. The Lord is the only
physician who can heal what is broken in your spirit. It isn't weak to
go to Him in your sickness; it's the wisest move you can make.

And as God, He heals far more than the surface-level injury. He is
a God who not only can mend the broken situation you're facing but
also tenderly treats the underlying heart issues that go along with it.
What manifests as fear may really be a lack of trust in God. What
surfaces as anger may be poisonous roots of bitterness that need to be
cut away. Your impulse to isolate may point to shame or regret that
God seeks to wash away. Bring to Him your losses with trust, knowing that as He mends your circumstances, He is also treating far more
serious issues in your spirit.

Lord, reveal to me the issues of my heart that You want to address
as I walk through this valley with You. You are the great physi-
cian. Heal me!

> He delivered us from such a deadly peril, and he will deliver us. On him we have set our hope that he will deliver us again.
>
> —2 CORINTHIANS 1:10

I know so well the pain you're feeling. The hopelessness. The wondering. *Will I ever laugh again? Will I ever love again? Will I ever sleep through the night?* You've lost something or someone you cherished. You're angry because it's unfair, afraid because it's unfamiliar, and fragile because the questions come from so many directions that you don't know how to ask for help. You feel like you're fumbling around in the dark. Friend, let me remind you: Light is always near! God is with you. No situation, emotion, or doubt can separate you from God's radical love for you (Romans 8:38–39).

When I feel helpless, it often helps me to remember the simple, core truth of the gospel: Jesus saved me from eternal punishment, from every one of the billions of sins I'll commit in my lifetime. And if I can trust that, I truly can start to trust that He will deliver me from this. Not take it away or fix everything that's broken, but deliver me—heart, mind, and soul—through this painful reality. He isn't a one-and-done savior. He will deliver you from this dark valley you're in. He is with you always, until the end of the age (Matthew 28:20).

If life feels hopeless, remember that Jesus is the ultimate deliverer. He carries you mightily through grief, shame, heartbreak, and evil. Take a moment to reflect on the specific ways the Lord has delivered you, and give Him thanks.

He found him in a desert land,
    and in the howling waste of the wilderness;
he encircled him, he cared for him,
    he kept him as the apple of his eye.

             —DEUTERONOMY 32:10

Moses sang this song of praise in the desert. When he faithfully answered Yahweh's call to rescue the Jewish nation from slavery, he left home to live in an unknown, barren place and lead the grumbling Israelites for forty years. Although he suffered much on the decades-long journey toward the promised land, the Lord provided for him. He encircled Moses in His sturdy, comforting arms.

I've never been hugged more than in those first months following Ben's death. I mean full embraces, the kind of hugs where I lay in my safest people's arms and wept. At first I felt embarrassed, but as I learned to accept their tender, physical invitations, I felt remarkably safe even as I fell apart in their arms. God grieves over your heartache, too, my friend. His arms are wide open and ready to encircle you. He will continue to care for you and provide for you. Your inheritance as His beloved child is secure. You are the apple of His eye.

Close your eyes, and picture yourself in a barren desert. Then picture Jesus—strong, calm, kind—standing next to you. Now imagine His sturdy arm around your shoulders, and exhale. He knows the route to the promised land. Let Him lead you.

Day 28

> Aaron died there on the top of the mountain. . . . And
> when all the congregation saw that Aaron had perished,
> all the house of Israel wept for Aaron thirty days.
>
> —NUMBERS 20:28–29

Thirty days for mourning—it's such a specific amount of time. Cultures around the world, including ancient Israel, have dedicated specific time frames for intentional mourning. Enduring the aftermath of death or loss slows our thinking and our capacity to operate normally. Don't be surprised by this. Don't fight it. Don't shame yourself or try to outrun it. Lean into the slowdown. This won't be your pace forever, but it's your pace now. Author and theologian C. S. Lewis knew this well: "No one ever told me about the laziness of grief. Except at my job—where the machine seems to run on much as usual—I loathe the slightest effort. Not only writing but even reading a letter is too much. Even shaving. What does it matter now whether my cheek is rough or smooth?"[2]

Thank God that He knows you need to slow down right now because you need rest. You are drained dry mentally, spiritually, emotionally, and physically. You need the presence of God to fill you back up. Allow yourself the time to mourn whatever you've lost. Let yourself sit still. Be unkempt and be sad. Your life has gone off track. It's vital to take some time in neutral before trying to reroute so you don't end up more lost.

Give yourself permission to rest today. Cancel plans if you can; let the to-dos wait for another day. Just rest.

Day 29

> While bodily training is of some value, godliness is of
> value in every way, as it holds promise for the present life
> and also for the life to come.
>
> — I TIMOTHY 4:8

Training of any kind is challenging. It always requires work that strains before it strengthens. We accept this willingly when it comes to physical exercise and nutritious eating. We endure the difficulty because we have faith in the result. Training is taxing at first, but the result is a stronger, more capable body.

For all our commitment to physical training, it's easy to neglect spiritual growth. Godliness requires training, and the training ground often comes in the form of trials. If you are in Christ, the Lord allows suffering not to punish you but to promote you. To build you into a greater, humbler, holier ambassador for His kingdom. Don't be discouraged or distrust God when life forces you to strain some spiritual muscles. The reward is immeasurably more than you can imagine.

Though it feels unnatural, praise God for the spiritual muscles He's building in you during this struggle. Thank Him that He doesn't waste trials but uses them to build a more resilient, secure version of you.

> Rejoice always, pray without ceasing, give thanks in all
> circumstances; for this is the will of God in Christ Jesus
> for you.
>
> —1 THESSALONIANS 5:16–18

Our default setting isn't as often to praise God as it is to question Him. Our natural tendency is to despair, withdraw, and doubt; we know He has power to change our circumstances and alleviate our pain, and we wonder why He hasn't done so yet. And we're right! The Lord has infinite power to reroute this devastating path you're walking. But whether God works miraculously in your situation or not, He is always working on your character.

Any time the Lord allows you to struggle, it's because He can already see the magnificent fruit on the other side. When you rejoice, pray, and thank Him even in your low valleys, that is when your heart is the most open to receive His divine work of sanctifying your soul. His ultimate will is to lead each one of us to become more and more like Christ, even in struggle. Pray for what you need in this trial, knowing God can surely provide it. And even in your lack, look for ways to rejoice in Him, because as you do so, His supernatural peace, which transcends understanding (Philippians 4:7), will fulfill and sustain you in more powerful ways than you can imagine.

> What is one small thing—physical, relational, spiritual—you
> can rejoice over and thank the Lord for today even in the
> midst of your hardship?

Day 31

You keep him in perfect peace
   whose mind is stayed on you,
   because he trusts in you.

—ISAIAH 26:3

A tightrope walker crossing a deep cavern is laser focused, steadfast, and unwavering as they take small steps back to land and safety. Their mind is fixed absolutely on the wire, not unaware of the peril below but intentionally concentrated on being connected to the wire at all times.

Like the tightrope walker, your soundest strategy for navigating a dangerous world is to stay fixated on Jesus' strength and victorious sovereignty and then to move slowly, trusting that He can uphold you. The perils you're facing are still very real, and your anxieties certainly merited, but Christ's perfect peace will transcend and quiet those fears in every moment that you keep your focus on Him and not the rocks below. Keep your gaze on Jesus. And then take one more small step forward.

Lord, I am so keenly aware of the danger surrounding me. Help me keep my gaze completely locked on You so I have the courage to walk trustingly through this day.

> I form light and create darkness;
>> I make well-being and create calamity;
>> I am the LORD, who does all these things.

—ISAIAH 45:7

Like me, are you eager to claim God's promised blessings but quick to overlook the fact that He creates darkness and calamity too? You should claim the promises of God's Word! They are true, and as His child, they are yours. But when darkness or calamity comes, we wonder, *Why would a good God create such a thing?*

Though we can't understand it fully, "sometimes, God permits what He hates to accomplish what He loves."[3] Though He never allows suffering to punish us or to coerce us into dependence on Him, He repurposes suffering to enrich our faith and draw us into deeper, more intimate and sustaining relationship with Him. Your loss, your sickness, your lack—it's neither a mistake that God has made nor an aggression against you. But it can be a catalyst for greater relationship with and trust in your heavenly Father, if you let it. He is "the LORD, who does all these things," for your good and for His glory (Romans 8:28).

Bring to God your frustrations and resentments over what He's allowed in your life. Be specific. Scream or rage silently, whatever you need in order to release your disappointment toward Him. He is a safe place for your anger.

> The Lord God has given me
>   the tongue of those who are taught,
> that I may know how to sustain with a word
>   him who is weary.
> Morning by morning he awakens;
>   he awakens my ear
>   to hear as those who are taught.
>
> —ISAIAH 50:4

The Lord touches and speaks to His children in an infinite number of ways. I'm convinced one of the most intimate ways He meets us in our suffering is through the loving words and presence of other believers. Each of us is made in His image, and each of us has life to speak into our brothers and sisters who are hurting. There is celebration in communities united in joy, but there is great intimacy, compassion, and kingdom power in communities united by pain.

Allow the Lord to teach you and shape your heart to be one who, like Jesus, knows how to deeply empathize with the pain of others. Let Him expand your capacity for compassion so you can listen to, cry with, pray for, and encourage those who hurt as you do. You can recount to them the peace and endurance you are receiving from the Holy Spirit. You are one of God's greatest tools to heal the broken hearts of others. Allow Him to use you to lavish love on His other hurting children.

Could anyone in your life use encouragement or solidarity from you right now? How can you support them today by sharing something that God's done in you or for you this week?

Those who cling to worthless idols
　　turn away from God's love for them.
But I, with shouts of grateful praise,
　　will sacrifice to you.
What I have vowed I will make good.
　　I will say, "Salvation comes from the LORD."

　　　　　　　　　　　　—JONAH 2:8–9, NIV

You need help right now. That's no secret. You may need physical help keeping up your home, car, or family. You need emotional support systems or safe places to openly grieve. And more than likely, you need professionals trained in mental health to guide you through the psychological mess that is grief. This may mean therapy. It may mean psychologist-prescribed medications. Use the tools that therapists and doctors can safely provide for you.

Sadly, some will condemn Christians for turning to clinical practices as part of their healing journey, claiming, "All you need is Jesus." And while it's absolutely true that He is the one source of complete soul, body, and mind healing, God has gifted us with counselors, doctors, and other people with skills who can radically contribute to your healing. Don't dismiss the powerful tools this world has to offer. As long as you keep these blessings in their rightful place—secondary to Christ—they are very helpful! Just be wary of letting blessings become idols. Never put your faith in those things, but rather, pursue their aid with your faith resting in nothing but Jesus and His redeeming love for you.

Thank God today for the incredible gifts of counselors, doctors, pastors, and wise friends. Continue to pray that if you start to rely more on those people than on the Lord in your healing, the Holy Spirit will make it clear to you.

Three times I pleaded with the Lord about this,
that it should leave me. But he said to me, "My grace
is sufficient for you, for my power is made perfect in
weakness." Therefore I will boast all the more gladly
of my weaknesses, so that the power of Christ may rest
upon me. For the sake of Christ, then, I am content
with weaknesses, insults, hardships, persecutions, and
calamities. For when I am weak, then I am strong.

—2 CORINTHIANS 12:8–10

Your strength is likely fading. Do you feel insufficient to bear the pain? Stuck? Hopeless? Out of options? As backward as it sounds, you are in the most powerful place you can be. We often assume weakness is our greatest threat when Scripture is so clear that it's not. As Paul said, the humble acknowledgment of our weakness actually sets the table for rich connection with the Lord. Your greatest point of access to His divine power is not when you feel strong and capable but when you admit and surrender to your need for Him.

Builders demolish unstable structures in order to build a stronger foundation. I know you are torn down, friend. Now rest in your rubble. Though all you may see is debris, Christ, your Redeemer, has the power, tools, and plans to build something altogether new. Something more glorious than before. Your broken pieces, in God's hands, will become your absolute greatest strength.

Admit to God how weak you feel. Tell the Mighty One you
need His strength to endure as He forms you into a new, even
more beautiful creation.

Put on then, as God's chosen ones, holy and beloved,
compassionate hearts, kindness, humility, meekness,
and patience.

—COLOSSIANS 3:12

You have every right to be angry. God never wanted us to bear the insufferable weight of devastating loss. We were designed to exist in a kingdom of goodness, love, and unbroken connection. We were made for righteous, eternal fellowship, and when the evil of this world compromises that, we should rage against it. Jesus did (John 2:13–17). Don't suppress or blow past the tragedies and troubles you face on this side of heaven. Grieve them honestly, deeply.

But be careful that your anger doesn't control you. Don't let your discontent turn to bitterness and steal the peace that comes from walking closely with the Lord. You have a choice: Will you put on patience even in the excruciating process of grieving? Will you forgive anyone (others, yourself, even God!) you're harboring bitterness or resentment toward? These choices won't change your circumstances, but they will transform your perspective, your attitude, and your heart as you endure difficult times.

Confess any bitterness or resentment you're feeling to God today. Don't hold back. Then call on Him confidently to imbue you with compassion, kindness, humility, meekness, and patience as you seek healing.

Day 37

> He has also set eternity in their heart, without the
> possibility that mankind will find out the work which
> God has done from the beginning even to the end.
>
> —ECCLESIASTES 3:11, NASB

Grief leaves us feeling empty, as though there are gaping holes in places and experiences that used to make us feel full. Empty, like nothing and no one in all creation can fill the cracks that the one you love has left. Charles Dickens wrote, "Can it be that in a world so full and busy, the loss of one weak creature makes a void in any heart, so wide and deep that nothing but the width and depth of vast eternity can fill it up!"[4] Certainly, losses don't get replaced by God but are redeemed by Him.

So, don't grieve without hope. What Dickens said is true: Only eternity can fill the fissures of emptiness and loss you're feeling. Only Jesus, the One from whom all joy, hope, and peace come, can redeem what's gone. He doesn't replace your loved one, of course, but the Messiah honors and grieves the holes with you. He is willing and able to fill your heart with His perfect love when the one you love is gone. Rejoice! Because God's love can never be lessened and can never be lost.

Holy Spirit, fill the broken, empty places in my life with Your comforting presence. My losses are irreplaceable, but You are the restorer of all good things. Be near to me today.

For our sake he made him to be sin who knew no sin, so that in him we might become the righteousness of God.

—2 CORINTHIANS 5:21

I'm not sure I had ever read this verse until I was in my valley. And if I had, it certainly hadn't had the life-changing gospel impact it should until I was desperate for hope of any kind. And this hope changed me: Not only did Jesus pay the full debt for my sin, but He actually *became* my sin. Which means I'm not just ceremonially rinsed off or metaphorically clean—I'm remade into the full righteousness of Christ. You may understand what that means as it relates to eternity, but don't forget what it means for you right here, right now. When Jesus' perfect righteousness was credited to you, He granted you not just holiness but an invitation to the holy of holies. You have access to God and all His provisions at all times through the Holy Spirit. For your sake Jesus took on your sin so that, in turn, you could take on His power and His cherished position as a child of God.

Complete righteousness, freedom, and joy are yours today. You have access to all these things here on earth through Christ. Scripture calls us to "with confidence draw near to the throne of grace, that we may receive mercy and find grace to help in time of need" (Hebrews 4:16). Even as you struggle, revel in the magnitude of this transaction. Run daily to the throne of grace for what you need.

Praise You, Jesus, that You not only were the scapegoat for my sin but also are the giver of everything I need in order to endure today.

> I do not account my life of any value nor as precious to
> myself, if only I may finish my course and the ministry
> that I received from the Lord Jesus, to testify to the
> gospel of the grace of God.
>
> —ACTS 20:24

All of life is for God's glory—from the joys to the sorrows. We see this all throughout Scripture. Hannah's sorrow yet persevering faith as she begged God for a child though she was barren. Then her rejoicing when God gave her a son. Ruth's grief as a young, foreign widow. Then God's faithfulness to give her Boaz as a husband. They praised God in it all, but their suffering was all for His glory because others witnessed His generous, redeeming power in their broken stories.

When you continue to praise God and trust Him in spite of your pain, your voice becomes a megaphone for God's goodness to those around you. It's one thing to say "God is good" on the mountaintop, but the truth is somehow all the more powerful when spoken in the valley. In every season, you are a light in a dark world, a city on a hill (Matthew 5:14). But when your life looks so painfully dark yet you continue to worship the Lord, you become a powerful beacon that onlookers can't dismiss. Stick with Christ through the rough spots in your story; you are a crucial voice for those around you to hear God's.

I pray that, in this darkness, Your Spirit will equip me to shine all the brighter so others will witness Your mighty power in my life.

Day 40

Be still, and know that I am God.

—PSALM 46:10

Slow may not be what you want right now, but slow is what you need. I know you want to race beyond this season, to be done with it at last. But don't run away from this, friend. Now isn't a time to flee. Keep on doing the good and worthy work of properly healing your wounds. I know it's painful and uncomfortable, but you can't begin to heal until you fully feel.

When you slow down and allow margin to honestly acknowledge and process what you're going through, you make space for the Holy Spirit to speak to you, comfort you, and lead you. When you accept the heartbreak for what it is and don't immediately start making plans for how to fix things, you find space to invite God in to restore you in supernatural ways. Lysa TerKeurst wisely said this: "When you suffer, slow becomes necessary. Slow becomes good. . . . When you live slow for a season, the Son has access to the parts of you normally covered up by everyday put-ons."[5] You are so strong and capable most of the time, but right now what you need is surrender and slowness. Be still. Let the Lord in. Let Him work. Rest, beloved.

Spend a few minutes now in stillness—physically, emotionally, spiritually. Do whatever you need in order to slow down and connect with God today.

Day 41

> I perceived that there is nothing better for them than
> to be joyful and to do good as long as they live; also that
> everyone should eat and drink and take pleasure in all
> his toil—this is God's gift to man.
>
> —ECCLESIASTES 3:12–13

Though Jesus was "a man of suffering, and familiar with pain" (Isaiah 53:3, NIV), He was also the giver of abundant life. Life to the full (John 10:10). I know your life feels anything but full right now, but don't let your pain steal away the everyday joys of a life lived with the Lord. Your grieving is inevitable. Your lament, crucial. Our almighty Father's heart breaks, too, with unconditional compassion for His hurting children. But never let the Enemy shame you for continuing to chase joy. Especially as you grieve, seek out small, daily pleasures. Take moments to remember and immerse yourself in the beauty the world around you has to offer. This simple practice will help protect you from being overcome with despair.

Don't be afraid to smile or laugh again. And please never succumb to guilt or the lie that you're betraying your loved one who's passed by being happy. If the tables were turned, wouldn't you want joy for them? God's faithfulness is on display in every corner of the glorious creation. His voice is calling in a playful song, volume cranked to ten. His love dwells around loud, bustling tables. Don't miss these ordinary joys just because you're suffering. Even as you hurt, eat. Drink. Be joyful. Do good. It will do you good.

What is one small thing you can do today that will bring you joy and momentary lightness? Make time and go do it!

> Abraham lifted up his eyes and looked, and behold,
> behind him was a ram, caught in a thicket by his horns.
> And Abraham went and took the ram and offered it up
> as a burnt offering instead of his son.
>
> —GENESIS 22:13

You have faithfully followed God into uncertainty, into taxing battles and rocky valleys that feel dark, unfamiliar, and hopeless. But don't lose hope yet! The Lord has made a promise to you—sealed with the holy blood of Jesus—to go with you and to never leave you or forsake you (Deuteronomy 31:6). This is always true: As a child of God, indwelt by His Holy Spirit, you are never truly alone.

You may feel trapped in your situation. But let this be a comfort: God sees all that's behind you and all that's before. And just as He provided the ram for Abraham in place of his son, Isaac, so He will provide for you in this situation that seems void of escape or solution. Jesus will always act in your life when you choose to trust Him with it. He is sovereign God, forever for you, never against you. He may very rarely show up early, but He is never late in your moment of need. Trust Him. Wait for Him. He has the perfect timing, the perfect plan.

In what way do you feel trapped or stuck without a solution? Call out to God specifically for His perfect provision, for His perfect ram for you, and wait expectantly for His move.

Day 43

Though the fig tree should not blossom,
  nor fruit be on the vines,
the produce of the olive fail
  and the fields yield no food,
the flock be cut off from the fold
  and there be no herd in the stalls,
yet I will rejoice in the LORD;
  I will take joy in the God of my salvation.

—HABAKKUK 3:17–18

Since the Fall in the Garden of Eden, tragedies, suffering, and death have been natural consequences of sin. But God isn't punishing you. He isn't angry with you. He wants to rescue you. He listens for your call and reminds you of the salvation He's prepared for you.

But you have a part to play too. I never realized how powerful my "yets" were until my tragedy and suffering hit. I didn't know sacrificial gratitude could change my entire mindset. I learned quickly that my hurting hallelujahs were music to Christ's ears. It was when I learned to wail and worship in the same exhausted breath that I felt God the nearest. Worship is choosing to love Him even when you can't see His goodness on display. Your losses are weighty, but one day—in this life or the next—they will be restored. His joy and salvation are forever, and they're waiting for you.

Make Habakkuk's prayer yours today. Grieve the bare trees and vines in your life; lament what you've lost. And also, rejoice in a loving Father who will lead you back into fullness of life.

Behold, God is my salvation;
  I will trust, and will not be afraid;
for the LORD GOD is my strength and my song,
  and he has become my salvation.

—ISAIAH 12:2

God is your strength and your song. You understand what strength is because right now you feel so weak. God is also your song. Think about this. What does a song do, friend? It takes the painful, confusing, and frustrated emotions you often feel and weaves them into a lyrical story. It takes your jumbled feelings, articulates them, and affirms them as legitimate, worthy. And then it puts these lyrics to a melody that makes sense of confusion, even bringing beauty from pain. It reminds you that you are not alone. We all can embrace a shared human experience and break the isolation we feel simply through a song.

God never expected you to struggle alone to make some sort of melody out of the tragedy you've been dealt. All He expects is for you to come to Him. Let the Lord make your hurts into a song of hope. Sing with Him as you struggle, and know that He is with you, the Master Composer.

Take as much time as you can today to be in God's Word and in His presence, and ask Him to start turning your hurts into a song of hope. Take note of what that specific time of abiding and connecting with Him does for you.

Day 45

> Others suffered mocking and flogging, and even chains
> and imprisonment. They were stoned, they were sawn in
> two, they were killed with the sword.
>
> —HEBREWS 11:36–37

As much as we long for it to be so, human life in a broken world isn't fair. We are right to believe that the Lord is righteous and just, but justice in His kingdom doesn't always look like fairness in our world. This will always be a point of deep struggle for me. But I must remind myself that God doesn't ask us to understand. He simply asks us to trust Him amid—and in spite of—the circumstances that feel terribly unfair.

Many of the people whose stories are told in Scripture faced trial and tragedy, some as consequences of their decisions but many because of a hostile world. Jesus never promised anyone who follows Him an easy or a fair life. In fact, He promised we would suffer on His behalf (John 16:33). But He also promised us a perfect eternity. He promised us the Helper, the Holy Spirit (John 14:26), and to be with us always, until the end of the age (Matthew 28:20). I know you hate this pain, but don't turn from God in it. Run to your Savior, and let Him hold you in all the unfairness life may bring.

Lord, none of this seems fair. Remind me that You are good
and just. Remind me that faith is stronger than understanding.
Enable me to trust amid the unknown through Your Holy Spirit.

Thus says the LORD,
he who created you, O Jacob,
 he who formed you, O Israel:
"Fear not, for I have redeemed you;
 I have called you by name, you are mine."

—ISAIAH 43:1

Remember as a child how you'd wake in the night, sweating and terrified by a nightmare that felt so very real? Who did you call to hold you and reassure you? In that moment of panic, what you needed most was a safe authority figure to speak truth to you about what was real and what was just a dream.

God is the perfect Father, who created you and calls you by name in the midst of your nightmares. He is the eternal parent who reminds you in your fear that your current pain and sorrow are scary but are not your final reality. Though your suffering is very real right now, this world isn't your ultimate home. It isn't your forever existence. He has called you to a greater destiny, a better country, a place where you are fully awake to the real love, glory, safety, and perfection of a redeemed life in Jesus' presence. He is here to hold you in your nightmares, child, to take your eyes off the painful reality of this world and fix them on the beautiful reality of His kingdom to come.

Speak this truth to yourself today: "He will wipe away every tear from [my] eyes, and death shall be no more, neither shall there be mourning, nor crying, nor pain anymore, for the former things have passed away" (Revelation 21:4).

Day 47 CONNECT

> Confess your sins to one another and pray for one
> another, that you may be healed. The prayer of a
> righteous person has great power as it is working.
>
> —JAMES 5:16

The Christian life was never designed to be walked alone. As followers of Christ and members of the church, we are called to live and worship together as a family. We are called to humble ourselves and serve others but *also* allow others to serve us. Part of humbling ourselves is laying down the prideful impulse to bear our burdens alone. God created His church as an interdependent body, many parts united to make a healthy, functioning whole. Lean on the other members of the Christian family when you are weak and broken.

Carrying the weight of your sorrow alone isn't noble; it's crippling. Hiding your needs from those who love you isn't brave; it's isolating. The prayers of righteous members of Christ's body have great power, and you need them desperately in your seasons of despair and struggle. Scripture tells us "And though a man might prevail against one who is alone, two will withstand him—a threefold cord is not quickly broken" (Ecclesiastes 4:12). Surround yourself with faithful friends to talk with, pray with, and lean on.

Who do you need to ask for help today? Consider how you can better rely on trusted people in your community.

Thus says the LORD: "Let not the wise man boast in his wisdom, let not the mighty man boast in his might, let not the rich man boast in his riches, but let him who boasts boast in this, that he understands and knows me, that I am the LORD who practices steadfast love, justice, and righteousness in the earth. For in these things I delight, declares the LORD."

—JEREMIAH 9:23–24

You are competent. And you are strong. You have endured and overcome many adversities. But when severe loss and despair strike, we often can't handle well what's in front of us. We have little to boast in. Hardship acts like smelling salts, waking us to our need, reminding us of our inherent insufficiency and thus undeniable need for God's presence, provision, and power. One of my church's central messages is this: "All God needs is your need." Of course, we hate feeling needy and insufficient. But you can find sweetness in your relationship with God in the strain of your circumstances.

Why? Because your need is so great, so heartbreakingly evident right now. How much more satisfying is water when you're hot and exhausted? How much sweeter is chocolate after eating something sour? How much richer is love after working through a tough conflict together? And how much more tender does God's love feel to us when we're broken? I can assure you, there is an understanding of, confidence in, and intimacy with God that is often only forged through suffering. We may hate our need, but don't miss this sweetness.

Lord, thank You that You never intended me to handle everything that comes at me in this life. Give me the courage and humility to admit what I can't bear on my own and lean more on You than ever before.

Job arose and tore his robe and shaved his head and fell on the ground and worshiped. And he said, "Naked I came from my mother's womb, and naked shall I return. The LORD gave, and the LORD has taken away; blessed be the name of the LORD."

—JOB 1:20–21

It's difficult for you to see anything but what's right in front of you in this moment, anything but the chaos and uncertainty that surge from every direction. You feel naked and fragile and are so keenly aware of what God has taken away. And it hurts Him to know the overwhelming depth of sorrow you feel.

Like Job, you, too, have a choice. You have a chance to widen your gaze from just seeing the pain you're in to also seeing the goodness that was and the glory that is to come. Look back over your life, and remember how the Lord has blessed you and been faithful to you, though you feel anything but blessed right now. Look forward to the redeemed, painless, eternally joyful future that you know for certain Jesus has secured for you. The goodness of the past and guarantee of the future don't change your pain right now, but they will establish in you a firmer faith. Focus your eyes on the reality of how deeply God loves you and how He brings much-needed hope into an otherwise-hopeless moment.

What is one thing about God's character—who He is rather than what He does—that you can praise Him for today?

> Let not your hearts be troubled. Believe in God; believe
> also in me.
>
> —JOHN 14:1

These words may sound like fantasy to you right now. Given the tragedy you're facing, your heart may feel nothing but troubled. You may feel so angry about what you've lost or how you've been wronged that the only One you know to blame for your trouble is God. I mean, He's totally sovereign, right? *You couldn't have stepped in for me this time?* Just know that it's okay to feel this way. I understand. And even more than that, Jesus Himself understands.

Of course, Jesus is fully divine, fully God, but as a human, He was betrayed and abandoned too. He not only was rejected by His immediate family and most of the Jewish people but also was actually separated from God. On the cross He cried out, "My God, my God, why have you forsaken me?" (Matthew 27:46). Because He took the punishment for the sins of the world, He truly was cut off by God so that we never ever will be.

He chose rejection by the Father, abuse, and death on our behalf. So, if you are angry with God because He seems to have betrayed you or abandoned you, then rage. Be mad at the Father, like children so often are. But then please, oh please, melt into the arms of Jesus, the only One who was actually left alone so that you never will be.

Praise Jesus today that He chose to be troubled, abandoned, rejected, so that you will never be separated from the love and power of God.

> [Jesus] said to them, "I saw Satan fall like lightning from heaven. Behold, I have given you authority to tread on serpents and scorpions, and over all the power of the enemy, and nothing shall hurt you."
>
> —LUKE 10:18–19

All parts of the Holy Trinity—God the Father, Jesus the Son, and the Holy Spirit—are at work in our suffering. What a comfort. But Satan, too, tries to weasel his way into our pain. The most human moments of our suffering are marked with feelings of anger, betrayal, bitterness, and despair. This is natural. Don't dismiss these feelings too quickly, as they are integral to honest grief. But also, be wary of the devil's appetite for your disappointments and fears. These open wide gates into your mind. Isolation and depression make you vulnerable to Satan's attacks and lies unless you actively oppose them.

Jesus saw Satan fall from heaven. Jesus is the seed that crushed the serpent's head (Genesis 3:15). And in Christ you can do the same! Especially in seasons of trial, fight the Enemy with the sword of the Spirit, which is the infallible Word of God (Ephesians 6:10–18). He can't lie to you when you know truth. He can't steal your life, because Jesus has stolen the power of death. He can't defeat you even in your weakest moments, because he has already been defeated. He can shoot bullets, but with the authority of Christ, you are bulletproof.

I praise You, Jesus, that because of You, Satan has zero power over me! I call on Your Holy Spirit to extinguish every arrow of deceit he attempts to fire at me today.

> He sent from on high, he took me;
> he drew me out of many waters.

—PSALM 18:15

Do you feel like you're drowning? Treading water day after day and getting no closer to the shore? Like every exhausted effort you make to stay afloat isn't quite enough? Like giving up and going down would be easier than continuing to fight the waves? You are not alone. You may not be able to see any shoreline of hope or relief right now as you look at the days and months ahead. So, I urge you, weary friend, look backward.

Set your mind on things behind, on all the past times you were struggling, floundering in water you didn't know if you could make it out of. Remember how many times the Lord has drawn you up from rough seas, painful seasons or experiences, and tenderly set you on dry ground. Let hindsight be your buoy of hope when you have no more strength to swim. Jesus has always been faithful. He is still faithful. Though you flounder in the deep now, keep calling out His name. I promise you, He is coming from on high, and with time, faith, and endurance, you will find yourself hopeful and safe on the shore once again.

Write these words on a Post-it note, and stick it on your bathroom mirror. Repeat them aloud each time you glance at them: "Jesus is faithful. Jesus sustains me. Jesus is my safety and my strength."

Oh, the depth of the riches and wisdom and knowledge of God! How unsearchable are his judgments and how inscrutable his ways!

"For who has known the mind of the Lord,
or who has been his counselor?"

—ROMANS 11:33–34

In light of where you are right now, I know that worshipping the Lord can at times feel nearly impossible. Even after I found the courage to go back to church, I couldn't sing for months without sobbing. It was too heartbreaking at some moments, too anxiety producing and overwhelming at others. I felt like the only one in the room in an emotional puddle on the floor. I felt more drained than filled up. But singing is simply one of many ways to worship. "Oh, the depth of the riches and wisdom and knowledge of God!"

No matter what your worship may look like as you grieve, my friend, it's all glorious music to God's ears. A whispered "Thank You" or "Help me." A tear-filled plea from your dark room in the middle of the night. Nodding along to a hymn or worship song too painful to utter aloud. Laughter at a friend's silly attempt to lift your spirits. Whatever way you acknowledge Christ and His perfect, incomprehensible sovereignty over your life is worship. It's music to His ears, joy to His heart, and the greatest glory to His name. I know well, God cherishes your broken hallelujahs. Not just when they are loud or impressive, but when they are simple and desperate and sincere.

Play a worship song, and sing, sway, raise your hands, cry, or just breathe. Don't force a feeling, but turn your attention to God, and worship as honestly as you can.

When the goodness and loving kindness of God our Savior appeared, he saved us, not because of works done by us in righteousness, but according to his own mercy, by the washing of regeneration and renewal of the Holy Spirit.

—TITUS 3:4–5

What can save you from this tragedy—your strength, community, the passing of time? All of these play a benevolent and critical role in your healing. But the only thing that can save you is your Savior. Your strongest efforts on your best days will feel good, and you should celebrate them. But as the apostle Paul knew, the greatest strength you'll ever experience will be Christ's in you when you are at your weakest. Paul, who wrote a quarter of the New Testament, lived until his death with what he called "a thorn in the flesh," which God never removed from him (2 Corinthians 12:7, NASB). But that thorn continually drove him back to God for supernatural strength to live out his calling, keeping him from relying on his own efforts in vain.

It took lots of time and committed daily prayer for my energy, my joy, my hope, to be powerfully regenerated and renewed. I spoke out loud and wrote in journals over and over again the specific things that felt too big for me to overcome on my own. I had to practice surrendering my trauma and my heartbreak regularly. And as I did, the Savior, in His loving-kindness, began to restore me. The Holy Spirit is doing a mighty work in your soul too. The regeneration and renewal of God's children never ends.

Thank You, Jesus, that You are not only the Savior of my soul but also the restorer and redeemer of everything painful and broken I face. Save me from anxiety today, Lord.

> We know that for those who love God all things work together for good, for those who are called according to his purpose.
>
> —ROMANS 8:28

Have people cheerfully reminded you of this verse? Have you prayed it, clung to it, or grumbled about it? I know well through my own suffering, God's promise to His people to work everything together for good is trustworthy and true. The trouble is that what we see as good is temporary and what the Lord sees as good is eternal. Your good and His good won't always align from your point of view.

In our pain, when we imagine good coming from suffering, we first imagine relief, retribution, or measurable reward. And those things may come. But when God promises to work everything together for good, the good He has in mind is not necessarily our comfort but rather the ultimate good of us becoming more like Christ. Your Redeemer is working every minute of every day for your greatest good, even when it feels so very not good in the moment. Even so, I pray God gives you glimpses in the here and now of the fruit of your suffering.

Ask the Holy Spirit to reveal some small goodnesses in your life to keep you hopeful today.

He also said, "It is finished! I am the Alpha and the Omega—the Beginning and the End. To all who are thirsty I will give freely from the springs of the water of life."

—REVELATION 21:6, NLT

There is a reason Jesus referred to the Holy Spirit as "living water"— this fundamental element that no human can live without (John 7:37–39). We quite literally can't live spiritually flourishing lives without God's holy power working in us. What you are facing is too big for you to endure on your own. Brokenness and death can be and have been defeated only by God.

We can't purchase living water as we can the water of this world. Your strength, your efforts, on their own can't buy the life-giving and soul-saving water that Jesus offers us through His Holy Spirit. His presence, comfort, and provision are free gifts, and His supply is unending and ever available to you. All you need to acquire it is to bring your need to your Savior. He is ready and able to give you all the sustenance you need—for today and for eternity.

Quit trying to pay for something you can't afford, to earn something that can only be gifted. Go to Jesus, who offers it for free!

> Are not two sparrows sold for a penny? And not one of them will fall to the ground apart from your Father. But even the hairs of your head are all numbered. Fear not, therefore; you are of more value than many sparrows.
>
> —MATTHEW 10:29–31

Take a moment to look away from the turmoil inside and fix your eyes outside, on the natural treasures of creation. The flowers, the rivers, the birds—they are all tangible reminders of God's sovereignty over everything in the universe. When you pause to look, you will see intimate reminders of how He cares for each plant and animal. You will see the intentionality and purpose in the spring rains and the cycle of the moon. Even in the seemingly stagnant days of winter, the Lord is busy working to refuel and regenerate nature while it enjoys the rest it needs.

If God gives this much attention and care to the earth and the animals, how much more attention and care He must have for you! Every one of your hairs is numbered. Every one of your tears is kept (Psalm 56:8). Every one of your days is precious to the Father, and every one of your desperate prayers is tenderly heard. Nothing comes to you without His knowledge. Though you're hurting, your Father is gently and consistently caring for you with even more love than He does the rest of creation.

Lord, thank You that every tiny detail of my life matters to You. Let nature remind me of that today.

> To the one who conquers I will give some of the hidden manna, and I will give him a white stone, with a new name written on the stone that no one knows except the one who receives it.
>
> —REVELATION 2:17

When you suffer, when you lose something or someone of great value, you may feel like you've lost part of yourself. All the blessings and relationships God gives to us are good things, things of productivity, service, and love. They are things that help make up who we are, but they don't define who we are. So, beware, friend, at the loss of something precious to you that you not lose sight of your one true identity—beloved, chosen, adopted child of the King.

Jesus said we would have trouble in this life (John 16:33). You will lose titles, relationships, and names that feel so deeply ingrained in your identity that you forget who you really are in Christ. The positions and roles you hold here on earth will ebb and flow as you move from one season to the next. But Jesus has given you the ultimate name—the holy, perfect, eternal name "child of God." This name *never* changes. Write that on a stone, post it on your mirror—whatever you need to do to remember. You are a chosen child of God, secure in His fatherly protection forever. You are seen. You are cherished. You are whole.

What part of your identity feels like it's shifting in this season of loss? Ask the Lord to reassure you of your identity in Him today.

Day 59

> One man was [at the pool] who had been an invalid for
> thirty-eight years. When Jesus saw him lying there and
> knew that he had already been there a long time, he said
> to him, "Do you want to be healed?"
>
> —JOHN 5:5–6

I know you've been praying. I know you've been waiting for what
feels like an eternity for an answer, solution, or explanation from the
Lord. Don't give up, friend! Like the lame man who waited for healing for thirty-eight years, be persistent in prayer and continue to wait
on the Lord for all that you need. God is rarely early, and the waiting
pushes you to deeper trust in and dependence on Him, but He is
never late. He is never cruel in delaying but rather is allowing you
space to grow deeper and deeper in reliance on Him, because a life
reliant on Him is a life of freedom.

Be constant in prayer and patient as you wait to receive all the
healing, hope, and goodness Christ is ready to pour out on you. You
never know the day or hour He will show up, like He did for the
lame man, and enable you to walk again. Don't stray from the pool.
Keep calling out for His divine touch, because He is the only one
who can heal you. You will be healed. He is coming soon.

Answer the question "Do you want to be healed?" with very
specific ways you long for Him to heal you and your circumstances today.

I called on your name, O LORD,
   from the depths of the pit;
you heard my plea, "Do not close
   your ear to my cry for help!"
You came near when I called on you;
   you said, "Do not fear!"

—LAMENTATIONS 3:55–57

All throughout Scripture the Lord instructs His people to fear Him. And sadly, so many have misunderstood this command as a caution to be afraid of God. Do you ever feel afraid to be honest with Him? Do you worry that if you really told the Lord or others how disappointed or distrusting you felt toward Him, He'd hang you out to dry? I get it! But that fear is *not* the fear of the Lord that Scripture calls us to. In fact, the Bible assures us God's perfect love casts out this kind of fear (1 John 4:18). Fear of the Lord means living in awe of His goodness and glory.

Your Father never wants you to fear coming to Him with your whole heart, your honest good, bad, and ugly. The God who walked this earth and suffered Himself isn't looking for polite prayers and passive requests from His people. Like Jeremiah, whose nickname was "the weeping prophet," call out loudly from the pit of your pain. Don't filter your disappointments or desires, knowing He is able to meet your needs wondrously well. Never lose your healthy, awe-filled fear of our all-powerful God, but also never fear to approach your Father in heaven. You are His beloved child.

What are you holding back from God? Name that wound, need, or pain specifically, and call out to Jesus for rescue and healing today.

Day 61

> I will ask the Father, and he will give you another Helper,
> to be with you forever, even the Spirit of truth. . . . You
> know him, for he dwells with you and will be in you.
>
> —JOHN 14:16–17

As Jesus neared what He knew was the end of His earthly life, He was thinking about you. He endured all kinds of suffering during His thirty-three years on earth—homelessness, hunger, temptation, betrayal, death of loved ones, accusation, rejection. He knew as the divine God and as a flesh-and-bones man that flawed humans could never endure life's hardships on our own. And Jesus had a plan for us.

Jesus told His followers two thousand years ago that we would have trouble. But He also told them, "Take heart; I have overcome the world" (John 16:33). In the same way you can't escape suffering on earth, so, too, can you never escape God's Holy Spirit once you are in Christ. The Spirit of truth and power that raised Jesus' crucified body from the dead indwells you and is forever present to embolden you to endure whatever hardship you encounter. Even on days when you feel far from God, His Holy Spirit will never ever depart from you. You can't wriggle away from Him.

Thank You, Jesus, that You have already given me the only superpower I need to endure life with hope. Help me feel the Holy Spirit so near today.

Day 62

I know, O LORD, that the way of man is not in himself,
that it is not in man who walks to direct his steps.

—JEREMIAH 10:23

Ohe of the lies the Enemy spins is that we are in control, that our way must be better, easier, or quicker than God's way. But whatever sent your life into a tailspin has jarred you to the discouraging realization that you have much less control over your life than you thought. Yes, God gives you free will to make your own choices, but He never intended for you to be the author of your own story. As your mind reels with what-ifs, maybes, and endless questions about what's to come, take still moments to remember and be thankful that it's the Lord who directs your steps. It's the Father who knows the number of your days.

No matter how strategic or capable you are, Christ is still sovereign over all events, all outcomes, all things. Don't let this truth leave you feeling handcuffed; let it bring overwhelming hope!

You don't have to handle everything yourself. Show up, and surrender your losses to the Lord. Lift your eyes instead of straining to see forward, and let Him direct your steps.

Allow yourself to feel the frustration of not being able to fix everything. Then ask God to replace those feelings of helplessness with supernatural peace.

I will give . . .
    a monument and a name
    better than sons and daughters;
I will give them an everlasting name
    that shall not be cut off.

—ISAIAH 56:5

I remember so clearly the first moment I was introduced as a widow. I was sitting at a work meeting and heard my colleague offer to the woman across from me, "Mattie's a widow too." All the blood rushed from my face at the name I wished desperately could be erased. It felt so permanent. I also had to give up some names I wished were still true, like wife, and names I had hoped to be true in the future, like mother. It was a long journey to identify what parts of my life I had to mourn or lay down in order to arrive at the one name that would always stay the same.

You, too, may be grieving parts of yourself that have been stolen. I know this is painful. I know it takes time, prayer, and work to process and accept a new version of yourself. But as you grieve and adapt, continue to remind yourself that your value has only ever come from one thing: the untarnishable name "chosen child of God." That is how who you see in the mirror stays beautifully the same. Your name as His beloved, righteous son or daughter can never be lost.

Write down in pencil the parts of yourself you feel you've lost, the parts of your identity you're grieving. Then write in ink above those things, *Child of God.* That is the only name that defines you.

Day 64

And though a man might prevail against one who is alone, two will withstand him—a threefold cord is not quickly broken.

—ECCLESIASTES 4:12

Friends and family can support you, but they can't save you. When we're drowning in grief, we need loved ones to buoy us and be the cords that help tether us to solid ground. But be wary of entrusting your ultimate healing to any imperfect human. It's dangerous and foolish to expect anyone to be the source of your healing besides Jesus Himself.

Yet we absolutely need loving community and counsel to lead us in perseverance and love us well. Christianity isn't a solo sport. The power of community is crucial for us to remain hopeful and resilient human beings, and it's even more crucial in times of hardship. When you're hurt, confused, and downtrodden, you need the support of faithful friends and the direction of wise counselors more than ever to combat Satan's schemes. You need hand-holders, house cleaners, and prayer warriors surrounding you. But remember their role as encouragers is to continually point your heart back to Christ, the ultimate hearer of your cries and healer of your soul.

If you are surrounded by a loving community, praise God for it! But also, be sure those making up your safety cord are always pointing you back to God's counsel.

He will tend his flock like a shepherd;
  he will gather the lambs in his arms;
he will carry them in his bosom,
  and gently lead those that are with young.

—ISAIAH 40:11

My friend, I want you to find relief in this assurance from Scripture. I want you to exhale and rest today because the Lord's love for you has never been and will never be because of your strength, performance, or ability to weather pain. Remember that while you are a citizen of God's kingdom, an active part of His body and a member of His chosen nation, you are also His beloved child. A parent's love for their child isn't measured or conditional. It doesn't hinge on how tough, faithful, or capable the child is. Those traits are good, and your Father created you with great potential to be brave and resilient. But His unchanging, soul-filling love for you is dependent not on your power but solely on His own in you.

Like the exuberant, welcoming father in the parable of the prodigal son (Luke 15:11–32), God rejoices over you whenever you run back to Him. He grins with delight when you ask Him to carry your burdens instead of striving to shoulder them all yourself. He is overjoyed when you trade in temporary trust in what you can do or what fate might bring for the enduring hope He offers you. Exchange your striving for His steadfast love, and find peace.

Meditate on this today: *I am unconditionally, radically loved by God.*

The steadfast love of the LORD never ceases;
  his mercies never come to an end;
they are new every morning;
  great is your faithfulness.

—LAMENTATIONS 3:22—23

When I'm asked, "What advice would you give to someone grieving?" the list is endless. But the most practical offering I have to those early in their journey simply is this: Twenty-four hours at a time. That's how God will sustain you. That's how you will overcome. That's how life will return. You can't deplete the supernatural love and provision God has for you. His grace, mercy, peace, wisdom, patience, strength, forgiveness, understanding, and every other attribute of His character is in infinitely greater supply than you could ever need and is available in twenty-four-hour doses.

Often, as an all-knowing, good Father, the Lord provides for us in ways we don't ask for or even realize. But He also calls us to be active in prayer. We have a role to play. When we create daily rhythms of telling God what we need, we deepen that relationship as we vulnerably trust Him with our desires. He knows exactly what you need and how empty your emotional tank is. He simply wants to hear your voice and feel your heart turn toward Him in trust that He will provide for you. This life passes just twenty-four hours at a time. You can survive another twenty-four hours, friend, and when you do, God's mercies will be new again in the morning.

What specific gifts, capabilities, or blessings do you need in order to get through the next twenty-four hours? Ask God for them, and praise Him that He can renew them in you every morning.

Day 67

When you pray, do not heap up empty phrases as the
Gentiles do, for they think that they will be heard for
their many words. Do not be like them, for your Father
knows what you need before you ask him.

—MATTHEW 6:7–8

Prayer is your most powerful weapon in all seasons—those filled
with joy and those marked by sorrow. Prayer is your direct line of
communication, communion, and friendship with the Lord. I know,
when confusion and pain cloud your mind, prayer can feel taxing,
like a one-way call with no one on the other end of the line. Maybe
you're at such a loss or overcome with such anxiety, you simply don't
know what to pray. You don't even know what you need from God.
Don't worry. Don't overthink coming to your Father and spilling out
your heart.

Think of the people you're closest to in life. You can communicate
a lot to them even when your words are very few because you know
each other so well. Jesus is the friend who is closer than even a brother
(Proverbs 18:24), so don't stop coming to Him with your tired, broken prayers. To Him, prayer is not about the words you speak but
about the honest sharing of your soul with Him. He wants to be with
you in the thick of it. So, never forget, God calls you to prayer not to
judge the mastery of your communication but to speak gently to
your fragile heart.

Talk to Jesus today just like you'd talk to your best friend.
Don't edit; don't plan; just give Him the honest update for
today, and let Him sit with you in it.

Blessed is the man who trusts in the LORD,
    whose trust is the LORD.
He is like a tree planted by water,
    that sends out its roots by the stream,
and does not fear.

—JEREMIAH 17:7–8

Seasons of drought come and go. But when your spiritual roots are in the right place, pain and disappointment won't dictate how you respond to the hard circumstances you face. Consider an arid plain where harsh conditions mark most every season. Why does one tree endure and continue to produce fruit while another withers away? The one that endures has its roots by a river. It gets its sustenance far below the surface from a stream that enables it not just to survive but to grow in a place where none should thrive. Its growth doesn't make sense from the outside looking in. The tree should be withering away!

It's not on you to bear good fruit in this harsh season of suffering. It's up to you to keep your roots in the water, by the stream. I promise, like the water sustains the tree, Christ will sustain you. Don't fear the desert. The Living Water can and will sustain you through anything.

What is one small way you can deepen your roots in the Living Water today?

If any of you lacks wisdom, let him ask God, who gives
generously to all without reproach, and it will be given
him. But let him ask in faith, with no doubting, for the
one who doubts is like a wave of the sea that is driven and
tossed by the wind.

—JAMES 1:5–6

I know you want to understand. You want an explanation for why
God let this tragedy befall you. And a promise that good will come
of it would be nice, too, right? I wished so desperately that He would
give me a magic road map to navigate the way forward. I wanted to
see what He sees, from beginning to end. I truly felt like understanding it all might finally give me peace and ease my doubts about God's
sovereignty. But even if He had revealed the entirety of His plan for
me, I couldn't possibly have grasped it.

Rather than seeking understanding as you continue to endure this
hardship, call on the Lord for wisdom, which He gives generously to
all His children if they ask. Wisdom won't give you answers to the
endless questions that plague you, but it will enable you to trust that
all your questions have been answered in the person of Jesus. Wisdom will assure you that your pain is not insignificant to God but
rather dear to His heart and held perfectly in His hands.

What explanations are you chasing—from yourself, others,
or God—that promise you a false sense of peace? Entrust
those to the Lord in prayer.

> Joseph's master took him and put him into the
> prison. . . . But the LORD was with Joseph and
> showed him steadfast love and gave him favor in
> the sight of the keeper of the prison.
>
> —GENESIS 39:20–21

If you're like me, you don't want to imagine an almighty God who allows one of His people to be falsely imprisoned. You may long to believe the appealing but false idea that your degree of faithfulness determines the degree of blessing or hardship in your life. While the Lord says His intention is never to hurt you, Scripture makes clear His priority to draw you closer and closer to Him. The result is that you lean on Christ more than you do on yourself and you trust in His kingdom promises more than you trust in the world's point of view.

Could God have spared Joseph from a false accusation and unjust imprisonment? Of course. But rather, God met him in his suffering, was unrelentingly faithful to him, and brought him comfort and even favor while in chains. And when the Lord did eventually rescue Joseph, He placed him on a path to be the second-in-command over all of Egypt, the right-hand consultant of the pharaoh. Trust what you can't make sense of right now. Let the Almighty make you, like Joseph, a bright light in your undeserved darkness. You never know how crucial your prison season might be to the grander story the Lord is writing.

Do you feel frustrated or slighted, like you didn't get what you deserved from God? Admit those feelings, and talk with God about them.

Day 71

> Let us draw near with a true heart in full assurance
> of faith, with our hearts sprinkled clean from an evil
> conscience and our bodies washed with pure water.
> Let us hold fast the confession of our hope without
> wavering, for he who promised is faithful.
>
> —HEBREWS 10:22–23

What is a true heart before God? It's broken, honest, and fully exposed. It looks longingly and hopefully for what you know He can provide but you can't see evidence of yet. It admits things to God in prayer that you'd be too afraid to speak aloud in a church building. People warn you to watch your tongue because words can't be unsaid, yet with God, everything unsaid is already said. He knows every broken, bitter, even scary intrusive thought that comes into your mind regardless of if you confess them to anyone or not.

Maybe you picture revenge on someone who hurt you or caused this pain? Maybe you're fighting back suicidal thoughts? Maybe you're still angry with the one who passed? A true heart brings everything to Christ in prayer—the good, the bad, and especially the ugly—because He adores you and because His Word is *the* truth that has power to speak back to those lies. Because He can be trusted to hold every thought with mercy, grace, and understanding. You're already washed clean. Nothing can change the Father's radical love for you.

Have you been battling condemning or intrusive thoughts? Speak them aloud to the Lord. Pray that He would show you scriptural truths to speak back to those thoughts. This is the first step toward freedom from them.

The one who sows to the Spirit will from the Spirit reap
eternal life. And let us not grow weary of doing good, for
in due season we will reap, if we do not give up.

—GALATIANS 6:8–9

Y ou may think of doing good as serving others in need, but doing
good also means sowing in your own heart. Your soul is the only soul
you can truly care for fully. God has given you your soul, and it's
yours and yours alone to ultimately take care of. So, how do we care
for our souls and fill up our tanks? Worship.

Action may have to precede feelings at first. In times when you
feel depleted, like there is zero left in your emotional tank, be diligent
to practice small spiritual rhythms like praise, worship, and prayer
that will pour back into your spirit. All of these actions will position
you to receive hope and will prepare you for the spiritual fruit that
God is sowing in you as you struggle.

In time, you will trust and praise God wholeheartedly again.
You're able to endure when you surrender your struggles to Jesus.
You're able to surrender when your hope in Christ is bigger than the
hell you're walking through. So, don't give up. Don't grow weary of
doing good—of worshipping God and pouring into yourself. In due
season, you will reap all the joy and peace you've lost.

Spend five minutes in private worship today, whatever that
looks like for you. Just you and the Lord.

Let those who suffer according to God's will entrust their
souls to a faithful Creator while doing good.

—1 PETER 4:19

If you were rescued at sea, a shipwreck victim of a ferocious storm,
would you rush to take control of the wheel of the rescue ship? It's
more likely you would settle down in the safest place possible and
leave the navigation to the captain. The wisest move you can make
when life throws you into stormy situations is to surrender to someone with far greater expertise and capacity to handle it on your behalf.
Let the captain be the captain.

If you'd trust the captain on the sea, how much more reason do
you have to trust the omnipotent God in your roughest times? Not
only is He a sovereign Father with perfect control over and plans for
how your painful season will play out; He is also Jesus, who has suffered just as you are suffering. He's been on the ship in the middle of
the storm. He understands how scary the waves are. God is your
captain and your companion. Entrust your soul, your plan, and your
fear to Him, friend. He is able and faithful to protect you and steer
your ship to safety.

What are you white-knuckling in this season out of fear or a
need for control that you can surrender to your captain and
comforter, Jesus?

> The LORD our God said to us in Horeb, "You have
> stayed long enough at this mountain. Turn and take
> your journey. . . . See, I have set the land before you."
>
> —DEUTERONOMY 1:6–8

After four hundred years of slavery, Moses led the Israelites to safety in a desert place called Horeb, where they stayed somewhat comfortably for a year on their journey to the promised land. After that year, God called them to move on. The trouble was, the next cities God called them to were full of powerful aggressors and enemies. Do you think the Israelites resisted? Maybe considered staying in their incomplete but familiar life at Horeb? I think I would have. In fact, I'm vulnerable to the same thoughts right now. When we're afraid of what's next, it can feel easier to stay where we are than to move toward the fullness of the promised land.

When the shock and adrenaline of grief wear off, you may start to feel at home in your sadness, even comfortable in your despair. Like nothing is ever going to be as good as it once was, so why try? But grief, discomfort, pain—these aren't your destination. Don't become so comfortable in your pain that you get stuck there. Long-term lament can give way to full-blown depression if you're not careful to heed God's call to push forward, confident that He will ultimately restore you to life. As the Lord called the Israelites out of Horeb and into a better land, so, too, will He call you to move toward a more vibrant life again. Trust Him, friend. Listen to His call. Follow His nudges toward restored life.

*Lord, if You're leading me into a new season, a new place, new
relationships, help me be obedient. Don't let fear keep me stagnant
in my pain. I trust where You're leading me.*

He has made everything beautiful in its time.

—ECCLESIASTES 3:11

When you hear these words of King Solomon, do both hope *and* frustration rise up in your heart? Does it feel hopeful but also a little disheartening? It reminds me of what Isaiah tells us God does with our brokenness: He brings beauty from ashes (Isaiah 61:3). But how can so much brokenness, so much that looks ugly and tainted in our lives, ever be made beautiful? And why does it have to take so much time?

There's a centuries-old Japanese practice I love that helps me imagine Solomon's words here. *Kintsugi* is a traditional technique of repairing shattered pottery. Rather than discarding the broken pieces, potters use a shiny lacquer and gold or silver powder to reassemble the pot and fill in its cracks. In this way, *kintsugi* honors the piece's history, not by erasing it but by highlighting it, by mending the breaks and beautifying the cracks.[6] Your losses will always be part of you. Your cracks will always be visible. But with the Potter's perfect hands, you, too, will be made beautiful in His time.

Is there a specific thing in your life that feels ugly right now? Name it, and speak what is true over it: "One day, this will make me more beautiful."

> You shall walk after the LORD your God and fear him
> and keep his commandments and obey his voice, and
> you shall serve him and hold fast to him.
>
> —DEUTERONOMY 13:4

To physically walk after someone means to follow their lead, step where they step, and continue on to wherever they're heading. But following a leader feels safe only if you trust them and if they have the knowledge required to make the journey successful. Even then, it's hard to follow another when you don't know the destination, how long your journey will be, or what you'll need along the way.

But Jesus isn't a flawed human leader. He's never guessing which direction is north. When God asks you to fear Him as you follow, He doesn't mean "be afraid" as you might following other people. He's asking you to revere Him, to stand in awe of Him and trust Him *fully* because He is all-knowing and all-powerful. Revere God because He is ultimately in control of everything, the only safe leader. Do what He asks of you, because He always has your ultimate good in mind. Hold fast to Christ, and follow confidently on His heels when you feel weak and disoriented. There is no safer place for you, especially in seasons of pain, than faithfully following in the Almighty's footsteps.

Ask the Lord to clearly direct your decisions, conversations, and thoughts today, and ask Him for the courage to follow His lead.

> We are his workmanship, created in Christ Jesus for good
> works, which God prepared beforehand, that we should
> walk in them.
>
> —EPHESIANS 2:10

You are the pinnacle of God's creation. He is immensely proud of you because you were made in His own image (Genesis 1:27). He made you uniquely and purposefully and sent you into this world chock full of kingdom purpose, brimming with holy potential for a lifetime of good works. And in His grace, some of the good works He has planned for you are birthed out of bad circumstances. Just as Jesus was a great light in our darkness (Isaiah 9:2), so, too, may your light shine most brightly when you find yourself in dark places.

I wish that wasn't the case, and I believe God does, too, because I know He hates to see His children suffer. But know this: No amount of tragedy or difficulty can mar the stunning image of God within you. You are on the way to many of the good works the Lord has prepared for you. Trust me. Steward this hardship well; stand confident in your identity as God's intentional workmanship.

Meditate on the thought that you are made in God's holy image and empowered by His Holy Spirit. He has created you to do good works, according to His grace.

> Since we are surrounded by so great a cloud of witnesses,
> let us also lay aside every weight, and sin which clings so
> closely, and let us run with endurance the race that is set
> before us, looking to Jesus, the founder and perfecter of
> our faith, who for the joy that was set before him endured
> the cross, despising the shame, and is seated at the right
> hand of the throne of God.
>
> —HEBREWS 12:1–2

If you've ever run or biked any long distance in a race, you know well the physical and mental exhaustion that inevitably comes. *Endurance* is defined as "stamina to undergo an unpleasant or difficult situation without giving way."[7] And one key to not giving way is continuing to fuel your body. Maybe your spiritual, emotional, and mental muscles are fatigued from the hard race you've been running. Maybe you desperately need to refuel.

Like an endurance runner needs good nutrition, you need spiritual fuel as you run this arduous race. It's tempting to fuel yourself with things the world offers—busyness, food, drink, ambition, sex, or any number of other things that make you feel temporarily filled. Those things are empty and fleeting and don't provide real nourishment. The person of Jesus is the only sustainable fuel. Fill yourself up with Him at every turn, every chance you get, and I promise you that you will cross the finish line clothed in glory.

> If you're feeling empty and tempted to turn to an unhealthy
> coping mechanism for comfort today, go first to the Word
> and pray that Christ supernaturally fills that hole so you can
> endure healthily.

Day 79

Remember not the former things,
    nor consider the things of old.
Behold, I am doing a new thing;
    now it springs forth, do you not perceive it?
I will make a way in the wilderness
    and rivers in the desert.

—ISAIAH 43:18–19

It's easy to fall into the habit of gazing back at the familiarity and security of the past. Nostalgia feels comforting because you can nuance it to highlight the good and lowlight the bad. The past can feel deceivingly safer than looking forward to a future full of question marks.

But don't look just at what has happened in the past to determine what is possible for the future.

Treasure the past—hold those blessings close to your heart—but don't let the way things have been limit your thinking and your prayers about how God might work in your future. He is a wildly creative God. His ways seldom follow precedent. He is doing new things and making new ways for you all the time. Just because you haven't seen a river in the desert doesn't mean one can't be coming. When you look back, do so gratefully. When you look forward, do so expectantly. God's plans are far beyond your capacity to understand, and the ways He's working in your life may be altogether new to you.

Spend some time dreaming with the Lord today about your future. Ask Him for what you desire, but also ask for the imagination to anticipate something greater that He may have in store.

The threshing floors shall be full of grain;
　　the vats shall overflow with wine and oil.
I will restore to you the years
　　that the swarming locust has eaten.

　　　　　　　　　　　　　　—JOEL 2:24–25

God has many names, each of which reveals a unique facet of His character. You may know Him as Creator and Savior, Shepherd and Rock. You also must remember that He is the redeemer of all things—of you, of His perfect plan for humanity, and of creation. What or who you have lost can never be replaced. But God is not in the business of replacing earthly things, all of which will inevitably fade away; He *is* in the business of restoring everything and everyone that is broken, sick, dead, or lost back to a form even greater than the original. He makes all things new, not all new things.

Your life will be full again. Your tears will be made into smiles again. Your heartbreak will make space for bigger hope. Jesus didn't come to replace the people you'll inevitably lose in this life. He came to fill the empty space so full of Himself in their absence that you can continue to live with joy until you're in their presence again for eternity.

Thank You, Lord, that no one who is in Christ is ever totally lost.
I praise You that You are the redeemer of the universe, including
all my pain.

In my Father's house are many rooms. If it were not so,
would I have told you that I go to prepare a place for
you?

—JOHN 14:2

When you lose someone dear to you, there is comfort in knowing
they are now with Jesus in heaven. Just like the thief who proclaimed
Jesus as Messiah while hanging on the cross (Luke 23:39–43), those
covered by Jesus' blood take their first breath in eternity the moment
they take their last breath on earth. I know this is hard to imagine.
Even if you believe this is true in your mind, it may feel impossible
to picture.

Scripture assures us that what Jesus said about preparing for His
people a personal place, your own room, is true. Like an expectant
mother readying a nursery for her child to come, so the Lord is preparing a specific place in eternity for each of His sons and daughters.
Picture the things, colors, and spaces your loved one enjoyed in this
life. Now envision him or her enjoying those things, just in the most
vibrant, glorious way imaginable. Think of him or her there. Your
image certainly won't be exactly as heaven is, but it's still a true
glimpse of the overwhelming joy and sense of home that have become
his or her reality with Christ. Rest in that.

Picture your loved one reveling in the beauties of heaven.
Picture them doing what they loved on earth but in unfathomable HD color.

Rejoice not over me, O my enemy;
>   when I fall, I shall rise;
> when I sit in darkness,
>   the LORD will be a light to me.

—MICAH 7:8

Do you feel like you're at rock bottom? Like there's nowhere lower, lonelier, or less hopeful to go than where you are right now? If so, speak these words from the prophet Micah with confidence and celebration! That may feel crazy, but in God's kingdom, the valley *is* a place worth rejoicing over. Why? Because the lower you are, the higher He lifts you. It's a wild, mysterious, and wonderful truth.

The Enemy may see you as vulnerable, but it's in your humbled position of weakness that you'll find more power than ever before—Christ's power! You're never in a stronger position to rise up in grace (and, subsequently, thwart the Enemy's schemes against you) than when you know you need the Lord with every fiber of your being. As your self-reliance decreases, your reliance on God increases, and you allow Him maximum capacity to transform your heart and move in your life in powerful ways. Claim this verse, and know that it's trustworthy and true. You're about to come out of these ashes stronger than ever before.

I praise You, Lord, that at my weakest I am strongest in You. Jesus, the One who defeated death, live and work powerfully in me today.

Trust in the LORD with all your heart,
    and do not lean on your own understanding.
In all your ways acknowledge him,
    and he will make straight your paths.

—PROVERBS 3:5–6

This passage was immediately one of the most comforting *and* one of the hardest for me to accept in my grief. Why? Because it was Ben's favorite passage, one he included in every blessing, in every prayer for our family. What was so natural for him—to trust without question—became one of my biggest battles with God. *How can I trust You still when You let this happen? How could You possibly make a straight or good way out of this tragedy?* I wanted so badly to understand but ultimately had to choose the better way, Ben's way: to humbly trust.

Remind yourself daily to keep choosing trust and to turn to Christ with every fear and question you have, every decision you must make and every step forward you must take. When you do, His promise here remains true—He will eventually make your path straight. Like resetting a broken bone, the process of making your way straight again will be painful. Trust the Lord to carry you through the setbacks. Trust Him through the pain. He is resetting what has been broken so that your spirit and your faith will emerge even stronger than before.

How has it been hard to trust God lately? Talk to Jesus openly about what is making it so hard. Then remind yourself that difficulties are never impossibilities with God.

In his hand are the depths of the earth;
   the heights of the mountains are his also.
The sea is his, for he made it,
   and his hands formed the dry land.

—PSALM 95:4–5

It's impossible to understand the fullness of who God is, the complete sovereignty and purpose with which He holds every facet of your life. When you feel overwhelmed or uncertain about His hand in your life, I encourage you to look to creation. Really see and soak in the incredibly diverse, mysterious, seemingly chaotic world that God created. And remember, if He can hold all of it together in perfect harmony and rhythm, He can undoubtedly hold you in perfect harmony and rhythm. Nothing you face is out of the Lord's loving, intentional, capable hands.

Just as He cares for creation, He cares for you in your deep heartbreaks. Christ is the calm in the chaos of stormy seas and the Living Water you need when you traverse barren, desert seasons. In your fear and in your lack, Jesus is with you. At your worst and at your best, He is with you. When you struggle to believe, simply look at how He sustains the world around you, and remember, you are the prize of God's entire creation. Just as He faithfully sustains the entire universe, He sustains you.

Take a few minutes today to contemplate an element of nature—the tree outside your window or the birds in the sky. Thank God that He is so attentive to you.

Through him we have also obtained access by faith into
this grace in which we stand, and we rejoice in hope of
the glory of God. Not only that, but we rejoice in our
sufferings, knowing that suffering produces endurance,
and endurance produces character, and character
produces hope.

—ROMANS 5:2–4

Have you ever been at the back of the line of a popular ride at an
amusement park? Or stood in line for a show or another event for
hours on end because you knew the experience would be worth the
wait? Though you may despise the long line and grow restless, your
choice to endure ultimately awards you the prize you've anticipated
and set your sights on. You know the ride will run and the show will
go on. What felt excruciating to me about waiting in grief—waiting
on healing, on closure, on energy, on specific prayers—was that I
couldn't see a concrete finish line. I didn't know how long the wait
would be or where the end was. And neither will you. This is why
daily communion with God is crucial.

Waiting hand in hand with God builds endurance, character, and
hope. You may not be able to see an end to your waiting right now,
but one outcome the Lord always works in our waiting is hope.
Never think He's abandoned you as you wait. Jesus is in line with
you, beloved, sowing great trust and hope in you as you endure.

It's okay to lament the grueling grind of waiting. Share that
frustration with God today, and ask Him to sow daily, supernatural hope in you as you wait.

> This God—his way is perfect;
>> the word of the LORD proves true;
>> he is a shield for all those who take refuge in him.
>
> —PSALM 18:30

Gd's Word reminds us repeatedly that the Lord is our shield. But if you're here with me, you know all too well that God being our shield doesn't mean He deflects our hardship. So, if He doesn't promise to protect us from pain, what does He shield us from when we take refuge in Him?

First and foremost, Scripture calls us to "take up the shield of faith, with which you can extinguish all the flaming darts of the evil one" (Ephesians 6:16). All those damning and afflicting thoughts creeping in? All the regret or shame you feel about what you did or didn't do before tragedy happened? Those flaming lies can be blocked by trusting God and His Word. Learn Scripture to speak back to those lies.

I also believe God mercifully shields us from the future. Anxiety exists about the future. Peace exists in the present. Jesus even told His disciples, "It is not for you to know times or seasons that the Father has fixed by his own authority" (Acts 1:7). If you find yourself regularly worrying about what's next, call on God to help you stay trustingly in the present.

What lies of the Enemy or chronic anxieties do you need the Lord to shield you from today? Thank Him that His Word deflects and protects us from all things untrue.

> Why, my soul, are you downcast?
>   Why so disturbed within me?
> Put your hope in God,
>   for I will *yet* praise him,
>   my Savior and my God.

—PSALM 42:11, NIV (emphasis added)

Nothing about the way God created you—your mind, your soul, or your body—is coincidence. You have two hands, two eyes, and two ears. You have a mind and a heart that, though very different in function, often work together to give you rich spiritual connection with your Creator.

You have two hands for a reason—one to hold your pain and one to hold God's promises. You have two eyes—one to acknowledge the hard reality of your circumstances and one to remain fixed on Jesus, who will eventually restore everything broken. You have two ears—one to hear wise earthly counsel and one to listen for Holy Spirit discernment in how to proceed. You have a mind that seeks to understand and a heart that can learn to trust. Always be honest about the gravity of what you're facing, and also remember to give the Lord the "yet": *Yet* I will trust You; *yet* I will surrender to You; *yet* I will hope in Your name. The tension of wailing and hoping allows you to grieve with your full humanity.

Practice praying with both hands today. Lift one hand, and express to God your griefs and fears; then lift the other, and claim the hope you have in His promises and power.

A friend loves at all times,
and a brother is born for adversity.

—PROVERBS 17:17

It's crucial that you hear me remind you, my friend—you don't need to do this alone. You can't do this alone. You don't earn God's favor by shouldering the weight of your sorrows solo. You aren't loved more when you ask for help less. These are all lies I had to break free from. I thought my healing would depend on how strong I could be when really it depended more on what I was willing to hand over. Why? Because I needed so much extra time and energy to manage my mental and emotional pain.

So often the help you need is obvious, tangible: cleaning your home, picking up children or groceries, mowing your lawn. Sometimes it's mental or emotional: someone to cry with, tell stories with, sit in silence with. Often, my people loved me well by way of silly distractions: committing to watch a TV series with me, sharing funny mishaps from their work or about their kids. Friends and family may feel awkward or not sure how to help, but they're longing to. I promise. As best you can, articulate what you feel you need today—physical help, emotional help, or even lighthearted distractions—and let them love you however they can.

Who is a safe person to reach out to today to ask for extra help, encouragement, or some time together?

> Blessed is the man who remains steadfast under trial, for
> when he has stood the test he will receive the crown of
> life, which God has promised to those who love him.
>
> —JAMES 1:12

In God's kingdom, crowns aren't given to kings and queens, Olympic athletes, or Nobel Prize winners. In God's kingdom, people like you and me are gifted the ultimate reward—the crown of eternal life—not because of what we do but simply because of who we are: the chosen children of God!

As James reminds us, blessed are those who remain steadfast, who stand the test. God honors those who keep running toward Him when their feet are blistered and their muscles are cramping. More than those who appear to blaze through without struggle, it's the ones who stagger across the finish line faithfully—the sufferers—that are awarded a crown. Jesus has already won the race and broken all the records in your place. He earned the crown you could never earn on your own and then places it proudly on your head. Don't despair that you're injured, bruised, and limping. Stumble forward faithfully and with full trust in Jesus, and you will receive the most glorious reward.

Remind yourself today that you don't have to do this well or keep it together as you grieve. Thank Jesus for the freedom to struggle and yet be crowned with His glory.

> Abraham called the name of that place, "The LORD will provide"; as it is said to this day, "On the mount of the LORD it shall be provided."
>
> —GENESIS 22:14

The context of this passage is one of the wildest to me in Scripture. God called Abraham to sacrifice his only son, Isaac, on the top of a mountain as a show of trust in and obedience to the Lord. Abraham obeyed, and at the very last moment, God sent a ram to take Isaac's place. And I'm sure, with trembling, worshipping hands, Abraham called the mountain "Jehovah Jireh," a Hebrew name meaning "the LORD will provide."

You likely don't need a ram, but do you believe the Lord really will provide for you? What are you lacking physically, financially, relationally, mentally that you may be hesitant to ask Him for? Do it! Daily! The answer may be "Not yet" or "Not exactly," but the Lord who provides knows infinitely better than you do who to put in your path, how to satisfy your physical needs, when to give relief. He won't leave you stranded and unequipped. Trust is a daily battle in grief. Remember Jehovah Jireh—the Lord who provides.

Pray specifically for your tangible needs this week. Ask in detail. And then ask Jehovah Jireh for supernatural trust as you wait.

> I tell you, do not be anxious about your life, what you
> will eat or what you will drink, nor about your body,
> what you will put on. Is not life more than food, and
> the body more than clothing?
>
> —MATTHEW 6:25

I know this command from King Jesus feels so much easier said than done. Especially now, in uncertain and sorrowful seasons, you may be thinking, *How is it possible not to worry when so much has gone wrong? When so much is broken and out of my control? When I feel paralyzed, unable to move forward?* More of us battle anxiety now than ever before, so you may wonder, *Is this command still relevant, even realistic?* Relevant? Always. Realistic? Yes! Easy? Not at all.

Be diligent, and make the best plans you can as you face whatever is in front of you, but as you do, pray for the courage to hand over final control to the Lord. Learning to live openhanded with your needs and worries, surrendering them to Christ before relying on (or despairing over) your own plans, is how to fight anxious thoughts. Let your prayer be for trust to supernaturally take the place of worry. This is far more than just glass-half-full optimism. This is deliberately choosing to fix your eyes on Christ so that hope can outweigh worry when things aren't going as you planned.

Write down or speak aloud everything you're anxious about today. Even imagine the worst-case scenario. Then pray for the power to release what you can't control to Jesus and truly trust Him with your life.

Day 92

The LORD will fight for you; you need only to be still.

—EXODUS 14:14, NIV

We live in a culture that not only refuses to prioritize rest but also dismisses its importance at best and flat-out shames people for it at worst. And this command Moses gave to the Israelites as they stood before the tumultuous Red Sea is just as powerful and true for us today as it was for them. Be still. Let God do it His way. I know you want to do something—anything—to feel like you have some control over your situation. But you don't need control; you need the One who controls everything.

It may feel harder to rest while you grieve than when things are going well, because busyness helps distract you from your painful reality. If you're facing loss, you crave distraction. If an obstacle is in your way, you crave solution. If loneliness is plaguing you, you'll do anything to fill the empty space. But in order to rest, to regain strength, perspective, and hope, what you need to do is spend intentional time with the Lord. Be still, and know that He is sovereign God. Rest—physically, spiritually, and emotionally. You need to recharge. Be still, beloved, and trust that the Lord is fighting for you.

Sit with the Lord in a comfortable place. Rest with Him.

> Above all these put on love, which binds everything
> together in perfect harmony.
>
> —COLOSSIANS 3:14

Every morning when you wake up, you have a choice before you. What will you wear—sweatpants, work clothes, makeup, cologne? On days heavy with grief, it's hard enough to get out of bed, let alone get dressed. But with time, it gets easier. It's hard to put on a good appearance or good attitude when you're hurting, so how are you supposed to put on love (for yourself, for others, for God) when you're at your wit's end?

You put on love just like you put on everything else: You choose it—sometimes each morning and sometimes each moment. It's hard to love yourself when you feel like you're dropping the ball. It's hard to love others if they've played an active or passive part in your pain. It's hard to love God, knowing He could have kept this hurt from you altogether. But each day we do, the choice to wear love becomes a bit easier. I assure you, there is no greater medicine for sorrow, no better antidote to bitterness, no more powerful means of finding moments of joy again, even in your suffering. Choose love today, friend, because eternal love has already chosen you.

What is a small thing you can do to love yourself today, to accept the radical love that God has for you, no matter how you're feeling toward Him?

Day 94

Now we see in a mirror dimly, but then face to face.
Now I know in part; then I shall know fully, even as I
have been fully known.

—1 CORINTHIANS 13:12

One of the hardest parts of following Jesus is trusting Him with the parts of your story that you can't see. Trusting Him when your heart and mind feel tied up in knots that you don't know how to untangle. Trusting Him when it seems like no good could possibly come from the brokenness you're walking through. But keep your eyes open! Because you are indwelt by His discerning Holy Spirit, you will see glimpses of the Lord and His work in you as you faithfully endure this season of trial. But even when you do see God work miracles and answer prayers on your behalf, you are getting only dim glimpses of the glory that He has ultimately prepared for you.

Here on earth, you can never comprehend the full scope of His grand purpose for your life. You will never witness the endless ways that God protects you and directs you as you struggle to live well and maintain faith in Him. But cling to the goodness that you do see in this dim earthly mirror, and hold fast to the promise of the glorious things to come. Because the more you trust the Lord with what you can't see, the greater your anticipation and joy will be as you await the time when you'll be home with Christ to experience it all in full.

Holy Spirit, give me eyes to see the small goodnesses You're working throughout my day today. And teach me holy anticipation, how to excitedly imagine a day in Your presence with no pain or mourning or crying.

Day 95

> As you received Christ Jesus the Lord, so walk in him,
> rooted and built up in him and established in the faith,
> just as you were taught, abounding in thanksgiving.
>
> —COLOSSIANS 2:6–7

Sometimes when everything around you is falling apart, life can feel like a gamble at best and a dumpster fire at worst. Like the world truly is going to hell in a handbasket, as some say. *Is there anyone left for me to rely on? Is there any stable ground on which to stand?* The answer is Christ. If you've known Jesus for years, remember the love you had at first. Remember who wooed your heart and captivated your soul. If you're new to faith, what is drawing you to Christ now? It's probably not specific biblical principles or a pastor or even a faithful friend that's given you hope. It's the ravishing, self-sacrificing, adoring person of Jesus.

There is no safer place than drawing close to Jesus, whether He's a lifelong friend or a new one. Even though I'd believed in Jesus and talked to Him since childhood, I'd never known Him as intimately or relied on Him so constantly as I have since I was widowed. I started to relate to Him not just as the Savior who defeated death but as my leader, friend, and Lord who was with me and at work in everything I faced. If there is nothing in your world right now to trust in, look to the unmatchable gift of the security that comes from Christ in you. Walk close with Him today, confident and loved.

Meditate on the truth that Jesus chose to die and rise again for you. You are so incredibly loved and protected by the King of the universe.

> To him who is able to do far more abundantly than all
> that we ask or think, according to the power at work
> within us, to him be glory in the church and in Christ
> Jesus throughout all generations, forever and ever. Amen.
>
> —EPHESIANS 3:20–21

This is a powerful prayer to claim. This is an absolute truth about the sovereign capabilities of Christ, who is with you and for you. Claim it in prayer! Recite God's own declarations of Himself and His power back to Him, friend, and know that those words from His Word have power. Often times we turn to this passage when we have tangible requests: *Heal my sickness; fix my finances; stop this pain.* Our Lord is able to answer those prayers, according to His will.

But remember to pray not just for your difficult circumstances but also for Christ to change the condition of your heart. God is able to do far more abundant work in your soul than you can ask or imagine. Sometimes the greatest miracle the world can witness is a hurting heart empowered to love God, trust Him, praise Him, and proclaim His goodness even when He doesn't change your circumstances. Call out to Christ to change both your situation and your heart while you're in this valley. He is able.

Consider your heart and the work God might already be doing there. Pray that He would heal your heart as much as you pray that He would heal your situation.

Day 97

> For the moment all discipline seems painful rather than
> pleasant, but later it yields the peaceful fruit of
> righteousness to those who have been trained by it.
>
> —HEBREWS 12:11

Discipline doesn't always mean punishment. If you've ever started a new workout plan, made New Year's resolutions, or worked toward meeting a deadline, you know that. Discipline is an ongoing commitment to make changes or build habits we don't enjoy to achieve results we desire. As strange as it may sound, what results do you desire as you continue through this valley? Really think about it.

Of course, our struggles here on earth are rich opportunities for spiritual discipline, the fruit of the Spirit. But how else do you want to be transformed as you move toward healing? Do you want to be more financially capable? Seek a wise adviser. Do you want greater control over crippling mental health? Seek counseling. Are you a generally pessimistic person who wants to live more hopefully? Start a gratitude journal, and say thank you to someone every day. Do you want to repair a broken relationship? Start with one kind text.

The Lord loves you too much to let your pain be wasted. These days are full of potential for spiritual and practical development if you embrace the discipline required to grow.

> What is one practical way you want to grow through this
> valley season? Commit to pray for it regularly.

Thomas (also known as Didymus), one of the Twelve, was not with the disciples when Jesus came. So the other disciples told him, "We have seen the Lord!"

But he said to them, "Unless I see the nail marks in his hands and put my finger where the nails were, and put my hand into his side, I will not believe."

—JOHN 20:24–25, NIV

When Jesus promised the disciples, "I am with you always, to the end of the age" (Matthew 28:20), it was true for them and it's true for you now and always. The power of the Holy Spirit, which spoke the universe into existence and raised Jesus from the dead, will never depart from you. Even still, God's presence can be very difficult to feel. None of our five senses are acute enough to discern His presence in every moment.

When you struggle to feel God, ask Him for what you need as Thomas did. Jesus was asking him to believe in His resurrection—something only divinely possible. Thomas needed to put his hands on Christ's hands and in His side in order to believe Jesus really was the risen Messiah. Jesus didn't shame him but met his doubt with reassurance. He will do the same for you. Don't be ashamed to ask God to more clearly reveal Himself to you. The Holy Spirit can give both spiritual and tangible reminders that He is always with you.

If you're struggling to feel God's presence or are desperate to hear His comfort or direction, ask for clear, personal impressions from the Holy Spirit to reassure you.

Day 99

Have I not commanded you? Be strong and courageous.
Do not be frightened, and do not be dismayed, for the
LORD your God is with you wherever you go.

—JOSHUA 1:9

God gave this command to Joshua as he prepared to lead the Israelites in a series of grueling battles. This charge may seem like a tall order, but God was calling Joshua to tap into divine strength, not his own. Ahead of him was a long, long line of savage enemies, and once Joshua defeated one, another would file in and take its shot at the Israelites. But Joshua stood strong, kept finding strength and hope in God, and was successful *because the Lord was with him everywhere he went.* He prevailed against each enemy because God Himself prevails over evil.

So it is with you as you suffer. Hardship and loss evoke all kinds of mental and spiritual enemies that line up to assault you in your weakness and fear. You may be so un-strong and un-courageous that you're simply trying to put one foot in front of the other. Sometimes that is the bravest thing to do. Sometimes strength looks less like running and more like getting back up when you fall. Sometimes courage looks like taking the next blind step forward when you can't see where you're headed. Like Joshua, your survival and success depend strictly on how connected and surrendered you stay to God's power and God's plan. Do not fear or be dismayed. Keep your eyes on God, not on your enemies.

*Lord, every time I get fixated on the enemies ahead of me,
draw my eyes back to You and Your perfect faithfulness to me
as I navigate this day.*

The sunrise shall visit us from on high
to give light to those who sit in darkness
and in the shadow of death,
to guide our feet into the way of peace.

—LUKE 1:78–79

Scripture uses darkness to refer to anything or anyplace danger-ously lacking God's presence—the sin-stained world, the workings of evil, or individuals who are spiritually lost. And even those who know God and walk in His light still operate daily in the middle of a world cloaked in darkness. Things break, plans fail, and hearts crum-ble under the weight of universal suffering.

But the great gift of the good news is that though you must live in a world of darkness, God's light is always shining in it. Light is always stronger than the dark. The Holy Spirit shines within you, showing you the way. Christ is the sun, moon, and stars in a grim and direc-tionless world, and when you fix your eyes on Him, He will guide you with supernatural light and peace. When it's darkest outside, when all around you is black, that is the precise time when the stars are the brightest and most beautiful. Keep fixing your eyes on the light, and the Lord will guide you into the way of peace.

In simple, honest words, thank God today that in your dark season He enables you to see His light, His love, and His supernatural peace all the more intensely.

Day 101

You formed my inward parts;
    you knitted me together in my mother's womb.
I praise you, for I am fearfully and wonderfully made.
Wonderful are your works;
    my soul knows it very well.

—PSALM 139:13–14

When things are going smoothly in life, it feels easier to stay sturdy in our faith and our relationships. But when hardship comes and we feel the weight of mental and emotional pressure, our deficits start to take center stage. Our default sins, fears, and weaknesses are exposed. We become impatient, irritable. Maybe we start projecting our own disappointments or shame unfairly onto those around us? Maybe we seek comfort in destructive places?

It takes courage and wisdom to identify these struggles and then address them. As best you can, bring them to light through talking with the Lord and with trusted brothers and sisters in faith who encourage you, not shame you. But don't despair or be discouraged; don't be surprised those struggles are there. Don't try to hide these flaws from God or others, and please, oh please, don't ever believe your Father is disappointed in you. He doesn't make mistakes. You are fearfully and wonderfully made. God knew your flaws and struggles before you did, and He's here to set you free from them.

Confess the sins or struggles that have come to light recently. Thank God for the forgiveness that He already has extended to you, and leave the guilt behind.

I am like a green olive tree
    in the house of God.
I trust in the steadfast love of God
    forever and ever.

—PSALM 52:8

The olive tree held significant symbolism to David, the author of the psalm above. The olive tree was a sign of vitality and fruitfulness in ancient Israel.[8] Olives were essential to Israel's agriculture and economy, and they even carried medicinal properties. Olive trees meant prosperity, health, and security. And like you have, David experienced all those blessings during certain seasons of his life.

But he also experienced seasons of struggle, lack, and waiting on the Lord. Like the olive tree, which grows in dry, warm, often-barren conditions, David was fruitful not in spite of his seasons of hardship but *because* of them. His ascension to the throne wasn't easy or quick; it was the result of years of wandering and trusting God in the wilderness. With an average lifespan of five hundred years, olive trees are trees of patient endurance. You, too, are an olive tree in God's house. You, too, endure drought and long seasons of waiting, but because of that, you are also a picture of vitality and fruitfulness in the kingdom. Hang in there, little olive tree. You will bear much fruit.

Lord, like David and the ancient olive trees, help me hold on. Let me trust the slow and taxing process of being sanctified through suffering, trusting You fully even as I wait.

Day 103 WAIL

My joy is gone; grief is upon me;
  my heart is sick within me.

—JEREMIAH 8:18

These words were spoken by one of Scripture's most faithful prophets. This cry of true lament isn't a sign of Jeremiah's lack of faithfulness. Exactly the opposite: This heartbroken cry of despair came from the prophet's godly desire for the abundant life that he knew was accessible to God's people. Jeremiah knew the life-changing joy of walking obediently with the Lord, and he was grieved for what was broken and twisted in the world around him.

From the beginning in Genesis, we learn we were made for Eden—perfect, loving unity with God and with one another. But we live in a sinful world, marked with chaos, darkness, and brokenness. Our good God has placed in us a desire for goodness, so it's right to grieve what is wrong. It's an expression of faith to proclaim, "This broken world isn't enough! It's not fair!" It honors God when you express that He's made you for more. Don't hide your heartbreak from God. Bring it to Him, loudly, painfully, and in full. He is the one who made you to desire uninhibited fellowship with Him. He joins you in your lament. Grieve and draw near to your Father.

Take some time today to release your anger, fear, or disappointment aloud to God. Imagine Him placing an arm around your shoulder and agreeing with you in your lament.

Day 104

You hem me in, behind and before,
    and lay your hand upon me.
Such knowledge is too wonderful for me;
    it is high; I cannot attain it.

—PSALM 139:5–6

Though you are stuck in a single moment in time, your heavenly Father is beyond time. Though you can face only what is immediately before you, He holds your past, present, and future in His mighty hands. It's natural to wish for the past and worry over the future. Our finite minds long to see the whole scope of God's plans at once. However, peace comes only when you keep your feet rooted in today. Leave what has been and what's to come to Christ, and be present in whatever today has for you.

The Lord hems you in—encircles and protects you. He is the shield at your back and the light at your feet. Your past sins and failures are forgotten, and your future unknowns have been known to God since the foundation of the universe. He is so close to you. He dwells within you. His Spirit surrounds you like a spiritual bodyguard. Stand firm, knowing that Christ stands with you and for you every day. Like a weighted blanket, let His peace lie gently over you. Let Him quiet your worries and soften your stress. He is behind and before you. You need only to be still.

Lord, help me accept the past as past and entrust the future to You. Let the power of Your Spirit surround me and fill me with peace that transcends understanding.

Day 105 WORSHIP

Offer to God a sacrifice of thanksgiving,
    and perform your vows to the Most High,
and call upon me in the day of trouble;
    I will deliver you, and you shall glorify me.

—PSALM 50:14–15

One of the most profound lessons of my valley journey is that joy and pain are not mutually exclusive. It has become the refrain of my life in many ways. But this truth didn't come easily. My first wedding anniversary came a mere three weeks after Ben's death. The torrent of emotions is unexplainable. But as I clutched the bouquet of paper flowers he'd left me, watched our wedding video, and wailed with tears, I felt this life-changing truth in a visceral way. I was devastated and broken, yet the joy I felt, seeing his face and knowing how deeply I'd forever cherish that day, was supernatural. I was heartbroken and I was thankful, in so many tiny ways.

What do I have to be joyful about right now? you might wonder. It may not be big, like a wedding day. It may be that friend who dropped everything to come help you, the sunshine and soft breeze that made you feel alive again for a moment, the song you hadn't heard in decades that brought back a memory and a smile. These small things are results of God's enormous grace. He is always working to sow peace and hope in your heart, especially as you struggle. Recognize these gifts of grace and thank God for them! From gratitude rise little waves of joy that will bless you even in the midst of pain.

Write down or say out loud three specific things you are thankful for this week.

Hannah answered and said, "No, my lord, I am a woman despairing in spirit; I have drunk neither wine nor strong drink, but I have poured out my soul before the LORD."

—I SAMUEL 1:15, NASB

How many times have you said to someone, "I tried, but I just couldn't hold it together"? Or "It was awful; I totally broke down"? I don't know when our culture started characterizing vocal, tearful expression of our emotions as weak or inappropriate, but that's not the message we get from Scripture. Hannah was in such visceral despair over her barrenness that she had to reassure the priest she was not drunk but grieving. She was pouring everything she had out before the God she trusted.

The way you will survive this is to remove the filter. Lament, cry, scream out because you are broken and mortal life isn't fair. Of course, we need to know our context and try as best as possible to be in safe places with safe people when we let ourselves be this vulnerable. But to shame yourself for losing it or breaking down is only robbing you of a deeper level of processing and healing. Hannah mourned. Jesus wept (John 11:35). You can too.

Repeat this with me today: "I have honest feelings where I want to throw my hands up in utter frustration and yell about the unfairness of it all. To deny my feelings any voice is to rob me of being human."9

In the beginning was the Word, and the Word was with
God, and the Word was God.

—JOHN 1:1

There is a centuries-old question in the church: "What is your only
comfort in life and in death?" The answer begins this way: "That I,
with body and soul, both in life and in death, am not my own, but
belong to my faithful Savior Jesus Christ."[10] This answer comes
directly from Scripture: In John 10:28, Jesus said, "I give them eternal life, and they will never perish, and no one will snatch them out
of my hand." And in 1 Corinthians 6:19–20, Paul wrote, "You are
not your own, for you were bought with a price." As simple and
unremarkable as it sounds, God's Word is where every assurance we
need can be found.

It's been said, "A Bible that's falling apart usually belongs to someone who isn't." This simple statement cuts to the heart of how faithful people endure lives marked by hardship. It gives an antidote for
the plagues of this life and a prescription for those who don't know
where to turn or what else to do. We learn the assurances and promises of our Savior in His Word. The Word will be your lifeline until
you go home to the Lord. Seek it. Devour it. Rely fully on it, and you
will find victory.

Spend ten minutes today reading the Bible or meditating on
one verse. Psalms offers a tender place for grieving hearts if
you don't know where to start.

> With the Lord one day is as a thousand years, and a thousand years as one day. The Lord is not slow to fulfill his promise as some count slowness, but is patient toward you.
>
> —2 PETER 3:8–9

This won't last forever. When another day feels unbearable, remember that Christ sees all your tomorrows and has a perfect plan for your ultimate flourishing.

God's patience extends to us even as we are impatient with Him. What feels agonizingly slow in coming—reprieve from the painful hardships you're facing—is actually coming at the right pace. And in the seasons of suffering that feel unending, know that God is there through all of it. He isn't holding out on you! He is working and sowing great beauty in you as you wait on Him. Just as it takes time to cultivate a flourishing garden, so God's redeeming work in your heart also takes time.

He is patient with us, so let's be patient with Him. Actively wait on the Lord and trust that though you feel stuck right now, this difficult season will yield some of your greatest spiritual treasure, both in heaven and on earth. Believing this when your heart is broken is a glorious act of worship because long-suffering and faithful endurance show the world that we are His no matter what.

What are you waiting for? Surrender the timing to the Lord in prayer, and praise Him that He is working for your good even now as you wait.

Day 109

> I consider that the sufferings of this present time are not
> worth comparing with the glory that is to be revealed
> to us.
>
> —ROMANS 8:18

Does Paul's statement leave you hopeful or angry? Does it feel at all realistic? Your suffering is so overwhelmingly present while the glory and eternal goodness that await you in heaven are so far away. But if you could fathom the grandeur of what is waiting for you, every devastation here would feel like a momentary detour on the way to eternal elation coming magnificently true. I know you can't understand the majesty of your heavenly reward, nor can I, but we can thank God for it. We can still long for it with assurance and anticipation when our suffering feels too much to bear. We can reorient our eyes to the joyous finish line.

But God never asks you to dismiss your hardship. He knows your suffering is heavy. Don't shame yourself for the toll it takes on you and the sadness it brings. Remember, it's not worth comparing, but it is worthy of carrying because of your love for what you've lost. Your hurt is worthy, but God has so much more goodness in store for you.

Holy Spirit, help me imagine the grandeur and intoxicating love that await me in Your uninhibited presence. Let that revelation relieve some of the heaviness of today's reality.

Day 110

Behold, the winter is past;
    the rain is over and gone.
The flowers appear on the earth,
    the time of singing has come,
and the voice of the turtledove
    is heard in our land.

—SONG OF SOLOMON 2:11–12

I've grown to love the coming of springtime. It often seems to come and go quickly, but after several long months of cold winter rain, the first signs of trees turning green and sleeping flowers blooming again take my breath away. I think this is in part because grief forced me to slow down, to really witness the earth's changes happen from season to season. But I think this appreciation came even more from my desperate need to see hope outside my own dormant story.

If it's hard to imagine beauty or new life in the months and years ahead, look to God's creation. If you're struggling to read His Word these days, look to the works of His hand. Look to the seasons. Every year, winter comes, but it's always followed by spring, when flowers bloom and the sun returns and the Lord's power brings life to earth once again. Let the seasons be your beacon of hope and a physical assurance to you that your God is not only powerful but also so very faithful. And if so faithful to the creation, even more mercifully faithful to you.

Think about the elements in nature that you love the most; think about your favorite memories in nature. If you can, spend some time today outside.

Day 111

> Teach us to number our days
> that we may get a heart of wisdom.
>
> —PSALM 90:12

What if godly wisdom is simply prioritizing the things that God prioritizes? Like the fruit of His Spirit. The people He tells you to love and serve. The practices He calls you to that may be inconvenient or mocked by culture. Pursue these things, and I believe wisdom will follow.

We've talked about the slowness of grief. Let this time of loss give you space to reassess and rearrange your priorities, to number your days and arrange your hours around the things of God that build wisdom in you. Of course, time with the Lord and His Word. But also, could you allot a little more time for rest? Jesus regularly took time away to reset. Could you plan to share one meal a week with friends or family? Jesus was often around abundant tables. Could you move your body a bit more? Jesus was always walking. Right now, as you look with tears on your life, you are learning to number your days. What do you want your precious days left to look like? Pursue what God prioritizes, friend, and you will gain a heart of great wisdom.

What's one thing God is calling you to prioritize? Set aside some time today to make a start on it.

His anger is but for a moment,
    and his favor is for a lifetime.
Weeping may tarry for the night,
    but joy comes with the morning.

—PSALM 30:5

The Lord isn't angry with you. Your loss and pain have come from living in a broken, imperfect world—not because you are being punished. Hear this truth with hopeful ears, my friend. Because of the life and work of Jesus, all God feels when He looks at you is delight. His momentary anger is instead aimed at this world permeated by sin since the Fall. Our Father rages against the sins that hurt you, even if those sins are your own, but His wrath will never touch you.

Like many, I felt angry with myself at times. I battled recurring pangs of regret after Ben's death. The slideshow of ways I could have stopped it played over and over in my mind. I beat myself up for months over the argument we had just a few hours before his fall. I blamed myself for choosing to stop at the restaurant where it all happened. Accidents happen every day, and people make sinful choices that hurt others, themselves, or both. But rest assured, God holds nothing against you. His supernatural joy, comfort, and peace are all He wants to offer you, beloved. Release your regrets. Draw close to Christ as you mourn. I promise you, His favor is unending.

Thank God that you are never the object of His wrath or disappointment. Praise Him that even though you weep in the night, joy will come. His favor is for a lifetime.

Day 113

> Let your light shine before others, so that they may see
> your good works and give glory to your Father who is in
> heaven.

> —MATTHEW 5:16

Jesus is calling all of us to shine our light in the world around us. This means sharing the gospel, telling of God's goodness, praising Him publicly, and proclaiming Jesus' redemptive work in your life.

But being a light also means sharing your darkness. Most people walk around with lots more darkness inside than you can see. No life is without struggle, and everyone around you is carrying secret heartbreaks, fears, addictions, or regrets that they work hard to conceal for fear of rejection. But isolation and shame aren't part of God's kingdom. That's not how He calls His body to operate. Be honest with others about your pain and darkness, and as you are, you give others permission to be honest about their struggles too. And from that place of vulnerability, a deeper connection and a truer love for one another will grow. It's such a tragedy that so many people think they're the only one who feels rejected, wounded, and alone. Let others know they're not the only one.

Lord, give me the courage to share my struggles honestly. May my vulnerability build stronger connections with others.

Day 114

> God gave us a spirit not of fear but of power and love and self-control.
>
> — 2 TIMOTHY 1:7

I know you feel weary and afraid. I know the pain is so big, so consuming, that it's hard to imagine feeling strong again. But the things you're feeling are just that—feelings. The fear, doubt, and anxiety are temporary, and though completely real and warranted in light of what you're going through, these feelings aren't your master. You aren't a slave to fear, dread, and hopelessness. These emotions don't have to control you.

Even when you have every reason to feel worried or afraid, remember, you have been purchased with Christ's blood and *set free*. You are now indwelt by His conquering, almighty Holy Spirit, the same Spirit who brings dead people to life. When you feel the most defeated, speak aloud and claim what is yours as God's child—power, love, and self-control. It's *Jesus'* power that resides in you, and it's at your very weakest that you can experience His strength most palpably. Don't succumb to feelings of fear, beloved. Rather, acknowledge them honestly, and then lay them at the foot of the cross.

What's bringing you the most fear and anxiety today? Be specific. Speak these things aloud, and ask the Holy Spirit to clear them from your mind as you surrender the outcome to Christ.

Be kind to one another, tenderhearted, forgiving one
another, as God in Christ forgave you.

—EPHESIANS 4:32

It's in suffering that this instruction, rooted in the command to love your neighbor as yourself (Mark 12:31), seems most difficult. When your wells of energy and focus feel constantly drained, it's hard to live from a place of compassion. But as with everything you face, the Lord brings profound beauty from ashes (Isaiah 61:3).

One of the fruits that come from seasons of suffering is increased compassion. Your pain gives you better context for the pain that others carry. Your capacity for patience, grace, and simple kindness toward others probably feels very low right now. Because of that, you're going to get it wrong. You're going to snap at your kids. You're going to feel hard toward people trying to help you. Forgive yourself. I know it's difficult, but pray for increased humility as you struggle to be tender toward others. One of the ways God is actively redeeming you right now is by using your hardship to foster humility. With time, prayer, and perseverance, you will begin to live with a greater sense of compassion for outsiders and patience for those in your inner circle.

Ask the Lord to reveal who you're taking your weariness out on, and then pray that He'll enable you to engage with them with greater patience and compassion this week.

Come, everyone who thirsts,
　　come to the waters;
and he who has no money,
　　come, buy and eat!
Come, buy wine and milk
　　without money and without price.
Why do you spend your money for that which is not bread,
　　and your labor for that which does not satisfy?

—ISAIAH 55:1–2

Right now, you are mentally and emotionally starving. Your world has been upended, and you feel empty. Run to the Living Water, the Bread of Life! Like someone physically starving, run to the one place that has sustenance to fill you back up and strengthen you. Don't reach for spiritual junk food or worldly fixes that, like sugar, will only give you the illusion of being full but inevitably leave you still hungry.

Hear me when I say, distractions and small things that bring you joy are wonderful! Eat a nice meal; watch something that makes you laugh; spend time with people who make you feel like yourself again. But be careful that you're not overconsuming or expecting these things to fix you. They are wonderful, temporary comforts. But Jesus is the Bread of Life, the Living Water. Let those enjoyable distractions be only an addition to true, daily dependence on Christ. Let the Lord fill your emptiness and all else be the cherry on top.

Ask the Lord to bring to light any spiritual or mental junk food you're grabbing for to heal what only He can heal. Repent, and praise Him that He freely and generously gives us all we need.

Day 117

I loathe my life;
I will give free utterance to my complaint;
   I will speak in the bitterness of my soul.
I will say to God, Do not condemn me;
   let me know why you contend against me.

—JOB 10:1–2

These honest words were spoken by the same man who was described as "blameless and upright, one who feared God and turned away from evil" (Job 1:1). These words are the lament of Job, a man who lived with such reverence for and faith in God's almighty power that he wasn't afraid to tell Him how disappointed he was with the suffering in his life. Job lost his wealth and all ten of his children and suffered great physical agony in essentially one fell swoop. Yet in his prayer of lament over his catastrophic losses, Job never cursed God but pleaded desperately for answers and for deliverance from the pain.

The Lord isn't scared of your doubts or questions. He isn't disappointed with you even when you're disappointed with Him. His answer to your prayers is sometimes "No" or "Not now," and even under His sovereign will, you will still suffer pain in this broken world. Don't hide your anger from the Lord. He, too, hates that you have to hurt. He weeps over your tears (John 11:35).

Bring your pain—with as much honesty as you can manage—to Jesus, knowing with divine assurance that nothing you can say or do will ever change the radical love He has for you.

Day 118

From his fullness we have all received, grace upon grace.

—JOHN 1:16

Some of the pain we suffer in life is the consequence of poor choices, but often pain comes through no fault of our own. The truth is, much of the pain that afflicts us isn't fair.

But the free gift of unconditional grace Christ gives us isn't fair either. We can do nothing to earn it, and Jesus gave up everything He earned so we could have His love and complete forgiveness for eternity. We should be jumping and shouting with praise that God operates not from a place of fairness but from a place of fatherly mercy. As much as we'd like there to be, there isn't a one-to-one ratio of our good works to God's blessings. Everyone in this life will suffer, fairly and unfairly. And on days when you're tempted toward bitterness at the unfairness of your pain, remember, too, how radically, generously unfair God's redeeming grace is. What God allows may not feel fair, but He is always good and gracious.

Remind me, Lord, as I groan at injustice in my life, that Your radical grace is also not fair. Let the truth of all You've given me soften the reality of this difficult thing You're asking me to carry.

Day 119

> God, who said, "Let light shine out of darkness," has shone in our hearts to give the light of the knowledge of the glory of God in the face of Jesus Christ.
>
> —2 CORINTHIANS 4:6

The glimmer of a candle or dancing flames of a campfire shine most beautifully at night. Though their quality never changes, we can miss in the sunlight what we marvel at in the dark. In our seasons of sunlight, we don't love God any less. But when life is running smoothly and our surroundings are bright, our reliance on Him isn't as obvious. We can forget our fundamental need for His love, grace, and direction.

But in your seasons of darkness, when your circumstances offer hardly any light or direction, Christ becomes your only way through. Only He can reveal His plan for you. When you have nothing, you realize God is all the provision you need. Though dark and painful in the moment, suffering brings the blessing of an intimacy with the Lord that's easy to miss in sunny seasons. His presence will often feel more palpable, more powerful, in the dark seasons of life than on the easy days. Look for Jesus. Cling to Him. Seek out His guiding light and follow Him through the darkness.

Ask the Lord to clearly illuminate the message of hope or nudge of encouragement you need today. Talk to Him throughout the day, and keep your eyes open to see what He's revealing to you.

> Being strengthened with all power, according to his
> glorious might, for all endurance and patience with joy;
> giving thanks to the Father, who has qualified you to
> share in the inheritance of the saints in light.
>
> —COLOSSIANS 1:11–12

The inheritance God has for you as His chosen, adopted child is a glorious one. An eternal feast and family more abundant than you can imagine are waiting for you. This is cause for great celebration and joy! But until then you'll continue to need His strength in order to endure life's hardships and His grace to patiently wait for what Jesus is preparing for you.

I know waiting is hard. Patience is a stubborn muscle to build. You may feel like you're waiting for healing, waiting for answers, waiting for what you've lost to be restored and what you long for to finally arrive. Patience doesn't come easily for us, and endurance can be taxing on your spiritual muscles, but trust me—good things are coming. Christ's healing in your life may seem a slow process, but His timing is never without purpose. Ask Him for the strength and patience to wait on what's next. Ask Him for joy that transcends your circumstances. And rest in hope, knowing He is refining you and readying you for the grand inheritance that awaits.

Lord, remind me that Your best work on my heart is done in the waiting. Pour into me divine strength and patience to endure this waiting season.

Day 121

Our God whom we serve is able to deliver us from the burning fiery furnace, and he will deliver us out of your hand, O king. But if not, be it known to you, O king, that we will not serve your gods or worship the golden image that you have set up.

—DANIEL 3:17–18

Daniel's three friends who boldly proclaimed the words above were standing in front of a blazing oven meant to incinerate them in seconds. And even then, they rejoiced that God *could* save them even when they didn't know if He *would* save them.

It turns out, God did save them from the fiery furnace that day, just as He will save you from certain hardships. But in the seasons of "but if not," resist the urge to turn away from your heavenly Father. Don't believe any of the lies the Enemy and the world will tell you: that God is not in control, not loving, not good, or that He's forsaken you. The times you really do get burned in the fire will be the hardest times to trust God, but we worship Him not because of what He does for us but simply for who He is to us. He is in the flames. The wounds are temporary, but He is always with you. He is still able to hear you, heal you, and redeem your pain.

Praise God today that He is in perfect, loving control of your situation. Ask for the reassurance that His will for your future is for your ultimate good.

Say not, "Why were the former days better than these?"
For it is not from wisdom that you ask this.

—ECCLESIASTES 7:10

The funny thing about remembering is that it can bring either thankfulness or paralysis. I looked back daily on photos and videos and told stories to friends about my favorite times with Ben. Reflecting on those beautiful, now somewhat rose-colored days that Ben and I had together felt like the only way to be close to him, and it was comforting. It's when that reflection becomes a roadblock that there's a problem. Solomon, the wisest man in all of Israel, warned against nostalgic comparison. That isn't wise, he said.

There is no easier time to aggrandize the past than when you're hurting or when you've lost something or someone dear to you. It's natural to look back. Reflecting to honor and appreciate the past is an important part of healing. But don't get stuck there. Don't let the cherishing of a previous season leave you bitter about your current season or unable to move into the next. Look back on the good days with gratitude, not grumbling. Cherish what you've had, but don't idolize it or cling to it foolishly. You can joyfully and tearfully remember the past and also live in and trust God with the present.

Are you clinging too tightly to the past? Grieve what you've lost as much as you need to, and visualize giving the past to God as a safe way of practicing letting go.

The thief comes only to steal and kill and destroy. I came
that they may have life and have it abundantly.

—JOHN 10:10

Many think this abundance refers only to measurable, earthly
things—health, wealth, success. And the Lord certainly does sometimes bless His children in those ways. But abundance in God's kingdom always flows from the internal to the external, from the spirit to
the circumstances.

An abundance of joy, peace, love, and hope comes by way of walking with the Holy Spirit, no matter what trial or loss you may be
facing. That's why Jesus taught, "Blessed are the poor in spirit, for
theirs is the kingdom of heaven. Blessed are those who mourn, for
they shall be comforted. Blessed are the meek, for they shall inherit
the earth. Blessed are those who hunger and thirst for righteousness,
for they shall be satisfied" (Matthew 5:3–6).

Even when earthly abundance is lost, don't let the Enemy steal the
spiritual abundance that is yours today and for eternity. Claim it
boldly, knowing that Jesus came, lived, and died so that you can have
a life rooted in abundant, inexhaustible hope.

Though you are meek, mourning, and poor in spirit, what are
one or two sources of abundance you can identify in your life
today?

Day 124

The LORD passed before him and proclaimed, "The LORD, the LORD, a God merciful and gracious, slow to anger, and abounding in steadfast love and faithfulness. . . ." And Moses quickly bowed his head toward the earth and worshiped.

—EXODUS 34:6, 8

This moment, hearing God introduce Himself, was undoubtedly one of the watershed experiences of Moses's life. He was anxious, excited, ready to lead his people forward and partner with God in work that would change the whole course of human history. He could have jumped and run out ahead of God. He could have tried to take this day into his own hands. But what did he do? He paused. He listened to the Lord's voice. He bowed. He worshipped.

I'm not sure I would have followed Moses's lead here. My impulse is to hurry to fix things. Waiting hurts, and action almost always feels better than sitting still. Especially in the early days of grief, I wanted a game plan. I actually asked my therapist for the best steps to heal as quickly as possible. But the first step is always to follow God's lead. Just as the Lord passed before Moses, so is He always going before you and reminding you who He truly is. Learn from Moses, and follow God even when you want to race ahead of His plans. The Lord is with you. He is powerful; He is steadfast and faithful.

Lord, reveal to me the plans and decisions I'm making that don't align with Your will for me. Give me the discernment and discipline to bring every choice before You and listen for Your voice.

> Let us consider how to stir up one another to love and good works, not neglecting to meet together, as is the habit of some, but encouraging one another, and all the more as you see the Day drawing near.
>
> —HEBREWS 10:24–25

I knew the danger of isolation. And though I began trying to rely on close, safe community, other unexpected or unwelcome interactions felt very overwhelming. I ignored text messages; I made up excuses to get out of things; I bolted down grocery store aisles to avoid an acquaintance. Besides my closest people, I didn't want to be around others when I didn't look my best and certainly didn't feel my best. But even more than that, I was afraid of telling the story all over again. I didn't want another pitying "I heard" or "I'm so sorry." I bet you've experienced this too.

It's hard to believe that people will ever see you just for you again rather than the thing that happened to you. It's hard to be around others whose lives may look cleaner, happier, or more blessed than yours. I didn't do this well at first, but I encourage you to ask God for the courage to step back into those day-to-day places. Call on your inner circle of safe people to run errands with you or go to an event with you when you feel fragile and overwhelmed. They can stir you up and support you as you take small steps back into life.

What's one thing you're longing to avoid this week that a dear friend could come to support you in?

And one of the elders said to me, "Weep no more; behold, the Lion of the tribe of Judah, the Root of David, has conquered, so that he can open the scroll and its seven seals."

—REVELATION 5:5

The next day he saw Jesus coming toward him, and said, "Behold, the Lamb of God, who takes away the sin of the world!"

—JOHN 1:29

Scripture says Jesus is both the Lion of Judah and the Lamb of God. But these are more than metaphors or simple teaching imagery. The strength of the Lion and the tenderness of the Lamb are supernatural pools of power to which you have full access at all times.

I felt the Lion's strength when finally cleaning out Ben's closet and car. I felt Him give me courage as I learned how to wail and lament, something I'd never done well before. He equipped me to face hard things in counseling and eventually to feel just enough confidence to date again.

I felt the Lamb's tenderness for me as I learned to forgive myself when I didn't grieve well. I sensed His mercy as I struggled with how to honor Ben's legacy and make a new one for my life. I was flooded with His grace as I reluctantly surrendered the things I couldn't control.

Christ is everything you need, in every moment. He has strength you could never muster and peace that defies logic in overwhelming moments. He, the Lion and the Lamb, is enough for you.

Thank You, Jesus, that You are my strength and my comforter. Give me strength for _____ and supernatural peace concerning _____ today, Lord.

> Elisha prayed and said, "O LORD, please open his eyes
> that he may see." So the LORD opened the eyes of the
> young man, and he saw, and behold, the mountain was
> full of horses and chariots of fire all around Elisha.
>
> —2 KINGS 6:17

When Elisha, God's prophet to the king of Israel, spoke these words, he and his young servant for whom he prayed were surrounded by a fierce Syrian army. They were surrounded by thousands of men, horses, and chariots, and the young man was rightly afraid. But Elisha, in his rich spiritual wisdom, saw a reality his servant couldn't see. The servant saw the physical army. Elisha saw the spiritual—God's army of angels who were ready to fight on their behalf.

This miraculous Old Testament story may seem unreal to you, like that doesn't happen for you and me today. But Scripture repeats to us that the spiritual world we can't see is real. That evil and holy beings are at war to draw us either from God or to God. We are all the young servant, rightly terrified by what we see. And what we see is real. But the Lord's army of angels and the power of the risen Christ are just as real. And they fight for your mind, your heart, and your hope just as they fought the army threatening Elisha.

Whatever physical reality you feel overwhelmed by today, remind yourself that the Lord is fighting in the spiritual realm for your mental and spiritual well-being.

As for man, his days are like grass;
  he flourishes like a flower of the field;
for the wind passes over it, and it is gone. . . .
But the steadfast love of the LORD is from everlasting to everlasting on those who fear him.

—PSALM 103:15–17

There are two ways we can read the verses above. We can read them without hope, accepting that our days here are brief and questioning whether anything really matters. Or we can read them with the radical, perspective-changing hope they offer: Our days here are brief in comparison with the eternal joy, love, and celebration that Jesus has secured for us.

If you could see the whole scope of your life—both earthly and eternal—from where Jesus sits, I bet you would sit back and rest. I bet you could understand and live out of the unshakable truth that who you are, your ultimate identity, isn't found in what you experience or what you have today; it's only in who God has made you to be and what He's prepared for you in heaven. Your current suffering is just one chapter in the complete life story the Lord has written for you. They are painful lines, lines that you wish weren't included at all, but in the grand scheme of what's in store, they will pass quickly, friend. While what you're going through is real, it's not your final reality. Hang in there. It will get better. Trust me.

Lord, help me view my pain and fears with an eternal perspective. Let the Holy Spirit remind me that every hardship is temporary and every wound will eventually be healed.

I am sure that neither death nor life, nor angels nor
rulers, nor things present nor things to come, nor powers,
nor height nor depth, nor anything else in all creation,
will be able to separate us from the love of God in Christ
Jesus our Lord.

—ROMANS 8:38–39

When you're in Christ, nothing in all creation can ever separate
you or keep you from His powerful love. Sometimes you'll feel closer
to Him than at other times, and sometimes you'll make choices that
may cloud your ability to discern the Holy Spirit. But you can never
be cut off from God. His love for you is flawless, indestructible,
everlasting—not because you're perfect but because He is.

I'm especially thankful that Paul emphasizes there is nothing in all
creation that can separate us from God. His list is exhaustive. Thus
we can know that neither loss nor lack, nor exhaustion nor fear, nor
depression nor anxiety, nor addiction, nor shame nor regret, nor
grief, nor any other suffering that may befall you, can pull you from
the Father's loving arms when you're in Christ Jesus. In fact, it's trials
that often push you more fervently toward Him and allow you to
experience His everlasting love in even richer ways. You're always safe
and secure with Jesus. He is the one you will never ever lose.

*I praise You, Jesus, that Your hold on me and love for me are
forever and unbreakable!*

> I sought the LORD, and he answered me
> and delivered me from all my fears.
>
> —PSALM 34:4

I know well the power of praying over the details. Don't be afraid to spell out specifically to the Lord what's on your heart or what you need deliverance from. Don't overgeneralize or dilute your desperation for the Lord's help as you come to Him in prayer. Keep claiming healing because you know He is abundantly able to do exactly as you ask and more (Ephesians 3:20). When you seek Him, He will always answer in His way and in His timing.

In the meantime, don't get hung up on what your picture of deliverance looks like. After God delivered the Israelites out of slavery in Egypt, they wandered in the desert for forty years before reaching the promised land. But that season was an incredibly significant time for Israel in learning who God is and who they were as His children. Deliverance from your problems rarely looks like removing the problems. Rather, deliverance often looks like releasing you from the grip of trauma and restoring you to the possibility of new life after it.

Call out for the exact deliverance and resolution you desire from God. Then surrender that desire to Him, trusting that He's working on your heart as He's working on your situation.

Return, O LORD! How long?
　　Have pity on your servants!
Satisfy us in the morning with your steadfast love,
　　that we may rejoice and be glad all our days.

　　　　　　　　　　　　　　　—PSALM 90:13–14

I believe God's heart aches with yours as you ask, "How long? How long?" He knows you want answers. He knows you're longing for relief. And it will come, friend. I wish you could see your story the way God does: redeemed and complete, with all the dark chapters ushering in even greater light in the ones to follow. All of Scripture promises us a better day is coming. And we should cling to that eternal reality. But the here-on-earth reality is that sometimes we have to take a much longer, more winding road than we'd like to get to that day.

Suffering is something no human will escape, but this life can be more than just a grind toward eternity. As you wonder when this journey through the valley will end, call out to God to give you supernatural capacity for joy and hope right in the middle of your suffering. Remember, in the persevering and the waiting, the Holy Spirit is more than enough to sustain you. Come to Him each morning because His mercies, His power, and His grace are new every day. God knows exactly how much strength, faith, and hope you need in these twenty-four hours, and He is faithful to give it.

Name and lament all you're waiting for or lacking right now. Then ask the Holy Spirit to infuse your grief with supernatural patience and trust even though you don't know how long you'll be in the valley.

All the words of my mouth are righteous;
   there is nothing twisted or crooked in them.
Take my instruction instead of silver,
   and knowledge rather than choice gold,
for wisdom is better than jewels,
   and all that you may desire cannot compare with her.

—PROVERBS 8:8, 10–11

In our digital world, we can seek advice and direction from millions of outlets. Some are extremely helpful. Some are faulty. In this time of struggle, confusion, and uncertainty, you are understandably craving guidance as you navigate something that feels utterly new and overwhelming. The Lord didn't design us to experience the good or the bad of this life alone. Keep seeking quality guidance from people equipped to help you in practical ways.

Be mindful, though, of replacing holy discernment with human insight. Through the Holy Spirit, all truth and wisdom have come to live in you! You have access to His guidance every day. Ask for God's wisdom to lead you in choosing who to consult with; listen for His guidance on what advice to pay attention to. Pray after you talk with friends, family, or counselors, and let the Holy Spirit affirm whether what they've offered you is true or not. With Jesus as your guide, your way *will* be straight and sound.

Ask the Holy Spirit to show you who are safe, godly counselors in your life and who are not. Ask Him to open wide any doors that can be helpful to your healing and close any that are not.

Do not be anxious about anything, but in everything by prayer and supplication with thanksgiving let your requests be made known to God. And the peace of God, which surpasses all understanding, will guard your hearts and your minds in Christ Jesus.

—PHILIPPIANS 4:6–7

This sounds lovely on paper, doesn't it? If only we could simply choose to get rid of this anxiety and quiet these worries! You may be diligent in surrendering your problems and your pain to the Lord. You may be coating every part of your broken situation in prayer. Yet the anxiety still persists. "Do not be anxious"? That is so much easier said than done!

But instead of focusing on how to rid yourself of anxiety, focus on handing the anxiety over to Jesus. Visualize doing this. Communication with Christ through prayer is your primary means for fighting anxiety, but consider adding another holy weapon to the mix. Continue in prayer and supplication to God at all times, but don't forget the power of thanksgiving. Intentional gratitude is one of the most powerful antidotes to anxiety. Write down or speak aloud everything, large or small, that you're grateful for throughout your day, and thank God for each thing. Make thankfulness a habit, and you'll be surprised to discover supernatural peace slowly quieting the voices of anxiety in your mind.

Begin taking notes on a pad or in your phone today. And throughout the day, write down as many things as you can, big or small, that you're thankful for.

> Everyone then who hears these words of mine and does them will be like a wise man who built his house on the rock.
>
> —MATTHEW 7:24

You've likely heard the parable of the house built on the rock. It's one of the first taught to children in church for good reason. Whatever beliefs you establish in your early years will inevitably affect the way you experience life and inform the worldview you develop. So, hear me: Jesus is the *only* solid foundation to build your life on. All other things, even good things, in this world will eventually collapse under the weight of sin and suffering.

No matter what you've built your foundation on thus far, whatever faithful or faulty bricks you may have laid, friend, you can always rebuild. So, how do you know what your foundation actually is? When you feel worried or overwhelmed, try to notice where you first turn for comfort or direction. To others? To social media? To the news, a book, or another numbing escape? Pay attention when your mind starts to run and your heart rate rises, noticing where you tend to look for stability. In those moments, try, if even for one minute, to go to God in prayer before seeking other sources of wisdom or comfort.

The next time you feel anxiety start to flood in, pause for one minute or more and speak aloud with Jesus before turning elsewhere for help.

> Any one of you who does not renounce all that he has
> cannot be my disciple.
>
> —LUKE 14:33

This was just as daunting a call to the twelve disciples as it is to us. Nearly everyone Jesus called to follow Him had to give something up in order to do so. James and John had to walk away from a thriving family fishing business. Matthew had to quit a high-paying government job to go live and work with the other disciples, who hated him. Peter had to leave his wife and sick mother-in-law to go with Jesus. And the Lord warns us we may have to do the same.

I know whatever or whomever you've lost may feel like sacrifice enough. But as we move through grief, God will call us to lay down other things in order to heal. What are you clinging to for a sense of safety, security, or hope? Do you need to renounce the need to control? Anger or unforgiveness that's crippling your progress? Rightful sadness that's spiraled into despondency? The cost of growth with God is sacrifice. It won't be easy and it won't feel good. It's okay to grieve the comforts you may be called to let go of. Just as He did for the disciples, Jesus promises that what follows your faithful sacrifice is glorious new life.

Lord, as scary as it feels, please show me what I'm wrongly clinging to for safety. Help me lay it down and turn fully to You for healing.

Surely he has borne our griefs
    and carried our sorrows;
yet we esteemed him stricken,
    smitten by God, and afflicted.
But he was pierced for our transgressions;
    he was crushed for our iniquities;
upon him was the chastisement that brought us peace,
    and with his wounds we are healed.

—ISAIAH 53:4–5

If you have surrendered your life to Christ, then by His blood, you are healed, holy, and perfect in the Father's eyes. Jesus was pierced, crushed, killed, and then resurrected so you can have unending and complete access to God—His grace, His love, His power, and His presence. This is the gospel.

But don't forget that not only did Jesus bear the weight of your sins and sin nature on the cross; He also has borne all your griefs and sorrows. Jesus Himself was a man of grief and sorrow. He lost loved ones to death. He was homeless and hungry, and His life was regularly in danger. Jesus came to save you for eternity, but He also came so He could fully understand you and your pain right here and now. He is the suffering servant, the great high priest (Hebrews 4:15). He knows the depth of your hurt, and He is far more equipped to carry it than you are. Surrender your griefs and sorrows to the One who came, lived, and died so He could hold your hurt for you. He is gracious and able.

Pour out every grief and sorrow, every worry and fear, to your suffering-servant Savior today. Know that He empathizes so deeply and can hold all your brokenness on your behalf.

Day 137

HOPE

Behold, my servant whom I have chosen,
   my beloved with whom my soul is well pleased.
I will put my Spirit upon him,
   and he will proclaim justice to the Gentiles.

—MATTHEW 12:18

In the same way Jesus came to empathize with us, understand us, and ultimately take on the weight of our sin and suffering, so, too, did He come to transfer His own righteousness to us. Father God spoke similar words of praise and affirmation over Jesus at His baptism and transfiguration (Matthew 3:17; 17:5). He was perfectly pleased with His Son's holiness. Jesus earned as a man what no other human has ever earned or will ever be able to earn. Then, when He willingly endured the cross and by the power of the Holy Spirit defeated death, those words became the chorus God now sings over you.

Jesus gifted you something that only the Son of God could buy: perfect acceptance and belonging as a child of God. When the Father sees you, He is well pleased. No matter how you struggle or sin or how poorly you have handled this difficult season in your life, your heavenly Father sees Christ in you. And in you, child, He is well pleased.

Release any words, thoughts, or actions keeping you in shame right now. Rest in the truth that God sees you and is pleased with you.

When my soul was embittered,
     when I was pricked in heart,
I was brutish and ignorant;
     I was like a beast toward you.
Nevertheless, I am continually with you;
     you hold my right hand.
You guide me with your counsel,
     and afterward you will receive me to glory.

—PSALM 73:21–24

On the days you feel most bitter, despairing, or pricked in heart, remember these brutally honest words to the Lord. Asaph, the psalmist, was drowning in sorrow and hopelessness. Yet he continued to cry out to his one Living Hope.

Asaph didn't hide from his anguish, nor did he hide from God as he grieved his awful circumstances. The only thing he knew for sure was that the Lord was continually with him—holding him, guiding him, and walking with him every step of his life, which would eventually end in glory. All of this is true for you too. Don't ignore the pain that feels insurmountable right now. Cry out to the Lord in the midst of it, and remember He is holding you, guiding you, and walking with you toward glory just as He did Asaph. This season isn't the end. You are never alone. And God will never let you go.

Wail with the Lord today; don't hold anything back. Then rest, knowing He is holding on to you with divine protection and love.

Do you not know that your body is a temple of the Holy Spirit within you, whom you have from God? You are not your own, for you were bought with a price. So glorify God in your body.

—1 CORINTHIANS 6:19–20

We've talked so much already about keeping our spiritual selves strong, about mental and emotional health in seasons of suffering. But what about your body? Have you even had time lately to think about what you're eating or how you're treating your physical needs? I know, for me, care for my body was one of the first things to fall to the wayside as I learned how to grieve. A lifelong exerciser, I couldn't work out for months—six, to be exact. My regular healthy diet gave way to whatever was in front of me, and wine became a crutch more often than it should.

If you feel like your physical health is falling last on the list right now, don't shame yourself! You're drained and hurting, and it's so hard. But try to remember, your body isn't just an arbitrary box for your emotions, mind, and spirit. It's a temple, made and given by God, and a tool that can help you heal when you care for it well! If you can't work out, take a walk. If you can't cook, ask someone to bring a healthy meal rather than ordering takeout again. Buy bath bombs, a massage gun, or a nice lotion to keep your skin and muscles feeling good. Grief reveals itself physically in our bodies. When we care for them, we're equipping ourselves to better care for our minds and spirits too.

What's one way you can care for and relax your body today?

> We do not have a high priest who is unable to sympathize with our weaknesses, but one who in every respect has been tempted as we are, yet without sin. Let us then with confidence draw near to the throne of grace, that we may receive mercy and find grace to help in time of need.
>
> —HEBREWS 4:15–16

I remember the first young widow I met after Ben died. Because of my age, I felt so isolated, like the only twentysomething in the world suffering this particular loss. Then this woman said, "Me too." I talked and she listened. Then she told me her story as tears welled in my eyes. That was it. No solutions were offered, just presence. Often what we need most when we're struggling is simply a listener. Someone to sit with us who truly understands and can empathize and affirm what we're feeling without fixing it. We need a friend.

What's beautiful about Jesus is He's not just your powerful rescuer; He's also the gentle, understanding friend who has stood right where you are. Felt what you feel. But relating to Jesus as a friend can be easier said than done. I get that. One way that helps me really feel His closeness is visualizing Him with me—sitting on my porch with me as I pray, wrapping His arm around my shoulders as I cry. It helps me to pray out loud, eyes open, rambling, just like I'd talk to a friend. No rehearsed or formal prayers. Just talk. Call on your powerful, compassionate, personal friend Jesus. He has already endured and overcome what you're facing. Let Him be with you in it.

Close your eyes, picture the man Jesus sitting with you exactly where you are, and ask Him to pour peace and rest into your mind today.

As the rain and the snow come down from heaven
     and do not return there but water the earth . . .
so shall my word be that goes out from my mouth;
     it shall not return to me empty,
but it shall accomplish that which I purpose,
     and shall succeed in the thing for which I sent it.

—ISAIAH 55:10–11

You have a chance to learn a simple yet powerful lifelong practice as you struggle: Invite the Lord into your suffering, and call out to Him for healing. Prayer and surrender are how you will find life again.

As you try to surrender your circumstances and your sorrow in prayer, you may feel at a loss for words. You're living with an onslaught of worries and feelings, and you may not know exactly how to talk to Him. Then don't rely on your words. Pray God's own words back to Him. There is more power than you can imagine in praying the infallible truths of Scripture back to the Lord and trusting them to be true in your life in Jesus' name. And when His words are sent out, prayed honestly, they don't return empty. They accomplish all that He purposes. When your words feel scattered or empty, go back to Scripture. Call out to Christ with the very truths He's given to you in His Word, and believe that He will honor them.

Select what you need most today, and make it your prayer:

Peace: Peace I leave with you; my peace I give to you. Not as the world gives do I give to you. Let not your hearts be troubled, neither let them be afraid. (John 14:27)

Belief: Immediately the father of the child cried out and said, "I believe; help my unbelief!" (Mark 9:24)

Endurance: We do not lose heart. Though our outer self is wasting away, our inner self is being renewed day by day. (2 Corinthians 4:16)

> He said also to the man who had invited him, "When you give a dinner or a banquet, do not invite your friends or your brothers or your relatives or rich neighbors, lest they also invite you in return and you be repaid. But when you give a feast, invite the poor, the crippled, the lame, the blind, and you will be blessed, because they cannot repay you. For you will be repaid at the resurrection of the just."
>
> —LUKE 14:12–14

In this valley of sorrow, we often feel mentally, spiritually, or emotionally depleted and messy. We look exhausted and feel anything but desirable. We can't imagine looking our best, let alone dressing for a grand, formal event. Not in this condition. But Jesus is calling us to His table.

It's on these days, though, friend, the ones when you are dirty, downcast, and weak, that Christ's heart invites you nearer. He came, lived, and died to redeem your ugliest days just as much as your beautiful ones. The Lord sees the whole of who you are, and He thinks you are wonderful. Everything you hate when you look in the mirror right now is not a wound to be ashamed of but rather a reminder that all your brokenness is robed in Jesus' beauty. Right now, as you are—disheveled, dirty, and despairing—God calls you to His table. You are a child and guest of the King. Never forget, you are beautiful to Him.

Ask God to remind you each time you think negatively about yourself today how gloriously radiant and beautiful you are in His eyes.

Answer me quickly, O LORD!
My spirit fails!
Hide not your face from me,
lest I be like those who go down to the pit. . . .
Make me know the way I should go,
for to you I lift up my soul.

—PSALM 143:7–8

When you are physically lost, where do you turn? What do you do? Don't you reach for your phone to call a trusted friend or open your Maps app? Maybe you stop and ask someone who knows the area for directions. Whatever recourse you choose, the first thing you do is stop so you don't continue on in the wrong direction.

So, too, as you navigate this uncomfortable, unfamiliar emotional territory, you must make the same effort to stop and ask the Lord for direction. The more you try to blindly forge ahead in this painful season, the greater risk you run of getting even more lost. Jesus is your trusted friend. He is your pathfinder. He knows this place you're in backward and forward, and He has nothing but your best interests in mind. Call on the Lord as your tired spirit and human discernment fail. Go to Him, in prayer and in the Word, to be sustained with steadfast love and divine direction each morning so that, through the guidance of His Holy Spirit, you may learn the way you should go.

Lord, give me supernatural direction today in my spirit.
Give me divine nudges toward the things I should do and
the people I should connect with as I go about my day.

I have fought the good fight, I have finished the race,
I have kept the faith.

—2 TIMOTHY 4:7

My senior year of college, I decided—somewhat on a whim—to run a half marathon. Though I was very diligent in my training, the race itself proved far more difficult than I expected. The course in Nashville is hilly—up and down nearly every mile—and I didn't have anyone running with me. I remember the long climb up Music Row at mile six and thinking, *There's no way!* I stopped at the next water station, downed one of my Go Gel energy pouches, and then realized I needed a tool, something to keep my mind from losing hope or breaking down before my body did. So, I started praying. Every mile, I chose a different person in my life to pray for while I trudged on to the next checkpoint. This took my mind off my physical pain. It helped me focus on a single mile at a time, rather than the long haul I had left. This strategy saved me!

Just like the struggle of that race, grief requires strategies. We must learn the tools we need to readjust our focus, renew our energy, and revamp our hope in the middle of an uphill battle that may feel impossible. That's why these spiritual practices matter to me. That's why I hope you're already learning to utilize them daily. Wail when you need a quick stop. Connect and worship so you can reenergize yourself. Hope because you know you can do the one mile in front of you. This is how we remain steadfast through the valley and continue toward the crown God has for us.

Intentionally practice all four of our rhythms in some small way today.

> I still have many things to say to you, but you cannot
> bear them now. When the Spirit of truth comes, he will
> guide you into all the truth . . . he will declare to you the
> things that are to come.
>
> —JOHN 16:12–13

Do you feel like it's the times you most desperately strain to hear God's voice that He seems silent? Know He is always listening, always there. But even if He is withholding answers from you, it's never out of cruelty or a lack of interest in your pain. The Father longs to constantly communicate with His children. But when your mind is clouded with grief and your body plagued with exhaustion, you may not be ready for what's next. You may not have the capacity to fully receive God's words, His direction, or His tender attempts to lead you. It simply may not be the right time yet. God isn't absent or dismissive.

Jesus warned the disciples that telling them everything would be too much for them to bear, so why wouldn't He also shield you in the same way? If the answers you're asking for aren't coming, call on the Holy Spirit, who is your Helper, to speak assurance, peace, and patience to you in place of anxiousness. It may feel like God is silent, but trust what He's doing. Trust His timing. Let His Spirit sit with you and calm you as you wait to hear what's next.

Lord, I want answers and need direction. If I'm not ready for that today, calm my heart and enable me to trust as I wait.

I tell you, do not be anxious about your life, what you will eat or what you will drink, nor about your body, what you will put on. Is not life more than food, and the body more than clothing? Look at the birds of the air: they neither sow nor reap nor gather into barns, and yet your heavenly Father feeds them. Are you not of more value than they? And which of you by being anxious can add a single hour to his span of life?

—MATTHEW 6:25–27

How does this passage seem obvious for birds yet unthinkable for humans facing lives full of loss and brokenness? I know it's hard. And I also know it actually *is* impossible for you to will yourself not to worry. The more you try to expel the anxieties from your mind, the more you inevitably focus on them. So, what are you to do?

First, pray. Go to Jesus daily, and ask *Him* to replace your worry with hope. Second, shift your vision. Reorient your focus from the worry to the One who has written every one of your days in His heavenly book (Psalm 139:16), the One with the power to order your steps. This isn't blind optimism; life demands far more than a glass-half-full point of view. This is consciously choosing, when anxiety creeps in, to take your eyes off the distraction of your worry and fix them on the person of Christ, who promises you refuge, provision, and peace.

Direct your focus to Jesus today by filling in the blank as many times as you can—either in a journal or in the margins of this page: Jesus is _____ (examples: kind, strong, a comfort, sovereign, a healer).

Day 147

Restore our fortunes, O LORD,
   like streams in the Negeb!
Those who sow in tears
   shall reap with shouts of joy!

—PSALM 126:4–5

You may not fathom it now, but the Lord has streams in mind for your future. He has plans to bring life back into your barren heart, not to replace what you've lost but to restore your days of joy. With every tearful day that passes, the Lord really is expanding your capacity for joy. I know that may sound crazy right now, but because you've grieved deeply, you will also come out of this with the ability to love more deeply, to live with greater compassion than before.

I've never been more comforted by a sunset than I am now. I've never savored a slow lunch with a friend or a sunny walk along the river like I do today. I wouldn't have entered my new marriage at thirty-two with the patience, grace, and profound appreciation I have today had I not gone through the depths of the valley. While being remarried certainly doesn't replace my life with Ben, my grief has, in endless ways, increased my ability to rejoice in the daily gifts of my marriage to Connor. God isn't in the business of replacing what is lost. From the beginning of the world to its glorious end, He is in the business of restoring our joy.

Lord, though I can't imagine it now, I thank You for the days of joy and restoration that are ahead for me. Revive and restore me in ways only You can.

You prepare a table before me
    in the presence of my enemies;
you anoint my head with oil;
    my cup overflows.

—PSALM 23:5

David praised God for a bountiful table, anointing oil, and an overflowing cup when his life was absolutely falling apart. When he wrote this passage, he was stuck in the valley of the shadow of death. Like a helpless sheep, he had no power to escape his painful circumstances, yet he chose to acknowledge the Lord's blessing right in the middle of his hardship. It would have been easy to focus on his lack of safety or security in this season. But the psalmist chose to set his eyes on the gracious God who cared for him even in his suffering.

There are endless negatives you could focus on in your own valley season. And those threats, hurts, and problems are very real and warrant caution and much prayer. But remember, even in the worst of your struggle, even in the presence of your enemies, God has a place for you at His table, where you can focus on the small joys and blessings that He still has for you. Sit hungrily at the Lord's table, with eyes open and hands ready to receive the little words, signs, or moments of goodness He has to fill you up today.

Pray for the desire and ability to focus on the small blessings and joys God has for you today rather than on all the negatives.

Day 149

> Peter opened his mouth and said: "Truly I understand that God shows no partiality, but in every nation anyone who fears him and does what is right is acceptable to him."
>
> —ACTS 10:34–35

If you're honest with yourself, do you like the idea that God is totally impartial? Can you accept that the people who had a hand in the tragedy that broke your heart—or those who made your healing journey harder and more painful—are fully forgiven? Do you believe that God's mercy is just but hate how it often feels unfair? Those feelings and thoughts are natural.

Because you are made in God's image, you are wired to desire justice. You are built with a hunger for goodness and a hatred for evil. But whoever has harmed you, intentionally or inadvertently, isn't yours to indict. It isn't up to you to determine the consequences of their actions. No matter how you feel toward them, you must trust that their actions and their hearts are in the Lord's hands. The only posture that will bring peace when someone has harmed you is forgiveness. They may not deserve it, but neither do you deserve God's endless forgiveness without the work of Christ. His mercy may not feel fair, but it's His to distribute. Pray for the desire to forgive and for the courage to extend to whoever hurt you the amazing grace that Christ extends to you. Forgiveness will always set you free.

Is there anyone in your life, including yourself, whom you're harboring anger or resentment toward? Ask God to soften your heart and help you forgive.

> Because he himself has suffered when tempted, he is able
> to help those who are being tempted.
>
> —HEBREWS 2:18

Since the Fall in the Garden of Eden, humanity has encountered endless temptation. Alluring opportunities of every kind are thrown in your face as you strive to live obediently in a world that champions selfishness and instant gratification. It's hard enough to resist sinful desires when you're strong and confidently walking with God. But it can feel almost impossible to do so when you're weak, depleted, and struggling to hear His voice because of the pain you're in.

Did you know Jesus felt that too? Matthew 4 tells us that after Jesus had fasted forty days alone in the desert, Satan himself came to tempt Him. How did He withstand? What did He model for us when we're weak, alone, and tempted? He quoted Scripture in response to all three of the devil's temptations. He fought with God's Word when His body and mind were too depleted to fight using anything else. As you struggle, follow this mighty example Jesus set for us.

Whatever you feel tempted to run to or are struggling to withstand, vocalize it to God and a trusted friend. Then find some specific scriptures to speak and pray aloud when that temptation comes.

For God alone, O my soul, wait in silence,
for my hope is from him.
He only is my rock and my salvation,
my fortress; I shall not be shaken.
On God rests my salvation and my glory;
my mighty rock, my refuge is God.

—PSALM 62:5–7

*R*ock. *Fortress. Refuge.* What do all these words have in common? They are a physical place—a place of security, stillness, and protection. I know, more than anything, you want a solution to the circumstances that are confusing and hurtful right now. You want an answer or an explanation to help you make sense of it all. Keep bringing those desires to the Lord in prayer, for not a word you utter is ever lost or forgotten by Him. He honors all your prayers and will answer them in His way, in His timing.

But what you need more than solutions and answers is a place to run to—a place of security, stillness, and protection. The Lord is that place. He is the rock, the refuge. When you're not enough and when answers aren't enough, I AM is enough. He is the fortress that you can rest and find safety in, even as the war continues to rage around you. Running to Him isn't running away from reality; it's running to the only One who can offer you perfect peace and relief in spite of your circumstances.

What would it look like for you to spend some time with the Lord today, not asking Him for anything but simply dwelling in His loving, safe presence?

Brothers, I do not consider that I have made it my own.
But one thing I do: forgetting what lies behind and
straining forward to what lies ahead, I press on toward
the goal for the prize of the upward call of God in Christ
Jesus.

—PHILIPPIANS 3:13–14

Do you have a tendency to dwell on the past? To obsess about the ways your life used to look when disaster seemed unlikely or far off in the distance? Nostalgia in and of itself isn't a bad thing. But when celebrating the past becomes a roadblock to the future, you put yourself at risk. You get stuck. You become blind to the ways the Holy Spirit is working in your life right now and can miss the growth and greater freedom God wants to lead you into.

One of my favorite quotes from C. S. Lewis says we are too content "to go on making mud pies in a slum because [we] cannot imagine what is meant by the offer of a holiday at the sea."[11] Absolutely, life was easier, felt safer, before you were thrust into this place of unknowns, pain, and fear. But if you're content to stay stuck in the slum, you'll miss the glory of the holiday at the sea. Don't you want to discover the strength of your character? See the power of your faith and feel intimacy with God as He stretches you into a more resilient, secure you? Press on with the Lord, my friend! The beauty that lies before you is worth the struggle.

Lord, give me the courage to be present with the ways You choose to stretch me today, that I may continue to grow toward renewed life.

Oh, taste and see that the LORD is good!
    Blessed is the man who takes refuge in him!

—PSALM 34:8

It may be hard for you to feel like God is good right now. You may be looking all around for evidence of His loving-kindness, yet all you might see are things He could have done to stop this affliction but didn't. But remember, you can see only a tiny fraction of the whole picture. And perhaps the sense of taste can offer some insight.

If you try a new recipe, you start with lots of individual ingredients, some of which you may like on their own and some of which you may not. Raw onion may be completely offensive to you, but as you cook it down, combine it with all the other ingredients, and follow the instructions, this unappealing ingredient becomes part of a delicious final product. But without the instructions, you may dismiss the onion as unpleasant, even cruel, to offer on its own to someone who's hungry. You can't see all the instructions for this life. You can't see the steps ahead that will take a bad-tasting season and use it to make a beautiful final product. The Lord has the instructions. He is preparing the final product. Trust Him that, with time, you will be able to taste and see that His plans for you actually are so, so good.

Lord, I hate this season right now. It tastes so bitter. Help me trust You and stay hopeful that this suffering is part of making me a richer, more beautiful soul.

Rejoice in hope, be patient in tribulation, be constant in prayer.

—ROMANS 12:12

How can I rejoice when there is a huge hole in my life that can never be filled? How can I be patient when I'd give anything to fast-forward through this devastating season? How do I stay constant in prayer when my mind, focus, and energy are completely zapped? The answer is, with Jesus' help.

Staying constant in prayer doesn't mean you stay on your knees all day long, skip work, and avoid responsibilities. Prayer can be as simple as whispering His name, in both heavy and lighter moments. Just a quick "Thank You, Jesus" or hushed "Help me, Jesus" can sustain you throughout a tough day. I was asked in an interview once how grief changed my prayer life. I realized immediately that prayer now felt to me like a constant text chain with God, rather than a long, formal letter. Prayer became a constant, somewhat-casual conversation. Rejoice when you're able to smile at an old memory. Call for Christ's peace when you struggle to fall asleep at night. Briefly but regularly include the Lord throughout your day. And when you do so, His Spirit moves and works in you. Continue to worship God through tiny prayers in both the joys and the struggles of each day.

Every time you feel overwhelmed or fearful today, whisper these simple words: "Help me, Jesus. Thank You, Jesus."

Day 155

I will gather those of you who mourn for the festival,
    so that you will no longer suffer reproach. . . .
And I will save the lame
    and gather the outcast,
and I will change their shame into praise
    and renown in all the earth.

—ZEPHANIAH 3:18–19

Though it feels all-consuming, brokenness is temporary. The suffering you're enduring isn't the ultimate end of the story. This promise God made to Israel—and subsequently to all believers—has remained true: He will gather you and turn your shame to praise. You might see the beginnings of this restoration in your days on earth, but you will for sure see its fullness at Christ's return when *every* bad thing will be redeemed, *every* lament will become shouts of praise.

But while you live in the in-between, everything broken, painful, and unfair that befalls you on earth is a reminder that God made you for more. He made you for unconditional love, perfection, and communion with Himself, and nothing this world has to offer can satisfy that desire. When nothing else feels worth rejoicing over, celebrate what you know will come true. Celebrate that your right now will never be the end of your story. Thank the Lord that your pain is temporary and that your shame and sorrow will one day be turned to glorious praise.

What specifically are you grieving or longing for right now? Speak these things aloud, and allow yourself a few minutes to imagine how they might be restored, because mourning isn't the end of your story.

The heavens declare the glory of God,
    and the sky above proclaims his handiwork.

—PSALM 19:1

The first things we learn about God in Scripture are in the creation story in Genesis 1 and 2. We witness His power, His wisdom, His intentionality, and His intimacy with all He creates. And just as we see His fingerprints in Genesis, so can we still see His power, wisdom, intentionality, and intimacy in the world around us. Have you ever watched the tide rise and fall at the beach? This isn't a random occurrence. It doesn't happen because of a strong wind. It happens every day as a result of Earth's intricate dance with a single moon orbiting nearly a quarter million miles away. The system is beautifully designed and divinely maintained. Unfathomably grand yet made possible through the working of a billion tiny details.

This is how God works for your good. He is employing the same mastery and intention right now as He restores and restructures the fractured pieces of your life. Your loss isn't too big. Peace and purpose aren't too far away. He sustains the cosmos and also knows every hair on your head (Matthew 10:30). He is intentionally preparing good things for you right now, even if you can't see them, even in your worst circumstances. Let the wonderful witness of the moon and sky remind you of that.

Find somewhere to gaze up at the sky tonight, and thank God that His purpose for your life is in both the big picture and the tiniest details.

Day 157　　　　　　　　CONNECT

> You are no longer strangers and aliens, but you are fellow
> citizens with the saints and members of the household of
> God, built on the foundation of the apostles and
> prophets, Christ Jesus himself being the cornerstone.
>
> —EPHESIANS 2:19–20

I know you feel vulnerable and exposed for many reasons right now. You may want to shrink back from loved ones, but isolation is not a comfort but a danger for you right now. Certainly, take your space to process and rest, but don't try to fight this fight alone. The Scriptures are filled with your faithful brothers and sisters who have gone before you, who faced similar difficulties, and who can offer you real comfort.

None of the figures of the Bible lived without struggle, fear, or despair. Joseph was imprisoned. Peter was overcome with shame. Martha and Mary grieved and questioned Jesus at the death of their brother. Daniel's young life was completely derailed when he was taken captive. Jesus Himself was betrayed, falsely accused, and abandoned. Stand on the strength of saints who have suffered before you, and borrow the faith of trusted people in your life when yours is weak. You aren't a stranger or alien. You have a whole household of believers who can stand with you and whose faith can buoy yours when you feel alone.

Find one story in Scripture of a sufferer who hoped, trusted, and persevered, and pray for a heart like theirs today. If you don't know where to start, read Hebrews 11, often called the Hall of Faith.

To us a child is born,
     to us a son is given;
and the government shall be upon his shoulder,
     and his name shall be called
Wonderful Counselor, Mighty God,
     Everlasting Father, Prince of Peace.

—ISAIAH 9:6

It's easy to say but difficult to believe: God truly is everything you need. You may long for more time, money, or support. You may not physically have the capacity to tend to the people in your care. *It can't be practical to rely on Jesus to literally be everything I need. Isn't that a blind, trite, cop-out answer?*

There's no explanation until you experience it, but Christ really is everything you need. It's true. He's been palpably present with me in times of crisis, like physical weights were lifted from my shoulders. He's brought Scripture to the front of my mind to calm whirling anxiety. He's been the only source of hope when everything around me was falling apart. He can so gently hold your pain: Wonderful Counselor. He gives you His strength when yours isn't enough: Mighty God. He reminds you that all wrongs will in the end be made right: Everlasting Father. He is a physical calm in the chaos: Prince of Peace. This may still sound crazy to you, but in prayer, boldly claim these names that God calls Himself, and expectantly wait for His counsel, strength, assurance, and peace to flow radically into your pain.

Pray to the Wonderful Counselor, Mighty God, Everlasting Father, Prince of Peace today and thank Him for being everything you need.

Day 159

> No, in all these things we are more than conquerors
> through him who loved us.
>
> —ROMANS 8:37

You are in the middle of a fight—a fight with anxiety, fear, and painful circumstances outside your control. Some days you may feel so hopeless that you imagine raising the white flag, simply giving up. On better days, you may feel determined that you won't let this loss or this conflict defeat you.

But the hard truth is that not only will most trials you face be out of your control but their effects will also ripple through your life for years to come. There isn't a singular finish line to suffering. The pain will soften but never go away completely. I know this may sound discouraging, but I hope it points you to the greatest hope, the Living Hope—Jesus. No matter what you face, the pressure isn't on you to conquer it or overcome it yourself. You are more than a conqueror; you are the chosen one of the Conqueror who has defeated sin, sorrow, and death. The only way to win this battle, to survive this pain, is to surrender it daily to the One who has already won everything on your behalf. You are more than the conqueror of your own suffering because Jesus loves you, chose you, and can conquer it in you and for you.

Whatever burden you're feeling pressured to carry on your own, call out to Jesus to carry it for you, to direct your next steps forward, and to comfort you with the knowledge that He is the conqueror of all things.

In my distress I called upon the LORD;
    to my God I cried for help. . . .
He sent from on high, he took me;
    he drew me out of many waters.
He rescued me from my strong enemy
    and from those who hated me,
    for they were too mighty for me.

—PSALM 18:6, 16–17

Even though we know the final war on sin, death, and suffering has been won by Jesus, none of us is free from the daily battles of being human. Battles with depression, despair, bitterness, betrayal, fear—mental and emotional battles so intense they're wreaking havoc on our physical bodies. You can believe Jesus will erase and redeem all your heartache in eternity while still feeling helpless to overcome your earthly struggles in the here and now.

Take heart in this scriptural imagery of how the Lord fights for you, friend. When you call to Jesus and surrender these battles into His hands, He comes down from on high and fights your enemies on your behalf. While language in this passage may be figurative, that doesn't make it any less true. Part of walking in faith is choosing to take God's Word at face value. Think about the magnificent power required for someone to rescue you from physical raging waters and strong enemies. Then how much more can Christ supernaturally and mightily defeat the spiritual forces coming against you if you hand the battle over to Him daily?

Name the specific battles you're fighting right now. Call out in Jesus' name for those enemies to be quieted, cast out, and defeated.

Day 161

Gracious is the LORD, and righteous;
    our God is merciful.
The LORD preserves the simple;
    when I was brought low, he saved me.
Return, O my soul, to your rest;
    for the LORD has dealt bountifully with you.

—PSALM 116:5–7

One of the most difficult things about suffering is that the scope of its damage goes far beyond its point of impact. Most all types of loss have a ripple effect.

Pain is difficult to compartmentalize. As hard as you may try, your grief will spill over into other facets of your life, and its echoes will be heard for years and years to come. But when your pain feels too big, I encourage you to look for the good in the simple things right in front of you. The small tasks that felt impossible a week ago but that you can manage now, the little glimpses of beauty in nature or loved ones around you, the gentle nudges and humbling reminders of God's presence. Look for these little gifts and thank God for them. Healing from loss will happen in a thousand individual moments, not in one grand instant. Meet Christ in the everyday, ordinary places. It's there that you will begin to find the bounty of healing He has for you.

Lord, help me see the little ways You've dealt bountifully with me so that I may constantly feel You close.

> He did not permit him but said to him, "Go home to
> your friends and tell them how much the Lord has done
> for you, and how he has had mercy on you."
>
> —MARK 5:19

Many of us have been taught to keep quiet when we are hurting, to downplay the ways we need help. If you are experiencing God in perceivable, supernatural ways, do you worry others may dismiss you or reject your experience? *Will they think I'm crazy?* Or if you are in a season when your dire pleas seem to go unanswered, you might wonder, *If I'm honest with others about the silence I'm feeling, will they start to doubt God's goodness too?*

Please relax. It's not your job to maintain God's reputation. He is Alpha and Omega. He can handle humanity's doubts and impatience with Him. But also, don't forget the power of an honest testimony of His good work. You don't need to know Scripture front to back or have theological training to share honest, personal experiences with others. The greatest work you can do for the kingdom (and a powerful practice to promote your healing) is to tell the truth about your pain and the truth about how the Lord is meeting you in it. Share both the answers and the questions you've found as you've walked with Christ. It's only when we're honest about where we are that we can begin to grow.

Talk to a safe and trusted person today, and share your honest questions about God or His response to your situation. Rest in the companionship of a caring listener.

Day 163

My flesh and my heart may fail,
> but God is the strength of my heart and
> > my portion forever.

—PSALM 73:26

Notice that this psalm reveals someone who was taking steps rather than sitting scared. This is a picture of a flawed human being who had courageously strained forward and failed. The psalmist had assessed his situation, prayed for direction and discernment, boldly put his best foot forward, and still failed.

There is a difference in waiting on the Lord and being immobilized by fear. Be careful not to equate the two. When your life gets upended for any number of reasons, you'll have tough choices to make as you attempt to grieve, process, and move forward. Always, always do so with fervent prayer and open ears, waiting for the Spirit's direction. But don't be afraid to take new steps when you feel led. Even if you fail, the Lord gives the strength to get back up and the provision you need to take another brave step. Walking with Christ doesn't mean you won't make wrong choices or fall on your face. It means that when you courageously try and fail, He will empower you and equip you to keep moving in the direction He's leading.

What next steps are you afraid to take? And what is holding you back?

Though he cause grief, he will have compassion
    according to the abundance of his steadfast love;
for he does not afflict from his heart
    or grieve the children of men.

—LAMENTATIONS 3:32–33

If you believe God is truly sovereign, then you know He could have stopped this tragedy from happening with a single word. You know He could have altered the outcome and spared you the pain. And you're right. But what you must also remember is that while the Lord is fully sovereign, He is also fully loving. Like a good earthly father, He assures us He never allows pain in His children's lives without reason. Punishment is never the motive for trials He allows to befall you. You are fully redeemed and righteous in His eyes through Christ. Punishment isn't a part of your relationship.

Because God's ultimate concern is the state of your soul and the Christlikeness of your character, pain becomes a vehicle to refine you and reroute you back to Himself. He wants the absolute best for all His children. And sometimes a parent's best teaching and greatest wisdom come when a child is uncomfortable or in pain. The Father's heart is never to hurt you, His beloved child. It's to protect you, guide you, and lead you into places of richer faith and flourishing.

Lord, help me believe this pain isn't a punishment from You. If I'm holding any distrust or bitterness toward You, forgive me and help me, Holy Spirit, to release it for good.

Day 165

> I do not ask that you take them out of the world, but that you keep them from the evil one. They are not of the world, just as I am not of the world. Sanctify them in the truth; your word is truth.
>
> —JOHN 17:15–17

These are some of the last words Jesus prayed to the Father during His time on earth, and these words were not just about the disciples but about you. With His death approaching, *you* were on His mind. You were the one He was praying for. And I believe God honored His prayer, beloved. As long as you call out to Jesus, He is ready and able to defend you from the Enemy and from the world.

The paradox of Jesus' prayer, though, is that even as He prayed for your protection, He also prayed for your sanctification—the process of being refined to be more and more like Him. More and more holy. Sanctification rarely comes without struggle. Jesus knew that through suffering you would become more like Him, yet at the same time, He also pleaded with the Father to keep you safe from evil. It's hard to fathom, but God works both in safety and in suffering when you actively walk with Christ. He allows hardship because it sanctifies you, but when you call on Him in Jesus' name, He is faithful to fight the Enemy on your behalf.

Lord, protect me from the Enemy and all evil in Jesus' name. Thank You that You don't waste my pain but miraculously use it to make me more like Christ.

> Behold, the LORD's hand is not shortened, that it cannot save, or his ear dull, that it cannot hear.
>
> —ISAIAH 59:1

Even if you're talking regularly with the Lord, it's easy to overthink prayer or slip into doubt. Maybe you're like me and the specific prayers you've committed to speaking out daily have seen months and months of no reply, no return. I've given in to discouragement when I felt my pleas were falling on deaf ears. I've gone through seasons when I've been exhausted with the effort prayer seems to require. But now, in hindsight, I see that not one word was missed. I see that each need and desire I surrendered was esteemed and held tenderly by the Lord. Even the prayers that He answered no to, He eventually gave me peace to accept.

Prayer may feel either impossible or unimportant to you right now. On one hand: *This is way too big, and I'll avoid being disappointed with or bitter toward God if I just don't ask for it at all.* Beloved, God can reach further and do grander things than you even know to ask for. On the other hand: *This is so trivial; I shouldn't even bother God with this.* Dear friend, His ear isn't dull. He hears every one of your exhausted whispers. Nothing is unimportant. You're never bothering your loving Father. Bring it all—the too big and too small—to lay at His feet.

What is something you've been hesitant to bring to God in prayer that you can honestly come to Him with today?

Day 167

> Behold, I am with you and will keep you wherever you
> go, and will bring you back to this land. For I will not
> leave you until I have done what I have promised you.
>
> —GENESIS 28:15

Right now, you may find yourself in a similar place as Jacob was when God spoke these words to him—wandering far from home. Like him, maybe you're facing the unknown somewhere in the middle of a daunting journey. I know it feels scary and unnatural to you, but you can rest in His plan for you, even in the unknown. His vision and power infinitely (and lovingly!) exceed yours. He knows the exact way forward, and He is with you every step of the way.

The promised land God has for His children—both the eternal one, heaven, and the promised land of less painful seasons here on earth—is coming. God may not fix what's broken the way you'd like. He may not lead you in the direction or at the pace you desire, but you are always moving in a good, right direction when you follow Christ.

Praise the Lord today that He alone knows what the upcoming promised land for you is and that as you seek Him, He is leading you faithfully there.

Day 168

> In the day of prosperity be joyful, and in the day of adversity consider: God has made the one as well as the other.
>
> —ECCLESIASTES 7:14

*H*ow can a good God make a bad day? you might wonder. *When the days behind me and the hours ahead look pretty void of goodness, much less blessing, where is God's hand?* But remember, God's Word is perfect truth. He doesn't mislead. And the truth here is, He doesn't play favorites. Walking with God never guarantees you will be free from suffering. While He has the power to protect you from any hardship, He also grants humanity complete free will, entrusting it to sinful people in a sin-filled world.

Every day He makes is right. It's filled with majesty, love, and reflections of His character. The bad days are no less filled with His purpose and redemptive work than the good days. When the bad days bring you down, there is infinite evidence all around you that God is still in control, still intentional, and still good. Open your eyes; He has made every day according to His design, if you're willing to see it.

Ask the Holy Spirit for divine clarity to see small signs and reminders of God's generous goodness to you at every turn today.

Day 169

The LORD is my chosen portion and my cup;
    you hold my lot.
The lines have fallen for me in pleasant places;
    indeed, I have a beautiful inheritance.

—PSALM 16:5–6

If you could see clearly right now, you could recall countless ways God has blessed you throughout the years. When the loss you're suffering now no longer consumes your sight, you will look back on the blessings around you now—however invisible they may seem in the moment—and be reminded that God truly is good. Here and now, your portion seems scant, your cup tastes bitter, and the lines of your life have fallen far from pleasant places. But your portion and inheritance are not of this world. God will continue to give earthly blessings, but Jesus Himself is your ultimate gift. He is your cup, portion, and inheritance, now and forever.

But what does that mean practically? For Jesus to be your portion and lot as you're fighting through the valley now? Here are a few Old Testament Hebrew names of God that I've clung to and continue to claim: Jehovah Tsaba, the Lord our warrior; Jehovah Rapha, the Lord who heals; Jehovah Rohi, the Lord my shepherd; Jehovah Jireh, the Lord who provides; Jehovah Shalom, the Lord is peace. All these names and more are what you have access to as a child with the inheritance of Christ. Use them in prayer.

Which one of these names of God do you most need to claim right now? Address the Lord with that name, and tell Him your specific needs.

WORSHIP

Day 170

> Be filled with the Spirit, addressing one another in
> psalms and hymns and spiritual songs, singing and
> making melody to the Lord with your heart.
>
> —EPHESIANS 5:18–19

Often when we think of singing songs to the Lord, we think of corporate worship. Large groups in a church or at a concert or retreat, being led in praise by a singer or band of some sort. And corporate worship is beautiful! The Holy Spirit loves to dwell among the melodic praise of God's people. But I encourage you—don't reserve songs of worship just for groups or Sunday mornings. Music is powerful. And in times of distress, the lyrical words of others can help you identify what you're feeling but may be struggling to express. Songs can help you communicate with God when you don't quite know where to start.

Scripture says, "Draw near to God, and he will draw near to you" (James 4:8). This is just as true in your car, in the shower, on a walk, or on your knees in your living room as it is on Sunday mornings. At times when your words fail you, psalms, hymns, and songs of worship are a perfect way to draw near to the Lord. You may not feel anything physical or hear Him speak to you, but the Holy Spirit provides supernatural strength and grace when you worship in song, even as your tears fall.

Take a few minutes today to listen to, meditate on, or sing worship songs.

In this hope we were saved. Now hope that is seen is not hope. For who hopes for what he sees? But if we hope for what we do not see, we wait for it with patience.

—ROMANS 8:24–25

I interviewed a man once who shared his experiences of grief after the murder of his nineteen-year-old son. He talked about how faith and hope are *not* the same thing. This puzzled me, so I asked him to clarify. "Faith," he said, "is believing something is possible. Hope is believing that it's possible for you."[12] You may believe that God has the power to heal, give divine peace, and redeem all kinds of broken things. You may recall that He promises to use everything for the good of those who love Him (Romans 8:28). But do you truly believe He'll do it for you?

Hope in God's kingdom functions less like a noun and more like a verb. We're not confident because we possess a thing called hope; we grow in confidence as we actively hope that what God says is possible is specifically possible for us. Maybe we see the beauty and healing in others' lives and make a point to tell ourselves, *That can be my story too.* Even if your outcome doesn't match someone else's, the sheer act of hoping in the meantime lifts your spirits and keeps you relying on the Lord. You may see your hope come to fruition here on earth, or you may not see it until eternity. But it's coming! God's hope may not be a hope that's seen, but it's a hope that's certain. Stand on it.

Ask the Lord for the patience and the courage to keep hoping, keep claiming, keep imagining a restored and joyful future, knowing He is faithful to provide it in His way, in His timing.

> Trust in him at all times, O people;
> pour out your heart before him;
> God is a refuge for us.

—PSALM 62:8

The psalmists use this word over and over to characterize God: *refuge.* He is a place of safety, protection, and security for His people. And certainly we seek refuge in God's Word, in prayer, in worship, in church. But consider that maybe the Lord is providing a refuge for you outside the typical spiritual box.

James tells us that "every good and perfect gift is from above" (1:17, NIV). For me, those gifts included some unexpected places of refuge. Like taking up golf, which I'd never played before, because Ben loved it and it made me feel close to him. Like offering to pick up my friends' kids from preschool because, for a moment, it filled the hole of thinking I'd never get to be a mom. Like meeting a new friend (whom I didn't feel like engaging) who ended up being a safe haven because she wasn't there for the tragedy part of my story. God is an omnipresent, infinitely creative, and caring God. Try not to close the door too quickly on the things and people He could be using to provide a little refuge for you.

Lord, make me aware of anyone, any place, any activity You're offering me that could be a sweet place of refuge for me.

Yes, and I will rejoice, for I know that through your prayers and the help of the Spirit of Jesus Christ this will turn out for my deliverance, as it is my eager expectation and hope that I will not be at all ashamed, but that with full courage now as always Christ will be honored in my body, whether by life or by death.

—PHILIPPIANS 1:18–20

When Paul wrote this letter to the church in Philippi, he was physically locked in prison for preaching the gospel. Yet he began this declaration by saying he would rejoice. Paul was confident in his deliverance, whether it came by way of freedom in life or freedom in death.

Do you think Paul was hoping for his physical deliverance? Do you think he was praying desperately that he would escape being beheaded and instead be free to keep spreading the good news? I'm sure he was. But he also rejoiced, even knowing his deliverance might be not physical freedom from prison but the fuller deliverance that comes for all believers when they go home to Jesus. Whatever you're facing may or may not be life threatening. But you can still rejoice because, in any circumstance, deliverance for you is assured, whether here on earth or in glory to come.

As honestly as you can, pray Paul's words over your situation: "Yes, and I will rejoice, for I know that through . . . the help of the Spirit of Jesus Christ this will turn out for my deliverance."

> When they got out on land, they saw a charcoal fire in place, with fish laid out on it, and bread. . . .
>
> When they had finished breakfast, Jesus said to Simon Peter, "Simon, son of John, do you love me more than these?" He said to him, "Yes, Lord; you know that I love you."
>
> —JOHN 21:9, 15

This breakfast scene is one of the times Jesus appeared to His disciples after His resurrection. The men were out fishing when they saw Jesus beside what Scripture distinctly describes as a *charcoal* fire on the beach. Why the detail? I think it's included because the Lord loves us so intimately, He is faithful to redeem the painful details of our lives. Just three chapters prior, Peter denied having a relationship with Jesus three times out of fear, while standing beside a charcoal fire (18:15–27). He was overcome with shame. And not only did Jesus meet him with forgiveness, but He also did so around the same kind of fire, so as to eliminate any shame that a fire might trigger in Peter in the future.

Painful details, whether stemming from shame or from an intimate reminder of the one you're grieving, cut deeply, like hundreds of sporadic paper cuts you don't expect. A smell, a song, a food—endless triggers continue to remind us of what we've lost. And what Jesus did for Peter, He can absolutely do for you. Whatever your painful details are, whenever they pop up, surrender them to the Lord, who is kind and able to redeem them.

What are some paper cuts or charcoal fires that you need the Lord to help heal?

The Spirit and the Bride say, "Come." And let the one who hears say, "Come." And let the one who is thirsty come; let the one who desires take the water of life without price.

—REVELATION 22:17

Think about how marvelously satisfying your first sips of cold water are after a strenuous hike or hot afternoon outdoors. Though you regularly consume water without much thought throughout your day, you seldom savor it unless you're overheated, dehydrated. Nothing about the water is different, but in parched moments, your desperate need makes you slow down to fully delight in the refreshment.

It doesn't matter how long you've been journeying through grief; it has a stubborn way of mentally, emotionally, and spiritually dehydrating you. You feel depleted, run-down, and lacking in the resources you need for recovery on your own. Let Scripture remind you: Jesus is the Living Water. Nothing can satiate your thirst for peace or rehydrate your faith like He can. And just like with physical thirst, the remedy is simple. Take Him in. Read His Word. Sit, and ask the Lord expectantly for His presence. Though He is the same every day, He will never taste more life-giving to you than in your seasons of hardship. Drink Christ in and start coming back to life.

What is one small way you can pause and savor Jesus' radical love and redeeming grace today?

Let me hear in the morning of your steadfast love,
    for in you I trust. . . .
Let your good Spirit lead me
    on level ground!

—PSALM 143:8, 10

Pain has a way of not just breaking your heart but disorienting your mind and ruining your plans. All of a sudden the steady path on which you were traveling feels uneven, unsafe, and unclear. Your footing feels off, and you're facing a major undesired detour. Though we were still in our first year of marriage, Ben and I had made beautiful plans—about future trips, about our personal dreams and how to get there, about the names of our future children. And in his death, I also had to face the death of each one of those dreams. I felt I had no destination to look forward to, and the very ground beneath me felt unstable.

It's scary to move in a direction that is unfamiliar, and it's natural to feel anxious following a God you can't see or touch or hear. But remember, the Lord isn't surprised or confused by any of these changes. He's known since the beginning of time the way you should go. He guides you along these new and rocky paths. He's walking every step with you. Follow Him.

Speak aloud the specific plans that have been ruined and the unknowns that have you worrying today, and surrender them to your trustworthy Father.

Day 177

Let your eyes look directly forward,
  and your gaze be straight before you.
Ponder the path of your feet;
  then all your ways will be sure.

—PROVERBS 4:25–26

When you're hurting, it can feel better to camp out in your past or paint prettier pictures of your future than to vulnerably sit in your broken reality. And you should remember and thank God for good things past, just as you should always bring Him your desires for the future. But your healing will come only from courageously and honestly facing the pain of the present.

Remember, He is "the same yesterday and today and forever" (Hebrews 13:8). The Lord is building on your past and preparing your future, but you must go at the pace He sets. Your emotions are worthy of the attention they need in order to heal. Right now, your present is painful. You may be reminded at every turn of what you've lost or what you're still waiting for. Don't try to outrun your hurt. The wounds you're bearing today need your acknowledgment so Jesus can bring His healing.

Sit in quiet prayer today, and ask Jesus what wounds you need to acknowledge.

Day 178

> Come to me, all who labor and are heavy laden, and I
> will give you rest. Take my yoke upon you, and learn
> from me, for I am gentle and lowly in heart, and you
> will find rest for your souls.
>
> —MATTHEW 11:28–29

I know you've been fighting. With your life out of sorts and your heart broken, every day feels like another battle, another mountain to climb. And you should be proud of your resilience and endurance! Just look at how far you've come, all that you've experienced, and the hard days you've weathered. The Holy Spirit's power is running in and through you, and without Him, even twenty-four hours would be too much for you to endure. But strength isn't your most precious weapon in this battle with suffering. Rest is. You need relief.

Even God, the almighty Creator, rested on the seventh day (Genesis 2:2). You weren't built to burn the candle at both ends. You can continue to withstand this hard season only if you prioritize moments to be refueled in Christ's presence. Bring your burdens to Jesus. Let Him carry the weight with you. Allow Him to set you free from fighting this battle on your own.

How can you create a little space for rejuvenating rest today?

> When they measure themselves by one another and
> compare themselves with one another, they are without
> understanding.
>
> —2 CORINTHIANS 10:12

Please try to resist the urge to compare right now! Facing the reality of what you've lost or what you still long for is hard enough without measuring your lack against others' abundance. You may see a house full of children while yours stays quiet and empty. You may see a healthy marriage while yours unravels at the seams. You may see physical health and fitness while you struggle to look and feel your best. And it's okay for you to lament what seems to come more naturally to others. But be cautious—unchecked comparison will always steal your joy.

There's no time more primed for envy than seasons of suffering. You have every reason to mourn what you've lost—people, things, relationships that others may still have—but remember, no one's story will play out the same. God blesses all His children in different ways, at different times. Try asking Him to replace your tendency toward comparison with supernatural compassion, both for yourself and for those around you.

Are you living in resentful or harmful comparison with anyone in your life right now? Confess it, and ask for God's mercy and power to see the beauty in your story.

Be strong in the Lord and in the strength of his might.
Put on the whole armor of God, that you may be able to
stand against the schemes of the devil. For we do not
wrestle against flesh and blood, but against the rulers,
against the authorities, against the cosmic powers over
this present darkness, against the spiritual forces of evil in
the heavenly places.

—EPHESIANS 6:10–12

Yⁱou're fighting so much right now—uncertainty, confusion, fear, doubt, depression, anxiety. But there is an enemy far more dangerous you must be aware of. The devil is ready to capitalize on your weariness and pain because he wants to deceive you in your weakness. Scripture calls him "the father of lies" (John 8:44). He knows your mind is clouded and weak right now, and he'll do anything to plant seeds of shame and self-doubt as you work to heal. *You're moving on too fast, dishonoring your loved one. You should be over it by now. You're responsible for this. You'll never be truly happy again. You'll always be the victim.*

If these lies or others are bombarding you, remember that Christ has already defeated Satan at the cross! Though he can attack you, he *cannot* defeat you. You can deflect his deceitful arrows with the truth of God's Word and the words faithful friends speak over you. When you fight back with truth, the Enemy can't knock you off your course toward freedom and healing.

Jesus, show me what lies I'm falling victim to today, and reveal the scriptures I can use to fight back when the Enemy attacks.

Day 181

I will set my eyes on them for good, and I will bring
them back to this land. I will build them up, and not tear
them down; I will plant them, and not pluck them up. I
will give them a heart to know that I am the LORD, and
they shall be my people and I will be their God, for they
shall return to me with their whole heart.

—JEREMIAH 24:6–7

God spoke these words through Jeremiah to the people of Israel
who had been exiled from their home. For seventy years they suffered
in captivity under evil Babylon before the Lord restored their freedom and returned them home to Judah. He knew the end of the
story, which, in their suffering, they couldn't fathom. He allowed
them to suffer in order to bring their hearts fully back to Himself,
but His plan was never to leave them in exile.

Grief, sorrow, long-lasting pain, can make us feel like exiles in
many ways. You may feel estranged from God or others. You may feel
like a slave to sorrow, worry, bitterness. You may feel like a foreigner
in your own life, one that looks unfamiliar and has been turned
upside down. But, beloved, God's eyes are on you for good. He will
build you up and replant you. He won't waste the pain you're facing
but rather will use it for divine purpose and, in the process, draw
your whole heart back to Himself.

Ask the Lord for supernatural hope in this season to believe
and remember that He won't leave you in exile but is drawing
you back wholeheartedly to Himself.

I bless the LORD who gives me counsel;
> in the night also my heart instructs me.
I have set the LORD always before me;
> because he is at my right hand, I shall not be shaken.

—PSALM 16:7–8

As we walk through life, aren't we most often looking forward? *What's around the corner? Where do I turn? What's the next right thing to do or choice to make?* But when tragedy strikes, your vision can become blurred. Pain has a way of blinding you, like you're trying to drive a car with ice covering its windshield. You're frustrated because you want to move forward, but you're scared to press the gas because you can't see where you're going.

This is why I love this visual of being in the dark of night and setting the Lord always before us. That's what we can feel like in grief—blind, stumbling, willing but unsure and a little afraid. But God can see every step, small or large, that's ahead. So, every decision, no matter of what significance, is worth bringing to the Lord in prayer. *Lord, should I go through his things yet? Should I commit to this event? Is this person safe to share with? Is it time for counseling or treatment?* When you set God always before you, He can instruct you in the major issues and the daily decisions that are easy to fear or avoid.

Talk with God today about one small thing and one major thing you're afraid or unsure of right now.

Can a woman forget her nursing child,
    that she should have no compassion on the son of her womb?
Even these may forget,
    yet I will not forget you.
Behold, I have engraved you on the palms of my hands;
    your walls are continually before me.

—ISAIAH 49:15–16

God hasn't forgotten you. He is keenly aware of your pain and the brokenness that feels inescapable right now. As a mother cherishes her child, so the Father adores you and has you constantly on His mind and His heart. His tears of compassion fall for you because the last thing He wants is for you to think He's abandoned you in your pain. It's completely the opposite! God's promise to never leave you or forsake you was made permanent by Christ's redeeming work on the cross. The nail holes in the palms of His hands confirmed for all time that you are a child of God. He is your Savior and Protector.

Everything that has fallen apart—everything that, to you, seems in shambles and unable to be redeemed—He is preparing to restore. Because He is for you and He has defeated sin and death, He will ultimately redeem your losses, and until then, He will sustain you while you wait for healing to come. He sees you; He knows you; He loves you.

Consider how powerful a mother's love and compulsion to help her child are. Now rest today, knowing that the Father's love and compulsion to help you are infinitely greater!

> As each has received a gift, use it to serve one another, as
> good stewards of God's varied grace.
>
> —I PETER 4:10

The last thing your pain feels like right now is a gift. At best it may feel a shocking disappointment, and at worst, a cruel betrayal. It's okay to feel those things. I know your heart is broken, and whether you believe it or not, God's breaks, too, for each tear you cry. He hates seeing you hurt. But unlike you, He has perfect, eternal vision. He can see your healed future, and nothing that is in His hands is ever wasted.

I remember the moment when I first profoundly felt that my story had power. As I sat across from a young woman over coffee, God used me to speak the hope over her that she couldn't see in her tragedy. She was a living, breathing recipient of the purpose God had called me to through my grief. Through God's loving power, you can steward your suffering to encourage and comfort others, to pour your hard-won compassion onto them when they need it. Godly purpose for your pain won't take the sorrow away, but slowly you will start to see what a powerful redemption story your life is. Your healing will be a gift to others down the road who can't see healing for themselves.

Lord, change my perspective on the struggles I'm navigating. Let my story encourage and empower others.

In your hearts honor Christ the Lord as holy, always
being prepared to make a defense to anyone who asks
you for a reason for the hope that is in you; yet do it
with gentleness and respect.

—1 PETER 3:15

As humans we delight in stories of those who overcome adversity.
We love an underdog who ends victorious in the face of a major
obstacle. And when you face suffering, you are living out an underdog story.

One of the many ways Christ draws hearts to Himself is through
the testimony, or story sharing, of His imperfect children, particularly those who are suffering. I know you can't see the end of this
valley yet. You may not even feel God working in or through you
some days. But your weakest moments are often your most powerful
testimony to His redemptive work. Because when you proclaim who
you know He is—good, loving, trustworthy—in the midst of your
difficult circumstances, God gets people's attention.

Be the story that inspires others. You are a chosen, capable, living
ambassador for the hope that can come only from Christ. You are a
reflector of His powerful light, light that shines most brightly in seasons of darkness. Though it can feel costly, even painful, to worship
in the valley, the Holy Spirit will enable you to be a witness to God's
power as you faithfully suffer. Be the underdog who, through the
work of Christ, overcomes and turns hearts and eyes to the Lord.

How can you share with someone today the ways—big and
small—you've seen God's goodness?

Day 186

> You have sorrow now, but I will see you again, and your hearts will rejoice, and no one will take your joy from you.
>
> —JOHN 16:22

I hate how the brokenness and sin in this world assault our joy. I hate that injuries, sickness, and accidents can steal away our happiness in a second. I wish that sorrow wasn't such a profound part of our journey toward eternity. Like Jesus and all the saints who have walked before you, you will weep and lament. But also like them, you have access right here, right now, even in the suffering, to joy unexplainable. The joy that comes from the Lord is unshakable. It has nothing to do with what's happening to you and everything to do with who died and rose for you. Scripture says, "The joy of the LORD is your strength" (Nehemiah 8:10).

You may have no reason to rejoice right now other than the fact that God Himself is for you, that you are chosen and cherished in |the hands of the Redeemer, who makes all broken things new (Revelation 21:5). But that is more than enough reason for joy. You can rejoice even as you weep. You can praise God even as you question His hand in your hardship, because joy comes from a deep, abiding reliance on the One who redeems everything.

Cry out to the Holy Spirit to flood your weary heart with joy today! Pray for open eyes to be delighted by small joys all around you.

Day 187

You shall sound the loud trumpet on the tenth day of
the seventh month. On the Day of Atonement you shall
sound the trumpet throughout all your land. And you
shall consecrate the fiftieth year, and proclaim liberty
throughout the land to all its inhabitants.

—LEVITICUS 25:9–10

This command to celebrate is literally part of the law that God gave
Moses to honor the Jubilee year. Every fifty years, the Jews were
required to pause their normal order of operations and rejoice. But I
imagine that whenever Jubilee came, the people had plenty to mourn
from those past fifty years too. It couldn't have been all trumpets and
feasts, right?

Some of the most anxious times for me in grief were the days and
weeks leading up to days of celebration—birthdays, holidays, and
anniversaries. Days that used to signal rejoicing but suddenly felt like
devastating reminders of what was gone. But like He did with the
Israelites, God taught me the power of pause and celebration. The
milestone days will feel heavier than others, but they're also an opportunity to consecrate—honor and cherish—what was and entrust the
days ahead to a God who will continue to deliver you from this grief.
Rejoicing may feel so unnatural, even irreverent. But God calls us to
jubilee, and when you celebrate, He will honor your obedience.

What's the next milestone day approaching for you? What's a
small way you can celebrate and honor it even as you grieve
what's gone?

When you pass through the waters, I will be with you;
   and through the rivers, they shall not overwhelm you;
when you walk through fire you shall not be burned,
   and the flame shall not consume you.

—ISAIAH 43:2

Notice, God doesn't promise to keep you out of the waters or the flames. He doesn't promise to keep you in a spiritual safety bubble and deliver you to eternity unscathed. The race you're running is a dangerous one because the world is broken. We will all go home to Jesus with scars.

But just as the Lord was with the Israelites as they passed through the Red Sea (Exodus 14:19–31), so Jesus Himself is with you now, delivering you to safety through very perilous conditions. Just as He was with Daniel's friends in the fiery furnace (Daniel 3:8–25), so He is with you. In order to find any peace in the middle of your own storm or fire, you must remind yourself, *God is with me.*

At times you'll feel afraid walking through deep waters and grow weary from life's flames. I hope this assurance of God's presence may soften your fears and quiet your anxieties even for just a moment. Because of Christ, you can't be defeated. Life will beat you up, but with Jesus at your side, it can't take you down. You are more than a conqueror (Romans 8:37) because He has already conquered everything on your behalf.

Call out to the Lord today, and ask Him to remove any feelings of panic. And remember, with Him, this won't defeat you.

Day 189

I rejoice in my sufferings for your sake, and in my flesh I am filling up what is lacking in Christ's afflictions for the sake of his body, that is, the church.

—COLOSSIANS 1:24

*H*ow can this be true? you might wonder. *Why ever rejoice in suffering?* What Paul spoke of in today's verse, Charles Spurgeon also knew well, claiming, "I am afraid that all the grace that I have got out of my comfortable and easy times and happy hours, might almost lie on a penny. But the good that I have received from my sorrows, and pains, and griefs, is altogether incalculable."[13] Still not convinced? Does it sound like someone covering up his suffering with faith Band-Aids? Striving to manifest some good because the bad is too painful to look at? What is this incalculable good that can come from sorrow?

I think what Paul and Spurgeon were talking about is the fruit of the Spirit—"love, joy, peace, patience, kindness, goodness, faithfulness, gentleness, self-control" (Galatians 5:22–23). This fruit grows through struggle—at least it did for me. I joke often that I was born without patience. I'm now grateful to know the beauty God sows in our waiting. Though I've always been kind, I'm not sure I was always compassionate. I'm thankful for the way my heart breaks for others and my ears open more quickly to them because of my suffering. The fruit of the Spirit has grown in me as I've traversed my weakness and brokenness, leaning on the Father's strength and not my own. The same is true of you. We become our best by enduring the worst. Expect great growth as you faithfully persevere. There is incalculably good fruit in this for you.

Lord, thank You not only that You comfort me in my pain but also that You use it intentionally to grow greater fruit in me.

> I will be found by you, declares the LORD, and I will
> restore your fortunes and gather you from all the nations
> and all the places where I have driven you, declares the
> LORD, and I will bring you back to the place from which
> I sent you into exile.

—JEREMIAH 29:14

God spoke this verse to the grieving Israelites living in exile. Though they had been stubbornly living for themselves and not for God, now because of their prolonged hardship, they were desperate for Him. Their ears were primed to hear His call back home. I love how C. S. Lewis described the decibel of God's voice in our suffering: "God whispers to us in our pleasures, speaks in our conscience, but shouts in our pain: it is His megaphone to rouse a deaf world."[14]

God is always speaking to us, of course, but He often turns up the volume when we're hurting most. He is raising His voice to call us back home, back to safety, back to Himself. Though none of us would ever choose exile, our seasons trudging through the valley, it's these times when we grow most in relationship with and love toward God. When life is loud and chaotic, He shows up as a good Father and shouts to us to make sure we hear Him. Listen for God's prompts in your spirit, your daily life, and the words and actions of others. He is shouting all the more clearly to you in your pain.

Ask the Holy Spirit to open your ears to hear the divine shouts of God to you today. Thank Him that He calls to you over the chaos.

Day 191

They have conquered him by the blood of the Lamb and
by the word of their testimony.

—REVELATION 12:11

We present our résumés to prove our competency to someone who doesn't know us well. We gain their trust with our qualifications, experience, and references. The same applies when you're looking for someone to comfort you, doesn't it? I want to confide in a person who's walked the path I'm walking. And the reverse will be true for you for many years to come, my friend. Your experience is an invitation for someone else to be seen and comforted. They need to know that you, too, have hardship on your résumé.

One of the most painful parts of suffering is that it can leave you feeling isolated. I often struggle to remember that thousands of others around the world have also been through what I'm facing. Solidarity is powerful medicine for suffering. You have the ability to break others' isolation and meet them with personal understanding and encouragement in their pain. It may sound pointless, but keep a record—a journal or simply a note in your phone—of the hardest days and the days of surprising strength and joy. Not only will they be good reminders to you of your own resilience, but they can also serve as hopeful evidence to others that they can survive too.

Make an effort to reflect on and record profound moments of both struggle and hope to encourage yourself and others who may need it.

> To the degree that you share the sufferings of Christ, keep
> on rejoicing, so that at the revelation of His glory you
> may also rejoice and be overjoyed.
>
> —I PETER 4:13, NASB

At the end of the day, if someone asked you what it is that God wants most from you and for you, what would you tell them? Obedience, holiness, evangelism, happiness, sacrifice? All of these things are true. But above all other things, He longs for relationship with you. He wants to wrap you up in His love and glory. He wants your crosses to drive you to His comfort. J. C. Ryle said it like this: "We forget that every cross is a message from God and intended to do us good in the end. Trials are intended to make us think, to wean us from the world, to send us to the Bible, and to drive us to our knees. Health is a good thing, but sickness is far better if it leads us to God. Prosperity is a great mercy, but adversity is a greater one if it brings us to Christ."[15]

God simply wants you. He wants intimacy and connection. Of course, He wants obedience and all the rest. But more importantly, He wants your heart. And sometimes hardship is what it takes to turn your heart fully back to Christ.

Set all pretense and performance aside, and spend time in honest and vulnerable prayer today. Talk with Jesus truly.

You shall therefore lay up these words of mine in your heart and in your soul, and you shall bind them as a sign on your hand, and they shall be as frontlets between your eyes.

—DEUTERONOMY 11:18

Author Randy Alcorn asked a man, "What [should we] do to prepare for evil and suffering?" His immediate answer? "Become a student of God's Word."[16] Darrell Scott, the man who answered this question, knows one of the most devastating losses any human can face. He lost his daughter in the 1999 Columbine school shootings. He has every reason to resent and distrust God because He didn't spare his innocent daughter's life. But Darrell was already a student of the Word when tragedy struck. He had built his life on the foundation of the truth of who God is.

Even as he lived out a parent's absolute worst nightmare come true, he stood firm, acknowledging God's sovereignty and calling out for the grace he knew only God could give. His faith didn't change the devastation and sorrow of losing his daughter. But this man endured unimaginable loss and was able to live in trust rather than bitterness because he knew God's Word and thus knew God's heart. Do you need a reminder of God's good heart for you? Become a student and lover of His Word. It's never too soon.

Spend ten minutes reading one of the Gospels. What does it tell you about the heart of God?

> Rejoice always, pray without ceasing, give thanks in all circumstances; for this is the will of God in Christ Jesus for you.
>
> —1 THESSALONIANS 5:16–18

Even as children of God, don't we spend countless hours wondering and stressing about what God's will is for our lives? Particularly in your current struggle or as you face difficult decisions, have you desperately cried out for discernment? *God, please show me Your plan in this!* And while it's always a delight to the Father when you run to Him and desire confirmation of His will, remember that He's spelled it out plainly for you in His Word: Rejoice, pray, and give thanks.

While these rhythms of worship may be easier to practice when life is going smoothly, they are crucial to you as you endure seasons of hardship. You may feel like there is nothing to rejoice over or thank God for. You may feel discouraged in prayer because something specific you asked for wasn't granted in the way you'd hoped. But trust me, and ask others who've faithfully suffered before you: Praising the Lord in the storms of your life makes you a radiant light for the kingdom. It draws you close to Jesus and enriches your relationship in beautiful ways. When you rejoice, pray, and give thanks even as you suffer, your spirit is buoyed with supernatural strength and hope.

Consider three things you can rejoice in and thank God for today. Write them down and carry them with you.

> These all died in faith, not having received the things
> promised, but having seen them and greeted them from
> afar. . . . But as it is, they desire a better country, that is, a
> heavenly one. Therefore God is not ashamed to be called
> their God, for he has prepared for them a city.
>
> —HEBREWS 11:13, 16

If you were to read the last line of a book first, would you be more willing to accept the ups and downs, the heartbreaks and conflicts, of the rest of the story? If you knew the prize that awaited you at the finish line, could you tolerate the aches and pains a little longer as you ran toward it? My prayer for Ben's bodily healing wasn't answered. And I'd imagine many of your prayers and desires remain in the "no" or "not yet" category too. So, can we still trust that God is making all things—our broken things—new?

The answer is always yes. But just as countless heroes of faith before us, we may not live to see the fruit of God's promise to restore us and our losses. God absolutely can redeem your suffering in discernible ways here on earth, and He very well might be doing just that. Praise Him when this happens! But sometimes the restoration won't come until you, too, are home in a better country. Some of your most painful experiences won't make sense until you can see them from an eternal perspective in the sinless, painless, tearless city Christ has prepared for you. When you can't see the good He's working right now, remember that His promise is still true.

It's okay to lament the discomfort of waiting for a better country. Take time to acknowledge your disappointments and desires today, and rest in the comfort that redemption is how your story will end.

> I, the LORD your God,
>   hold your right hand;
> it is I who say to you, "Fear not,
>   I am the one who helps you."

—ISAIAH 41:13

When we are afraid or in pain, one of the first physical reactions we have is to hold someone's hand. When I first walked back into my and Ben's house after his death, a friend grabbed my hand. As I sat in the front row of the funeral service with his parents, we held one another's hands. As I stood on our back deck with his best friends days later, we took communion and locked hands again. There is something powerful in simply holding on to someone you trust and borrowing some of their strength when you feel scared and weak. It's no coincidence that God reminds His people repeatedly that He is at their right hand.

Just as Jesus came to physically walk this earth to save you, so, too, is He here to walk side by side with you through every spiritual battle you face. His is the hand you can hold when your tank is totally empty. His is the hand you can hold when the next steps feel unbearable. His is the hand you can hold when all you want to do is close your eyes and be guided by someone who knows what lies ahead. Let your instinct be to reach for Christ, and let your hope spring from knowing He will never let go.

Close your eyes, and picture Jesus beside you, His nail-pierced, powerful hand reaching out for yours. Never forget this is your reality at all times, every day.

Will you even put me in the wrong?
    Will you condemn me that you may be in the right?
Have you an arm like God,
    and can you thunder with a voice like his?

—JOB 40:8–9

When the Lord spoke these words to Job, a man who had lost nearly everything precious in his life, God wasn't angry with him. He was correcting Job's sight. He was reminding Job of the grandeur of who He is. Job had been faithful through intense and undeserved suffering but at a certain point got understandably frustrated. We can all relate to this. I know you've wondered at some point, *Lord, wouldn't all of this have been better if . . .* Or *Why couldn't You have just done it this way?*

God doesn't blame you for your disappointment, nor does He hold it against you. But He will always remind you that He is perfect in His plans, kind in His sovereignty, and always working for your good and His glory. You may think you know better than God at times, but remember that, like a child in the back seat telling his parent how to drive, your directions would never get you where you need to go. Even when your heart is in the right place, remember Jesus' rightful place as the King of your life. You don't have to understand or like the way He's working, but let this remind you to humbly trust your God.

Lord, if I am resentful toward You in any way today, convict me and forgive me of that. Help me lay aside my frustration and fully trust You.

She had heard the reports about Jesus and came up
behind him in the crowd and touched his garment. For
she said, "If I touch even his garments, I will be made
well." And immediately the flow of blood dried up, and
she felt in her body that she was healed of her disease.

—MARK 5:27–29

The distressed woman who reached out for Jesus' cloak had been suffering an awful disease for twelve years. She was afflicted with an issue of chronic bleeding that not only pained her physically but also ostracized her socially from her friends, family, and religious community. She was outcast, hurting, and alone, and she knew in her desperation that the healing power of the Messiah was her last shot. Her only shot. Was there doubt in her mind that maybe Jesus wouldn't heal her? Probably. But what she brought with her is all you need to bring to Jesus, friend: a mustard seed of faith.

This woman had just enough courage to take the risk that Christ's robes *might* heal her. She wasn't a rabbi or a scholar and likely had had no formal education. But what she did believe was that Jesus could heal, and she acted boldly and faithfully, hoping with all her heart that it was true. All you need to do is reach out for Christ, desperate and hopeful for His powerful healing to touch your deepest, most broken places.

*Jesus, I am desperate. I'm grasping for Your supernatural power
today to heal me from _____.*

Why is my pain unceasing,
   my wound incurable,
   refusing to be healed?
Will you be to me like a deceitful brook,
   like waters that fail?

Therefore thus says the LORD:
"If you return, I will restore you,
   and you shall stand before me."

                          —JEREMIAH 15:18–19

Can you identify with Jeremiah's pain here? Known as the weeping prophet, Jeremiah was doing exactly that in this devastated prayer—he was weeping! He was crying out and questioning whether the Lord would heal his chronic rejection and sorrow. He even wondered if God's words had deceived him. Had he trusted in promises that might not ultimately be true? He held back none of his despair but was fully transparent in his anguish.

And what happened when he lamented fully and honestly to God? God drew near to him. God acknowledged his suffering and reminded him to come close, to return to Him even with his questions, frustration, and hopelessness, and that He would restore him. There is no prayer too dire and no pain too big to lay at your Father's feet. Don't be afraid to bring your whole broken heart to Him, all the beautiful, ugly pieces. Just continue to return to Him.

> Be totally honest with God about how you're feeling—about your situation or about God Himself. Say what you hate, what you're scared of, how you're disappointed. Say all that you need to.

> I am sure of this, that he who began a good work in you
> will bring it to completion at the day of Jesus Christ.
>
> —PHILIPPIANS 1:6

Before the foundation of the universe, God authored a perfect ending to your story. If you are a committed follower of Jesus, there is no valley low enough and no scene dark enough in the narrative of your life to keep your guaranteed happy ending from coming. Take a moment to really pause and consider that. It's like every time you turn on a romantic comedy, knowing that no matter what conflict occurs, the story *will* be made right and true love will win. The same is true with the story God has written for your life!

He began a happy-ending love story for you when He set the world in motion, and the day you accepted Jesus as your Lord and Savior, His blood ensured that that ending *will* come true. You can trust the Lord infinitely more than the writers of romance stories. You can walk through every dark and painful chapter of this life with confidence, hope, and expectation because Christ is completing His good work in you. The story gets better, if not perceivably in this lifetime, then undeniably and extravagantly for eternity. Nothing can thwart His plan for you, and no hardship here will be wasted. Every pain you experience will add to the beauty of your happy ending.

Thank God today that He is writing a perfect happy ending to your story. Praise Him that complete love, joy, and glory are what you're heading toward.

Day 201

My soul clings to the dust;
  give me life according to your word!
When I told of my ways, you answered me;
  teach me your statutes!
Make me understand the way of your precepts,
  and I will meditate on your wondrous works.
My soul melts away for sorrow;
  strengthen me according to your word!

—PSALM 119:25–28

What a beautifully broken yet hopeful prayer the psalmist offered here. He admitted that he was so burdened, like his soul was melting away. But even as he despaired, he pleaded with the Lord to supply everything he couldn't muster on his own. He knew that true peace and hope in the face of hardship can be revealed only by God, through His Word.

You can pursue endless how-tos and temporary fixes in this world as you struggle, but none will bring peace or embolden you with courage the way God's Word does. It's that plain and simple. The psalmist knew that. Like him, I encourage you—spend time in what many call God's love letter to us. His words of life are intended to give you life. He wants to teach you His statutes, to reveal to you His good works and His merciful heart, and to strengthen you by the power of His Holy Spirit as you meet Him in Scripture, in prayer, and in worship. This psalm is a humble and effective reminder of the power of Scripture in our struggle. Use it!

Pray this before reading the Word today: *Lord, give me life and strengthen me through Your words. Illuminate exactly what my heart needs in order to trust, understand, and cling to You.*

> While we were still weak, at the right time Christ died for
> the ungodly . . . but God shows his love for us in that
> while we were still sinners, Christ died for us.
>
> —ROMANS 5:6, 8

Don't miss the beginning of that sentence: "While we were still weak . . ." How good is God? We know that salvation is a gracious gift from God, one that we can never earn. But we're reminded here that He gave us that gift not when we were obedient and strong but when we were sinful and weak.

The Lord always shows up for you at the right time. He provides what you need when you have nowhere else to turn, and thus, He gets all the credit. And if He would give you the gift of eternal salvation when you were sinful, weak, and undeserving, won't He also gift you what you need in your pain? He will fill you up when your soul feels totally empty. And you can expect Him to provide the peace you need at precisely the moment peace feels impossible. You're never past the point of rescue with Christ. Because it's in your most hopeless moments that Jesus shows up with His most abundant love and grace.

Thank God today that He needs nothing from you but your need. Praise Him that, in your total lack, He shows up with abundant mercy and grace.

> She came and knelt before him, saying, "Lord, help me."
> And he answered, "It is not right to take the children's
> bread and throw it to the dogs." She said, "Yes, Lord, yet
> even the dogs eat the crumbs that fall from their masters'
> table." Then Jesus answered her, "O woman, great is your
> faith! Be it done for you as you desire."
>
> —MATTHEW 15:25–28

Do you relate to this woman? When you go to God, wail, and call out tearfully for something to ease your struggle through this valley, do you feel like a dog just hoping for scraps? The woman in this passage came desperately to Jesus for the healing of her daughter. And while Jesus' response may sound cruel or dismissive to us at first, He was asking this Gentile woman a very important question of faith. The Jews referred to Gentiles, or non-Jewish people, as dogs. Jesus was asking the woman, "Even though the Jews degrade you, do you believe you're still worthy of My blessing?" And He honored her bold yes.

What things make you feel less than or unworthy of the Lord's favor? Have you doubted Him too much? Are you hiding sins you're ashamed of? Have you come to God as a last resort in your pain? Whatever shame you feel disqualifies you from the Lord's blessing and healing is a lie. All God requires of us is our honest and humble faith. He needs us to admit our need, believing He hears us simply because He loves us. The outcome of your requests is in God's hands, but never doubt how much your needs and your prayers matter to Him. He is listening.

If you're holding on to any thoughts or regrets that are causing you to doubt that you're worthy of God's blessing, speak them aloud to Him today and ask to be freed from that wrong thinking.

I believe that I shall look upon the goodness of the LORD
 in the land of the living!
Wait for the LORD;
 be strong, and let your heart take courage;
 wait for the LORD!

—PSALM 27:13–14

Waiting is often where I struggle most. It seemed like every day a flood of questions would run through my head: *How long will this pain go on? When will _____ finally happen? When will I start to feel like myself again?* I knew in my mind the goodness of the Lord, but in the throes of grief, I longed to see His goodness with my eyes too. This is natural. Every season, good or bad, will require waiting of some sort because this earth isn't our ultimate home, and deep in our souls we know that.

But the waiting is important because it reminds us of the power and peace that come from reliance on the Lord. Scripture says that one of the muscles that suffering builds in us is the muscle of hope (Romans 5:3–4). As you wait, actively look for God's mercies that are hidden all around you—physical health, supportive community, a much-needed nap, even a delicious meal. As you patiently hope for resolution or reprieve from your struggles, as you long for the peace of eternity, hold tight to the small goodnesses you can see and be confident of the perfect eternity that's surely coming your way.

Ask the Lord for eyes to supernaturally notice all the blessings, encouragements, goodness, and beauty around you today. Then pay attention!

The Spirit helps us in our weakness. For we do not know what to pray for as we ought, but the Spirit himself intercedes for us with groanings too deep for words.

—ROMANS 8:26

Hardship has a way of making us feel helpless. It's not unusual to be at a loss for words when others ask you what you need or how they can help. You may genuinely not know what you need right now or have the capacity to figure it out, and that's okay. There's no quick fix here, and it can be hard to find adequate words to express your pain, your fears, or your needs. Maybe you're feeling that confusion and helplessness in prayer too. I get it. Even as a writer and speaker, I often found my mind blank and my tongue tied when I came to the Lord.

Remember Jesus' words on the cross as He suffered unimaginable pain: "My God, why have you forsaken me?" (Mark 15:34). This is groaning. This is a cry of someone in anguish at a loss for words. And in the same way Jesus called out to the Father, so, too, does the Holy Spirit groan on your behalf as you grieve. God's Spirit *in you* prays directly to His loving, fatherly heart *for you* when you don't know what you need. How powerful is that? How freeing is that? How kind is that? Sometimes the only words you need are "Intercede, Holy Spirit."

Take four deep, long breaths. Now close your eyes, and simply pray, "Come, Holy Spirit. You know exactly what I need. Prepare me to see it and receive it."

Because he holds fast to me in love, I will deliver him;
  I will protect him, because he knows my name.
When he calls to me, I will answer him;
  I will be with him in trouble;
  I will rescue him and honor him.

—PSALM 91:14–15

In one sense you know that these words are true of your soul for eternity. You know that Christ has already delivered you from sin, protected you from God's holy wrath, and ensured your name is forever written in the Book of Life. But don't forget, friend, that the Lord's deliverance and protection, presence and rescue, are all available to you in the here and now too. When you call to God in your suffering, He may be freeing you from threats you're not even aware of.

Of course, we pray that God deliver us from our pain. But He is also rescuing us from far more dangerous things: self-reliance, self-righteousness, and a deceitful prosperity gospel mindset. When we don't rely on the Lord, we're running on a dangerously inflated sense of our own competence. "Pride goes before destruction, and a haughty spirit before a fall" (Proverbs 16:18). When we compare how we grieve with others' grief, we compromise compassion and fall victim to our blind spots. When we believe our obedience can earn God's favor, we will always end up disappointed.

Keep praying for deliverance from your sorrow, but also ask God honestly to rescue you from pride, which leads to all sorts of heartaches and falls.

Lord, reveal any place I need to humbly reset my reliance on You.

> May the God of hope fill you with all joy and peace in
> believing, so that by the power of the Holy Spirit you
> may abound in hope.
>
> —ROMANS 15:13

Joy, peace, and hope are likely not the foremost feelings you're experiencing right now. As you grieve what's lost and wonder about what's to come, you're probably feeling more dread, despondence, or even despair as you navigate this painful season. But please take to heart that you don't have to wait forever to experience joy again. You can't change your circumstances, but you can change your perspective.

Yes, your pain is real, but you can shift your gaze to what is true about God. His goodness and perfect, loving control are still real too. Sure, you can't know how or when He'll redeem this loss, yet you can remind yourself of all the things He's redeemed in the past. You have a choice to fixate on what He's taken away or call to mind what He's already been faithful to give. Changing your perspective like this won't eliminate the reality of your painful circumstances and the sorrow that comes along with them. But it's the way to actively seek out real hope. Reminding yourself of God's faithfulness to you really can fill you with joy and peace even as you grieve.

Write down two characteristics you know to be true of God from Scripture that you can focus on today. Have hope, knowing His character never changes!

> Our citizenship is in heaven, and from it we await a
> Savior, the Lord Jesus Christ, who will transform our
> lowly body to be like his glorious body.
>
> —PHILIPPIANS 3:20–21

You are a citizen of heaven. More than from your status as a citizen of your country or city, your identity comes from your secured place in eternity. Your spirit is united with Christ's, and the Holy Spirit lives within your earthly body. And though one day your physical body will be fully restored and redeemed at His second coming, right now it continues to bear the burden of a sinful world—it continues deteriorating day by day.

This never feels truer than when you're suffering.

Whether you're struggling in your grief with physical depletion or poor mental health, your body bears the weight of all your stress and sorrow. Hardship will leave you physically run-down and cognitively weak. Don't shame yourself for this, my friend, but be aware of it as you struggle. Know that your body is working harder than you realize to combat the strain of stress and to sustain you through each day. Have grace for your not-yet-redeemed body, and call out to God for the strength and endurance you need until you go home.

Take inventory of any physical or mental deficits you're feeling today. Call out to God for supernatural healing and resources to treat those ailments.

> You have kept count of my tossings;
>> put my tears in your bottle.
>> Are they not in your book?

—PSALM 56:8

The psalmist David wrote these words as part of a great song of lament. Line after line, he recounted the oppressions, threats, and injustices he had suffered. Then he paused to remember that God remembered them too. God always remembers your tossings, your wanderings. He never forgets your wilderness seasons of worry, running, or isolation. He holds you tenderly and draws near to you as you struggle.

Likewise, the Lord collects your every tear and keeps them safely in a bottle. David's beautiful image here references a sweet ancient practice. In Roman times, it was common for those grieving a death to collect the tears of the mourners in a tear jar, a way to honor the love they had and grief they now bore for the deceased. It was a means of both celebrating and grieving, representing love, joy, loss, and remembrance. David knows well God's immense Fatherly compassion for His people and imagines Him holding our tears with reverence and tenderness in the same way. Your pain is recorded in His Book of Life and remembered for eternity. None of your hurt is forgotten.

Praise God today that He takes great care to note every one of your tears.

Day 210

Out of the abundance of the heart the mouth speaks.

—MATTHEW 12:34

The way your heart and mind work together is a very intentional part of God's creation. While your physical heart and brain work together to keep oxygen fueling your body, your spiritual heart is the soil from which your thoughts, words, and actions grow. Simply put, what you put in will determine what spews out. As Jesus' followers, we need to fill our hearts with the truth so that our thoughts, words, and actions will subsequently be filtered through truth as well.

When our hearts fixate on discouragement, discouragement will ripple out in our words and behavior. When our hearts fixate on fear, fear will be the language that we speak. Be intentional to fill your heart with God's words—His truth and His promises. Read them. Write them down. Repeat them to yourself. Go back to His words again and again. Even if your mind struggles to believe them right now, pour them into your heart. Eventually the hope at the root of their message will make its way into your thoughts, words, and actions.

Meditate on this passage so that it takes root in your heart and starts to reset your mind: "The peace of God, which surpasses all understanding, will guard your hearts and your minds in Christ Jesus" (Philippians 4:7).

One of them, when he saw that he was healed, turned
back, praising God with a loud voice; and he fell on his
face at Jesus' feet, giving him thanks.

—LUKE 17:15–16

The man in this passage is one of ten men with leprosy who were miraculously healed by Jesus. Leprosy was highly contagious and, as a result, forced its victims into physical, emotional, and spiritual isolation. They were permanently shunned and labeled unclean and inferior. Leprosy stole every joy from their lives. And by Christ's mercy, all ten of them were healed—yet only one thanked Him.

It's easy to get swept up in the excitement of a long-awaited blessing, a "yes" answer to prayer. Every mercy God gives us should be celebrated and enjoyed. But don't forget, as the Lord begins to heal what is diseased or broken in you, that one of the greatest tools to continue in that healing is thankfulness. Pause at every moment, small or large, when you can see God redeeming and working in your life, and worship Him. Awareness and thankfulness will help increase hope in and connection with God as you work through this season together.

What are three things, small or large, you can pause and thank God for today?

Thus says the One who is high and lifted up,
    who inhabits eternity, whose name is Holy:
"I dwell in the high and holy place,
    and also with him who is of a contrite and lowly spirit,
to revive the spirit of the lowly,
    and to revive the heart of the contrite."

—ISAIAH 57:15

When you are at rock bottom, remember, it's the Mighty One's greatest pleasure to lift you up. Jesus chose to descend from heaven in order to raise you from death to life (spiritually and, one day, physically at the resurrection). Though God is holy, perfect, and all-powerful, it's His joy to stoop down into your most broken moments and sit with you in your tears. He is on His throne at all times, but He is also dwelling inside you and walking through life's most devastating valleys with you. You are not alone.

Christ doesn't just comfort you while you grieve and then ascend back to His throne room in heaven, wishing you good luck. He is in this with you for the long haul. Slowly and faithfully, He will revive you. He will lift you out of despair and start to mend the fractures of your broken heart. Jesus is *the* Redeemer. Cling to Him, and He will carry you out of the darkness into a higher, holy place.

Thank God today that He is not a God who simply directs from above but a Messiah and Savior who descends with the sole purpose of lifting you back up.

Day 213

> If we live by the Spirit, let us also keep in step with the Spirit.
>
> —GALATIANS 5:25

This may sound like a simple instruction, but it takes intentionality and commitment to put it into practice. Particularly in times of struggle, it can be hard to walk in obedience to God. It's difficult to have patience with situations and offer gentleness to others. But the Lord calls us as His children to keep in step with Him. Think about when you played follow-the-leader as a child. Your single focus was doing what the leader was doing. So, consider this in your times of pain: What does God's Spirit do?

The Holy Spirit is gentle, not forceful. He nudges us to step here, speak this word, ask that question, remember this truth. Every day, pay attention to His soft prompts, and follow His lead. Stay so constant in prayer for God's help that your thoughts can't be separated from your prayers.

The Holy Spirit also reminds believers of the Word (John 14:26). So you, too, remind yourself as often as you can what God's Word says. It will seep into your heart and mind and carry you back to a place of peace even when everything all around you is falling apart.

Pray that the Holy Spirit shows you ways to connect with Jesus and the hopeful promises from God's Word today.

My mouth will praise you with joyful lips,
when I remember you upon my bed,
   and meditate on you in the watches of the night;
for you have been my help,
   and in the shadow of your wings I will sing for joy.
My soul clings to you;
   your right hand upholds me.

—PSALM 63:5–8

Nighttime can be some of the most distressing hours when you're hurting. For months I had a girlfriend on call on any given night to come stay with me. For years I kept the television on and built a fortress of pillows beside me so my bed didn't feel so empty. Falling asleep and the haunting dreams that often followed became a daily dread. Nighttime felt the easiest to get trapped in cycles of endless, anxiety-producing thoughts. That's why I love the vulnerability of this psalmist here to remind us that we need to meditate on the Lord as we lie worried in our beds. He says, "I get it; here's what works for me."

When you dread another sleepless or tear-filled night, meditate on God's Word as you lie down. Listen to worship music or a podcast of Scripture being read. Picture yourself physically curled up in the Father's arms in your room, in the shadow of His wings, just as a toddler would curl up in his mother's arms when he's sleepy and afraid. Cling to God in prayer. Think about the heart of Jesus for you, picture Him sitting with you, arm around your shoulder, and know that you're safe.

Find a specific passage, prayer, or song that makes you feel connected to and safe with the Lord. Repeat that each night this week as you fall asleep.

Day 215

Remember my affliction and my wanderings,
    the wormwood and the gall!
My soul continually remembers it
    and is bowed down within me.
But this I call to mind,
    and therefore I have hope:

The steadfast love of the LORD never ceases;
    his mercies never come to an end.

—LAMENTATIONS 3:19–22

But is such a powerful word. It's where you find strength to endure when you're weak; it's how you actively shift your perspective. Learn from this intentional, courageous *but*. The writer, Jeremiah, knew there's no good in sugarcoating your circumstances. He knew it doesn't serve you to try to gloss over the hurt, the doubts, the disappointments. He was honest about how hopeless and helpless he felt as he faced hardship, even admitting that he "continually remembers it."

But as he admitted his pain, he also called to mind God's faithfulness: "The steadfast love of the LORD never ceases." The reason he could get up in the morning and expectantly await a better future was that he was aware of his pain *but* he knew God wouldn't leave him in it forever. Hope doesn't eradicate the hurt, nor should your hurt blind you to the eternal hope that God's unchanging love for you offers. Tell the truth about your suffering, *but* let your pain always be accompanied by the Living Hope of Christ in you.

> *Lord, this hurts. But I know You're at work. This is harder than I know how to handle. But You are good.*

I will lead the blind
　　in a way that they do not know,
in paths that they have not known
　　I will guide them.
I will turn the darkness before them into light,
　　the rough places into level ground.
These are the things I do,
　　and I do not forsake them.

—ISAIAH 42:16

Notice the words used to describe God as our Shepherd through difficult times: *lead, guide, light, level.* Our Good Shepherd delights to lead His sheep to safety.

The Lord can safely lead you into uncharted territory because no territory is a surprise to Him. He can guide you through perilous places because He is your ultimate protector. He can bring light into places that feel totally consumed with darkness, because He is the Light of the world. He can bring your soul and spirit stability when everything around you is spinning out of control, because He is the Prince of Peace. Resist the urge to forge your own path. Instead, lean on Him for wisdom and direction, and He will do all of this and more for you.

What is the next step or decision that scares you? Surrender it to the Lord in prayer today; ask for His help and guidance.

If then you have been raised with Christ, seek the things
that are above, where Christ is, seated at the right hand of
God. Set your minds on things that are above, not on
things that are on earth.

—COLOSSIANS 3:1–2

One of the reasons we resent suffering so much is that it can be
hard to see the good that God is working through our discomfort.
Unlike when we exercise, pushing our physical bodies and seeing
measurable change, the spiritual muscles that suffering builds aren't
as easy to recognize. But just as the Lord will one day redeem your
physical self, resurrecting you like Jesus was resurrected, so, too, is He
redeeming your spiritual self, making you more and more aligned
with His Holy Spirit.

As you spend intentional time with the Lord, you may be surprised at moments of patience in situations that weeks ago would
have sent you into a tailspin. You may find yourself better able to take
control of rambling anxious thoughts and calm them with biblical
truth. You might start to more easily rejoice for those who have what
you wish you had. Thank God when you see these fruits of spiritual
refinement show up. When you choose to set your mind on spiritual
things, the things that are above, it will inevitably foster greater joy
and sturdier faith as you endure this suffering.

*Lord, thank You for strengthening my soul. Help me see the
beauty You're working in my heart through this suffering.
I praise You that You don't waste my pain!*

Have you forgotten the encouraging words God spoke to you as his children? He said,

> "My child, don't make light of the LORD's discipline,
>   and don't give up when he corrects you.
> For the LORD disciplines those he loves,
>   and he punishes each one he accepts as his child."

As you endure this divine discipline, remember that God is treating you as his own children.

—HEBREWS 12:5–7, NLT

Whether you are a parent or not, you know that often the kindest thing a parent can do for their child is to discipline them. Sometimes the discipline is correction of a wrong behavior or protection from something they're unaware is a threat. And sometimes it's the process of instilling a new skill or character trait. Though the child can't always see the tender, loving heart behind the discipline, the parent is willing to be misunderstood to ensure the good of their child.

Scripture repeatedly describes God as our Father. As your divine parent, He may see dangers in your path that you can't see, and however He's disrupted your life may be the best means of protecting you. God's sole motivation for working in your life is love. Nothing He does is to intentionally harm you. Even His actions, inactions, and interactions that feel like discipline are for your ultimate flourishing.

If you feel at all angry or distrustful toward God today, picture Him as your parent, holding you at the doctor's office as you endure a treatment that hurts. Thank Him that He is a wise, protective Father.

> On the evening of that day, the first day of the week, the doors being locked where the disciples were for fear of the Jews, Jesus came and stood among them and said to them, "Peace be with you."
>
> —JOHN 20:19

The evening referred to here is the Sunday night following Christ's crucifixion, death, and burial. His followers were terrified. The disciples had scattered during His execution for fear that they, too, would be killed because of their public allegiance to Him. Not only were they afraid for their lives, but they were also confused and disappointed, left disillusioned after their Messiah was slaughtered. *What will happen now? Can He still save us?*

The fact that the writer specifically noted they locked all the doors just points to their terror and hopelessness. You may feel afraid and hopeless too. Like the situation you're in or the shame you're surrounded by is past the point of redemption, so better just to lock yourself inside. No matter what plan has gone awry or what threats seem to be pressing in, Jesus can always meet you behind your locked doors. There's nowhere you can hide from His mercy or run from His presence. Even as you hide, call out to Him. He's ready to come stand with you. He's already offering His miraculous peace to you.

What fear, regret, or situation do you feel trapped by? Call to Jesus to come behind the locked doors with you so that His supernatural peace may be with you in it.

The people who survived the sword
found grace in the wilderness;
when Israel sought for rest,
the LORD appeared to him from far away.
I have loved you with an everlasting love;
therefore I have continued my faithfulness to you.

—JEREMIAH 31:2-3

Life can feel like a constant battle. Even in seasons of success and happiness, there is wave after wave of things to worry about and fight to maintain. And then tragedy happens, and all of a sudden, you're on the front lines of chaotic battle with a long list of enemies—despair, anxiety, bitterness, sorrow, fear—seeking to destroy you from every direction. Hold on tight to the Lord, friend. Call on God's holy name in prayer to keep your adversaries at bay and push them back behind enemy lines, where they belong. The Lord can defeat the internal foes that you can't.

And when the onslaught does temporarily subside, when God beats back your deepest fears for a moment, exhale. Rest. Let Him restore your weary soul and bind up your wounds. Find grace, still-ness, and renewed hope in the quiet wilderness with Him. When you seek the Lord, in battle and in recovery, He is always faithful to sup-ply what you need. This life *is* a constant battle, but He *will* continue His faithfulness to you.

God of Armies, I can't win this battle on my own. Appear to me; fight for me; help me push back these mental and spiritual enemies today.

Everyone who has been born of God overcomes the
world. And this is the victory that has overcome the
world—our faith.

—I JOHN 5:4

I know you long for victory in this battle you're facing. You're desperate for it to be over so you can rest. God hears your cries. His
promise to you is true: With faith in the resurrected Christ, we overcome the devastations and atrocities of this world. Hold tight to this
truth and speak it to yourself daily. Write it on a Post-it note and put
it somewhere visible so that when you feel the pressure to rely on
your own strength, you can turn back to Jesus.

God has more than sufficient power to change your circumstances,
heal your heart, and restore your faith. Continue to bring those
requests to Him, like the persistent widow whose wish was granted
because of her faithfulness over time (Luke 18:1–8). Sometimes the
Lord is preparing a greater victory than you see. Sometimes when He
seems silent or dismissive of your cries for change, it's because the
circumstances you're facing are working a beautiful victory inside
you—that only He can see. Trust in this promise. Trust in His process. He will see you through.

Jesus, I know You are all-powerful. Please help me overcome
this hardship, in Your timing and in Your way. You have
already secured my victory, whether now or in eternity. I
trust You completely.

> We were so utterly burdened beyond our strength that
> we despaired of life itself. Indeed, we felt that we had
> received the sentence of death. But that was to make us
> rely not on ourselves but on God who raises the dead.
>
> —2 CORINTHIANS 1:8–9

Have you ever noticed that the people most sound and secure in their faith are the ones who have suffered? It's because they have a track record of reliance on God. They have survived hardship because of what Jesus did in them, not because of anything special they were able to do themselves. One of the surest signs of spiritual maturity is not independence but full, hope-filled, peaceful dependence on the Lord in seasons of both security and uncertainty.

While dependence in our culture tends to connote weakness or inability, Paul knew that what God says is true: Dependence is our greatest asset. Scripture says that pride comes before a fall (Proverbs 16:18) but that God exalts the humble (Matthew 23:12). We can't soften the impact of death. We can't handle the torrent of grief. We can't save ourselves, spiritually or otherwise. We need *His* strength, direction, and wisdom in order to endure the hardships we'll face until we go home. Reliance on Him is freedom! And every trial you face offers you a sweet reminder that dependence on Christ is *the* way to live securely and free.

Meditate on this truth: True security comes not from independence but daily, trusting dependence on Jesus, our Lord and Messiah.

Day 223

The LORD is my strength and my song,
  and he has become my salvation;
this is my God, and I will praise him,
  my father's God, and I will exalt him.
The LORD is a man of war;
  the LORD is his name.

—EXODUS 15:2–3

You know well that Jesus is the only one who can save you, but do you remember that Jesus actually *is* your salvation? Yes, right now, as He sits at the Father's right hand in heaven, He is your living and active salvation. He saves you from sin, of course, but also from fear. He rescues you from depression and loneliness. He delivers you from regret, shame, and hopelessness. He frees you from the snares of dread and anxiety. He pulls you from the paralysis you're stuck in and equips you to take one small step forward.

Scripture describes the Lord as a man of war because He is always fighting for you. Jesus fought and won the ultimate war against sin and death on the cross, but even still, with every breath you take, tear you cry, and prayer you pray, He is at war for you. Jesus is your Advocate. The Holy Spirit is your Helper. God is the redeemer of all that you have lost. Run to Him, and let Him save you today, tomorrow, and forever.

Lord, You are my salvation. I need Your rescuing. Save me from _____ specifically today.

> Continue steadfastly in prayer, being watchful in it with thanksgiving.
>
> —COLOSSIANS 4:2

We've talked already and will continue to talk about the power of regular communication with God. In times of stress and struggle, prayer may feel like the natural response or it may feel more difficult. Either way, on either day, keep praying. Keep coming to Jesus' throne, beloved. But when you do, don't let your communion end with "Amen."

Be watchful throughout your day after you present your requests to God. A grave mistake so many believers make is to put their prayers in the rearview mirror. You give God your requests and then go about your day with your spiritual eyes closed. Don't let your prayers be out of mind, out of sight. Pray expectantly—eager to see the Spirit work in response to what you ask of Him. That doesn't mean His answers will be quick or look just as you'd like, but when the eyes of your heart are thankfully and expectantly watchful, you will witness His faithfulness in powerful, tangible ways. And when you do see a prayer answered, rejoice and write it down! Keep a "God winks" journal or note in your phone. Record God's yeses and good-nesses to look back on for encouragement on days He seems harder to see or hear.

Keep your eyes open. Make a note of what you prayed about today, and ask the Holy Spirit for discernment to stay connected to His presence throughout the day.

Day 225

> I will not restrain my mouth;
>> I will speak in the anguish of my spirit;
>> I will complain in the bitterness of my soul.
>
> —JOB 7:11

What if I told you that your heartbreak, anger, and true lament don't sound like whining to God's ears? No, in fact, they sound like worship to Him. Your refusal to accept suffering reflects the holy longing for heaven in your heart. You know you're not made for pain, sickness, and heartbreak, because you were made for sin-free life with the Lord. When you wail, you're acknowledging that you desire better because you know God desires better for you, His beloved child. You honor His design and His plan for humanity and creation.

I've always been an "I'm fine" or "It'll work itself out" or "Everything happens for a reason" person. And there's nothing wrong with keeping a positive perspective. But rose-colored glasses don't do much for grief. They actually can be downright harmful, over time concealing the open wounds that need to be felt and directly addressed in order to heal. Don't hold back your disappointment, your rage, at a life that hurts. God's heart is breaking right alongside yours. You won't be here forever. He truly will heal all broken things. But for now, don't restrain your mouth. Your lament and longing for more are painfully beautiful offerings of worship to the God who made you in His own image.

How do you need to lament? With tears or yells, through writing or drawing, music or physical exercise—whatever will be most helpful in expressing your emotions today, do with God, knowing His tears fall right along with yours.

> The Gentiles seek after all these things, and your heavenly
> Father knows that you need them all. But seek first the
> kingdom of God and his righteousness, and all these
> things will be added to you.
>
> —MATTHEW 6:32–33

I know you want answers, explanations, anything to give a little sense of resolution. We are rational beings and all too often confuse understanding with peace. But if God answered all your questions, would it change the way you feel? For many of us, the answer is yes and no. God is generous and kind; He is willing and able to comfort His grieving kids.

Right before Ben passed away, I was told he'd had multiple strokes while in a coma and there was no chance of life. It didn't make sense. Doctors didn't know why. I walked away shocked, devastated, and without a clear answer. A few days later, I received a text from the neurosurgeon: "Have some info you might want to hear." In God's kindness and her generosity, she took time to explain to me the cause of his strokes found in the autopsy. It didn't change anything; I went on with funeral plans that day. Knowing the cause wouldn't bring Ben back or make my next several years any easier. But that tiny answer did free me from wondering for the rest of my life. It was God alleviating one of many unknowns I'd have to grapple with. So, seek the assurances you need from the Lord, but don't place undue weight on understanding. Thank Him for the small answers or insights He gives, and then choose to continue trusting Him with the ones He doesn't.

What is one revelation or assurance of peace you can remember and thank God for today?

Day 227

> Bear one another's burdens, and so fulfill the law of
> Christ.
>
> —GALATIANS 6:2

This may feel like a difficult, even audacious, command in a time of suffering. What a bold request, expecting you to carry the weight of another's burdens when yours alone feel unbearable! Indeed, there is a necessary selfishness when you're under strain, in distress, or walking through grief. It's wise to slow down, to rest, and to attend more carefully to your wearied mind and heart than you would during easier seasons. Many call this self-care, and it can help keep you spiritually full even as you're emotionally empty.

But even when you're weak—especially when you're weak—what Jesus taught remains true: "Give, and it will be given to you" (Luke 6:38). I've experienced the way God blesses our care for and connection with others in difficult seasons. When we engage with and encourage those around us also struggling, it broadens our perspective. To send a meal or text, to reach out and simply check in with a friend in need, not only serves them but also shifts our gaze onto something other than our own pain for a moment. You may not have much to give right now, but what you give will in return be given to you by the Holy Spirit.

What is one simple thing you can do to send love or encouragement to someone today?

"The mountains may depart
    and the hills be removed,
but my steadfast love shall not depart from you,
    and my covenant of peace shall not be removed,"
    says the LORD, who has compassion on you.

—ISAIAH 54:10

*C*ovenant. It's not a frequently used word in our time and culture. But it's the term God used to explain His relationship with us in Scripture, both in the Old Testament and in the New. Though commonly understood to simply mean "promise," which certainly is part of its meaning, a Hebrew covenant was a legal binding agreement between two parties. So, when you are in Christ, God's covenant of peace with you means that you are eternally, spiritually *bound* to His divine peace. It's not going anywhere. Jesus is the Prince of Peace, and you can't be separated from Him.

But notice what isn't a part of God's covenant of peace. He never promises pain-free living. He never promises perfection on this earth or that your plans will go uninterrupted. In fact, He warns us that mountains may depart and hills may be removed—hardship will happen, and suffering is a reality no one escapes. But amid the chaos and the trials, your secure binding to God's divine peace can never be broken. At all times, you have access to *shalom*—internal peace, harmony, wholeness, prosperity, welfare, and tranquility.

Praise God that His covenant of love and peace with you can never be broken, no matter how hurt or broken you are. Ask to feel His peace today.

Day 229

In him was life, and the life was the light of men. The light shines in the darkness, and the darkness has not overcome it.

—JOHN 1:4–5

Jesus is the Light of Life. He gives us vision, hope, and courage for the next steps when we can't see where we're going. And as much as we'd love for His light to eliminate *all* the darkness at once, He often shows up more like a single beam pointing just a few feet forward. I think of using a flashlight or candle when the power goes out in my home. Its light is essential to function in the dark, but it doesn't come close to illuminating the whole room. It leads you one step at a time.

I believe this is how Jesus meets us in our suffering. He gives us vision when the lights are out to see biblical truths, people, and things that can sustain us in the middle of the darkness. As you learn to follow His direction, He will illuminate a path toward safe places where your energy and hope can be restored—support groups, a specific place of meditation or prayer, counseling, a mentor to walk with you through grief. Where is His healing light pointing you? Where can you spend some restorative time today? The darkness may be all around you, but His light is always shining. Follow it! The darkness *will not* overcome it.

Pray for the Lord to reveal one new safe place of healing today. Trust His direction, and spend time there.

> You believe that God is one; you do well. Even the
> demons believe—and shudder!
>
> —JAMES 2:19

You may have grown up believing in God. You may be new to relationship with Him. You may still be questioning whether the gospel is true or whether it's some sort of religious bandage for a life that's too full of suffering to be under the control of a good God. Regardless of where you fall, tragedy and trial have a way of forcing you to face the validity of whatever you're putting your faith in, or as C. S. Lewis said, "You never know how much you really believe anything until its truth or falsehood becomes a matter of life and death to you. . . . Only a real risk tests the reality of a belief."[17]

As you start to see how much our life and hope depend on Christ, do you realize He is living, present, powerful, and active right now in your suffering? Or do you think He came to save your soul for eternity but sits back to watch you struggle now? If you seek answers to your questions—bringing them honestly to God through prayer— you will find that Jesus is more than real. More than true. More than powerful and present in your pain. He is ready and able to redeem all of it. Ask the hard questions. Christ will lead you to the answers.

Speak honestly with God today about any doubts or struggles you have. Pray that the Holy Spirit reveals to you any wrong beliefs that are holding back your healing.

Those who trust in the LORD are like Mount Zion,
which cannot be shaken but endures forever.

—PSALM 125:1, NIV

In your heart of hearts, you are wired to desire these fundamental things: love and safety. This is the perfect environment that God created in the Garden of Eden, in which Adam and Eve could flourish and enjoy unhindered relationship with Him because they were perfectly loved and perfectly safe. This is also the perfect essence of heaven, which all believers will experience for eternity with Christ.

But until then, in this world marked at every turn by sin, lasting safety is hard to come by. Things break; people leave; disasters strike; even the greatest blessings, relationships, and seasons have an expiration date. Though our future is secure in Christ, much of our time spent on earth feels unsafe, unsteady, and out of our control. Tragedy especially leaves us without sound footing, feeling victim to the erratic winds of grief and often mentally and emotionally shaken. The only answer I know is to then cling to our God, who is utterly unshakable. He never changes. He never falters. He's never afraid. His plan for you and care for you are secure forever. He's the only unshakable refuge we have. Trust Him.

Make a list of anything that feels unstable or unsafe in your life right now in pencil. Then, above your list, write *God's Love and Safety in Christ* in ink. Put this note on your bedside table, on your bathroom mirror, or in your car—somewhere you'll see it regularly.

Let us run with endurance the race that is set before us, looking to Jesus, the founder and perfecter of our faith, who for the joy that was set before him endured the cross. . . .

Consider him who endured from sinners such hostility against himself, so that you may not grow weary or fainthearted.

—HEBREWS 12:1–3

During a race, people sometimes run as pacers. They have experience, endurance, and a full picture of the course from start to finish. They set the pace for other runners. They go ahead as a leader for the ones who may be weaker, slower, or more apt to struggle. They also serve to slow those pushing themselves too hard at the risk of losing the energy to finish. They've run the race successfully before and have chosen to help others do the same. You need pacers in your life during challenging times. Seek out trusted friends or family.

I'm thankful to say I found a few of those people and sought their guidance regularly. Even when it felt embarrassing, I was honest with them about my struggles so they could best lead me. They loved me, encouraged me, and, above all, always pointed me to Jesus, our ultimate pacer. Jesus ran His own human race, setting a perfect example of how to suffer well. But He also lovingly provides people in our lives to lead the way, spur us on, and ensure we make it across the finish line.

Take time today to have a chat with a trusted pacer in your life. If you don't have a pacer in this season, pray for the Lord to provide someone for you, even as you continue to follow His lead.

It was the will of the Lord to crush him;
   he has put him to grief;
when his soul makes an offering for guilt,
   he shall see his offspring. . . .
Out of the anguish of his soul he shall see and be satisfied;
by his knowledge shall the righteous one, my servant,
    make many to be accounted righteous,
    and he shall bear their iniquities.

—ISAIAH 53:10–11

While this prophecy about Jesus may seem cruel to us—*why would the Father want to crush, grieve, and kill His own Son?*—it's actually a portrait of God's kindness, His unfathomable, sacrificial mercy. From before the dawn of creation, God knew no one could ever be holy on their own, and holiness is required to spend eternity in His holy presence. So, in miraculous, humble sacrifice, God became human and took on our whole punishment so you and I will never have to.

This is radical, overwhelming, adoring, selfless, rescuing love. This is the love God has for you as you yourself suffer. The fact that He did this willingly should drive you to your knees. As Randy Alcorn so wisely observed, "Some people can't believe God would create a world in which people would suffer so much. Isn't it more remarkable that God would create a world in which no one would suffer more than he did?"[18]

Rejoice today in the truth that you are so cherished by the God of the universe that He chose to suffer more agony than you will ever have to.

> Let the peace of Christ rule in your hearts, to which
> indeed you were called in one body. And be thankful.
>
> —COLOSSIANS 3:15

What does it mean to let the peace of Christ rule in your heart? *It's nice imagery*, we might think, *but we can't will ourselves to feel peaceful*. When things around you are falling apart and life reminds you that you are so utterly not in control, how can peace rule?

The author, Paul, was intentional with his choice of words. The Greek word for "rule" here is *brabeuō*,[19] a term used to reference the job of an umpire or referee. In ancient games or competitions, the officiant would *brabeuō*—decide, determine, direct, arbitrate, control—the final outcome. And while you can't will yourself into a place of peace, Jesus, the Prince of Peace, who is living in you by way of the Holy Spirit, has the final say in deciding what emotions take the driver's seat of your heart. Do you believe He controls the final outcome? Call on Him to rule and determine. Let peace have a bigger say in your life than anxiety, bitterness, and fear.

Tell the Prince of Peace your anxieties. Thank Him that He has final rule over the commotion of your heart, and ask Him to pour into you His perfect peace today.

The young men who had been spies went in and brought out Rahab and her father and mother and brothers and all who belonged to her. And they brought all her relatives and put them outside the camp of Israel.

—JOSHUA 6:23

The story of Rahab is a wild one. Scripture tells us she made her living as a prostitute within a city called Jericho (2:1–21). Though she wasn't Jewish, she had heard of the miraculous works of the Lord and believed in Him. She even helped hide some Jewish spies, saving them from the brutal Jericho army. Because of her faith and aid to God's men, they promised to spare her and her family when they defeated and took over Jericho. Here we see their promise to Rahab upheld.

She got the rescue she wanted. She and her whole family were brought to safety. But how alone, how out of sorts she had to feel being with a new people, part of a new religion, in a new camp outside Israel. Her prayer for safety was answered, but she had to be disoriented and afraid. I find such comfort in Rahab's story. I've felt the Lord lead me to safety in new ways and with new people that were uncomfortable. Sometimes the ways God protects and delivers us can feel confusing, not what we would have chosen. Take hope in Rahab's story that even the awkward or uneasy places God takes us are for our protection and ultimate healing.

Do you feel God leading you toward places, groups, or people that are uncomfortable to you? Pray for the courage to trust His leading.

God is not a God of confusion but of peace.

— I CORINTHIANS 14:33

One of my cornerstone passages as I walked my own valley was Psalm 34:18: "The LORD is near to the brokenhearted." In fact, I clung to this verse, meditated on it, and claimed it as true before I ever felt it in a palpable way. Then I started asking God to show me it was true. I asked for signs and assurances from Him, even dreams, to give me peace and direction. And with time and prayer, they started to come.

I saw a group of seven turkeys (the first animal I ever hunted with Ben) trotting across my neighbor's yard on a very tough rainy morning, a confirmation from God that His presence was still near. I still occasionally see double rainbows on milestone days, assurances that God will never leave me. I had a handful of wildly supernatural dreams where Ben showed me around heaven and promised me I'd be loved and marry again. And as comforting as these signs were, I couldn't help but question, *Is this really God or just my own wishful thinking?* It's good to be careful what we assign as divinely given. Pray for Holy Spirit discernment if you experience things like this. But God promises He doesn't intentionally confuse us, so when signs and dreams are from Him, He will give you a supernatural peace.

Have you witnessed a sign of assurance or comfort that you're questioning? Ask the Holy Spirit for discernment and divine peace if that sign is from Him.

Day 237

> Count it all joy, my brothers, when you meet trials of various kinds, for you know that the testing of your faith produces steadfastness. And let steadfastness have its full effect, that you may be perfect and complete, lacking in nothing.
>
> —JAMES 1:2–4

I know you wish you could snap your fingers and remove the sorrow, heartbreak, hopelessness, and despair. I, too, wish grief were a quicker process. But nothing about redemption stories unfolds quickly. God isn't a quick-fix God. And healing doesn't come in a single moment. James was right when he encouraged his readers that trials produce steadfastness of spirit in those who walk with Christ. "Steadfastness" could also be translated "perseverance." Healing, hope, and the ongoing work of sanctification in your heart is a slow but miraculous process. It's a lifelong process through which God prepares you for the unfathomable glory of heaven. It's a process that demands perseverance.

We all wish we could fast-forward through the valley seasons of life. But as your Redeemer and perfectly sovereign God, He knows the power of slow endurance. He knows the beauty that can come only from patience, trust, and daily perseverance of the soul. Your time on earth is a marathon, not a sprint. I promise that as you trust the Lord to meticulously rebuild what is broken in you, you will be more glorious at life's finish line than you can imagine.

Ask the Lord to renew your mind with a long-term perspective on the sanctifying and beautifying soul work He is doing in you through this hardship.

> Only Noah was left, and those who were with him in the
> ark. And the waters prevailed on the earth 150 days.
>
> —GENESIS 7:23–24

Whether you grew up in church or not, Noah's story of the ark and flood is universal. He's a hero. One brave man, faithful when called by God, to repopulate all of humanity. But think about how scared, how skeptical he had to feel. I'm sure within the nearly five months closed inside a rank-smelling boat with thousands of animals and his family, Noah questioned why he had to be the one to endure this. Was this really a call of honor or a cruel joke?

We see Noah's remarkable purpose in hindsight. And even if he knew God was using him for good, I bet it didn't feel great at the time. Your pain isn't a cruel joke and certainly isn't a punishment from God. If you feel trapped, flooded, grasping for hope that sunlight and dry land are in your near future, pray for faith like Noah's. Pray for endurance and holy imagination to believe that there is a life for you marked by joy and vitality once the waters recede. Waiting in the flood is painful, but it's also a tool of divine purpose if you continue to endure faithfully.

Be honest with God today about how hard this uncomfortable flood season is, how much you hate it. And then pray for the trust and vision to hope for beauty ahead.

It is good for me that I was afflicted,
     that I might learn your statutes.
The law of your mouth is better to me
     than thousands of gold and silver pieces.

—PSALM 119:71–72

It's an unpopular message in our culture, but God's plans for you in this life aren't for you to become the best version of yourself. His plans for you, as He prepares you for heaven with Him, are for you to look more like Jesus and less like yourself (Romans 8:29). His will for you as His chosen and adopted child is that humility would overtake pride, that trust in Him would replace self-reliance, and that generosity would take the place of selfishness and a scarcity mindset.

Like with any good parent, God's ultimate goal is your growth and your flourishing. He wants you to live more like Jesus because He knows that's where you'll find security, joy, and solid ground in a world that continues to knock you down. Unfortunately, much of this growth takes place through struggle. More times than not, our most valuable lessons follow disappointment or failure. Certainly, affliction and loss in themselves aren't good, but our kind Father always uses them for our spiritual development if we let Him. God never desires pain for you, but He will use it to make you more and more like Jesus.

Thank You, Lord, that in my pain You not only comfort me but also use the worst seasons to make me more like Jesus.

Day 240

Why are you cast down, O my soul,
    and why are you in turmoil within me?
Hope in God; for I shall again praise him,
    my salvation and my God.

—PSALM 42:5–6

The psalmists set an important example for us as we struggle, because they didn't sugarcoat their pain. They brought their inner turmoil to God with boldness and honesty, yet they still stood firm on the truth that hope always comes only from the Lord. You may not feel like praising God right now, but like the psalmists, you can choose to praise even when worship isn't your instinct! God wants to be with you in your despair. He is your hope and your salvation on your worst days just as He is on your best. Don't hold back your pain or your praises from Him.

At the dawn of time, God created us in His image (Genesis 1:27). And because you're made in His image, you're also made with a deep capacity for feeling every kind of emotion—from ecstasy and joy to sorrow and anguish. In the same way that Jesus wept over the brokenness of His people (Luke 19:41–42), so, too, does He want you to honor the painful emotions you feel. This world is filled with suffering, and it honors God when you bring your heartbreaks to Him just as you bring your hallelujahs.

Practice this psalm's rhythm of lament and worship today, speaking out specific things burdening you and specific things you can praise God for right now.

Day 241

He is before all things, and in him all things hold
together.

—COLOSSIANS 1:17

We know that God is truly the Creator, the Redeemer of this world, the one sovereign God. Just as He works through people's goodness and obedience, does He also somehow work through evil, through the world's sinfulness? Because He is perfectly holy, He never causes evil, of course, but is He somehow in it? Charles Spurgeon said it this way: "Yet God was in it: 'This thing is from me, saith the Lord.' God had nothing to do with the sin or the folly, but in some way which we can never explain, in a mysterious way in which we are to believe without hesitation, God was in it all."[20]

All through Scripture God reiterated that He is *with* His people—in the storm, in the lion's den, in the fiery furnace. He's not afraid to get down and dirty with you in the messy parts of life. He's not absently gazing down from the throne of heaven. He is the Suffering Servant. He is the King who stoops to conquer. He is the Lord who kneels down in order to pull you back up. Though evil isn't from Him, He is with you. He is at work orchestrating it all for good. He is in it all.

Lord, nothing is out of Your hand, and You are in all things—in the good and somehow also in the bad. Help me trust You.

Then shall the young women rejoice in the dance,
  and the young men and the old shall be merry.
I will turn their mourning into joy;
  I will comfort them, and give them gladness for sorrow.

—JEREMIAH 31:13

The prophet Jeremiah wrote these words to a people who needed good news in a dark time. Because of their prolonged disobedience to God, some of them had already been taken into exile, and before long, Jerusalem would fall to the king of Babylon. Yet this is the redemptive final chapter of the story God wrote for them in that season. Even in the throes of their suffering, the Lord was reminding them that they were still His people, that restoration would come.

At the time of this prophecy, many of the people of Judah had turned from God or ceased to trust Him. But unlike humankind, the Lord is perfectly faithful. His plan was never for their exile to be permanent. His intention was always to bring them home to Jerusalem, into a season of rejoicing and new life, and back into right relationship with Himself. God's plan for you, His beloved child, includes suffering because this world is broken. But His plan for you also includes rejoicing, redemption, and new life, even if you can't see it now.

Lord, thank You that I will be dancing and joyful again someday. Give me courage and imagination to believe in the good that's ahead.

Rejoice with those who rejoice, weep with those who weep.

—ROMANS 12:15

This is one of the hardest commands for a sufferer to hear. How are you supposed to rejoice? How, in your flawed and broken human heart, can you celebrate another who has exactly what you've lost? How do you cheer for someone who has been blessed with exactly what you long for?

I feel this on a cellular level, my friend. Five months after Ben passed, my sister was engaged to one of his very best friends. *Joy and heartbreak.* Within a year of his death, seven of my girlfriends had their first babies. *Will this ever happen for me?*

It's exactly when you have reason to envy another that celebration will move you toward healing. It's an act of faithful worship to God when you can be joyful for another's abundance in your place of lack. The Lord works heart-level miracles when you show up for others in spite of your pain. Pray for the ability to rejoice with those who rejoice, even as you weep. Christ will empower you to do so, not out of your own strength but out of His.

Are you withdrawing from someone in your life, even envying them, because of how their life differs from yours? Pray for the ability to rejoice with them, even as you weep.

> He called his disciples to him and said to them, "Truly, I say to you, this poor widow has put in more than all those who are contributing to the offering box. For they all contributed out of their abundance, but she out of her poverty has put in everything she had, all she had to live on."
>
> —MARK 12:43–44

I know you feel depleted. Like you're running—if you're still running at all—on mental and emotional fumes. You may have too little capacity to give yourself what you need, much less to give to your church, to your family, to your friends. How can you continue to be faithful when you've lost so much and are living in crippling uncertainty about what's to come? Of course, Scripture calls us to serve others with our time, energy, and finances. But I believe what the Lord wants most from you right now are simply your broken hallelujahs. Your worship even in the weariness. Praise from tired knees that rises to heaven like the sweetest melody.

Like the poor widow's offering of only two coins, your most powerful offerings to God come when you have nothing left to give. You have every reason to be upset with Him or doubt His hand because He didn't defend you from pain the way you wish He had. And it's from that very place of disappointment that your praises to Him, trust in Him, and tear-filled testimony of His goodness will sound most loudly to the world. It's when you have nothing left to give but still offer your pennies of praise that you're the brightest light for the kingdom.

> With whatever energy you have left, offer a prayer of praise for how glorious, gracious, and generous your Father is to you. Thank Him for specific ways He has blessed you.

The LORD is my shepherd; I shall not want.
    He makes me lie down in green pastures.
He leads me beside still waters.
    He restores my soul.

—PSALM 23:1–3

Maybe you have heard or recited this passage often throughout your life. Maybe its words of comfort are brand new to you. David, the writer of this psalm, knew well the role of a shepherd. He himself was a shepherd before he was a king. He knew that, just like sheep, humans are utterly unable to tend to and protect themselves. Sheep are fairly weak and very vulnerable to predators. Without the direction and protection of a shepherd, they're helpless prey.

But in the care of a shepherd, they shall not want. They are provided for in every way—nourishment, water, rest. It's only when they surrender completely to the shepherd's lead that they're able to rest and be restored. It's when they obey his commands to lie down and fill themselves with water that they can continue on whatever journey is before them. Maybe your impulse is to go it yourself, but remember that you are fairly weak and very vulnerable—to discouragement, to despair, and to the Enemy, who wants to attack you in your pain. Listen to your Good Shepherd. Lie down, and let Him bring you rest and restoration so you can keep navigating this dangerous valley together.

Create a time and place to lie down in surrendered rest and pray for restoration in your Shepherd's presence.

Day 246

> Humble yourselves, therefore, under the mighty hand of
> God so that at the proper time he may exalt you, casting
> all your anxieties on him, because he cares for you.
>
> —I PETER 5:6–7

If this feels like another biblical paradox to you, I get it! Many of the truths of kingdom reality contradict what appears to be true in earthly reality. Humility isn't a virtue our culture promotes much these days. Meekness today connotes weakness, while Jesus claimed the meek "shall inherit the earth" (Matthew 5:5). Modesty is mocked, while pride and excess are celebrated. But God said a heart of humility is all He needs from you in order to exalt you. So, what does humility look like in suffering?

Humility looks like honest lament. Like not trying to pretend you're okay but rather laying all your tear-stained cards on the table before God in prayer. It looks like choosing trust in Christ over fear and grasping for control. It looks like asking for help when you need it. Rest assured, friend, there is no safer place than being in Christ's presence with a heart fully open, humbled, and surrendered to His loving, sovereign care. Your healing and resilience depend on His strength and wisdom, not your own. Come humbly before Him today, admitting everything you don't feel capable of on your own.

Take a deep breath. Humbly admit how powerless you are over your situation. Thank God that He is your almighty strength in everything you can't control.

Day 247

My God, my God, why have you forsaken me?
  Why are you so far from saving me, from the words
    of my groaning?
O my God, I cry by day, but you do not answer,
  and by night, but I find no rest.

—PSALM 22:1–2

Few truer prayers have ever been uttered than this defeated cry from Psalms. Its author, David, knew suffering well as he was hated and hunted by the ruthless and jealous King Saul. And though God was with David each day as he scavenged for food and sought shelter, his season of suffering in the wilderness wasn't brief. He waited on physical reprieve and safety for years as a runaway, fighting for his life. Of course he felt at times like God was nowhere near him, like none of his prayers were being heard.

But as we move through David's story, we see that God was always there. He provided a cave for him to take cover in (1 Samuel 24). He brought some strong warriors from the Gadites to fight with him (1 Chronicles 12:8). He provided the spoils from a destroyed town to sustain David and his followers (1 Samuel 30). Don't confuse your waiting with God's withdrawal. You may not hear His voice or see direct answers to your prayers, but God is always faithfully providing for and sustaining you. On the quiet days, remind yourself of His perfect faithfulness. He is never closer to you than when you expectantly wait on Him in the wilderness.

What is it you feel like you're waiting on? Like God is being silent about? Call out to Him to give you peace in the wilderness as you wait for His direction and rescue.

> The Helper, the Holy Spirit, whom the Father will send
> in my name, he will teach you all things and bring to
> your remembrance all that I have said to you. Peace I
> leave with you; my peace I give to you. Not as the world
> gives do I give to you. Let not your hearts be troubled,
> neither let them be afraid.
>
> —JOHN 14:26–27

We are complex and multifaceted beings, functioning with a divinely designed balance of heart, body, mind, and soul. In grief, each of these elements of our being feels the suffering. Your heart breaks because the world isn't fair. Your body is exhausted, pushed to its limits by mental and emotional stress. Your mind is clouded and unreliable. Your soul feels beaten down, weary.

It's at these times that we must lean into the Helper. Press into the power of the Holy Spirit, who lives and moves actively inside you. Scripture reminds us, "Where the Spirit of the Lord is, there is freedom" (2 Corinthians 3:17). Ask the Holy Spirit to bring to your mind scriptural promises to sustain your hope. Ask Him for physical and mental peace that transcends understanding and unstable circumstances. Perfect peace, which comes from God, has nothing to do with what's going on outside you and everything to do with who is working inside you. You need help in your heart, body, mind, and soul right now. Let the Helper do His work in you and set you free.

Holy Spirit, I am depleted. Fill my heart, body, mind, and soul with supernatural resilience, strength, peace, and hope as I go throughout this day.

> I will instruct you and teach you in the way you should go;
>   I will counsel you with my eye upon you.
>
> —PSALM 32:8

Part of what sets the Lord apart from other gods or higher powers that people turn to is His insanely intimate and personal nature. His Spirit literally dwells in His children and is internally instructing and teaching you daily if you're in Christ. If this idea feels new to you, here are practical steps that help me stay aligned with the Holy Spirit's leading.

Get into the Word. I know this feels like an old refrain from me at this point, but Scripture is the living, active Word of God (Hebrews 4:12). It's His voice on paper! The more you take in what He says, the more prepared you'll be to recognize His voice.

Pray. Ask God for the desire and ability to discern the Holy Spirit. He is actively affirming or rejecting your mind's desires, thoughts, and plans. Ever been told to trust your gut? When you're in Christ, your gut is the Holy Spirit speaking to you. Pay attention to peaceful as well as stomach-churning impulses. Ask the Holy Spirit if those impulses are direction from Him, and then follow. If you're still unsure, ask a faithful friend to pray for clarity for you as well. As you spend time with the Lord and pay attention to your body, you'll learn to discern where God is leading.

Don't know where to go in Scripture to start learning God's voice? Go to the Gospels—Matthew, Mark, Luke, or John—to take in the words of Jesus Himself.

> Bear with each other and forgive one another if any of you has a grievance against someone. Forgive as the Lord forgave you.
>
> —COLOSSIANS 3:13, NIV

No matter how much you love those around you (and hopefully you've found safe community), discord and misunderstanding will always flare up in difficult seasons. That's why I love this call to bear with each other. It means, though your relationship or interactions with someone may be strained right now, you can trust you're both in it for the long haul. If you know your relationship with your friend or family member is secure, you can be honest if they've been insensitive or done something to hurt you. Don't try to stuff down frustrations and end up withdrawn and resentful. Bring your grievances truthfully and graciously to close friends and family. And pray for clear vision and humility if someone brings an offense to you.

Of course, this doesn't apply to everyone you engage with. Don't waste your limited energy on those whose words or actions show that they have less than your best interests in mind. But with those you trust—your safe, long-haul community—know that honest communication and humble forgiveness will enrich your relationships in the end if you prioritize this rhythm of grace in a time of grief.

Have you been harboring unforgiveness toward or frustration with anyone? Find a time to gently approach it with them.

They drew near to the gates of death.
Then they cried to the LORD in their trouble,
  and he delivered them from their distress.
He sent out his word and healed them,
  and delivered them from their destruction.

—PSALM 107:18–20

Maybe you didn't know until now how real the feeling of being in "the valley of the shadow of death" could be (Psalm 23:4). The helplessness pressing in, the mental and emotional strength crumbling, the joy-stealing presence of despair, is all too much sometimes. I'm so sorry you're in this valley. But follow the lead of this psalm. Call for Him. Over and over, day by day, moment by moment, run to your merciful and powerful Shepherd.

Even though you feel utterly depleted, you can practice this one rhythm: Cry out to God, and let Him deliver you from this immediate moment of distress you're facing. Just this minute or this hour. Because when you call to God in desperation and trust, He will send out His Word and His Holy Spirit to sustain you for one more day, through one more breakdown, tough choice, or painful conversation. You may feel a settling peace or hear a gentle consolation, a verse may come to mind, or the touch or word of a loved one may comfort you. However it looks, He will deliver you one prayer, one moment, one day at a time.

Every time you feel overwhelmed or anxious today, pray this quickly: "Lord, I'm crying for You in my trouble. Deliver me from this moment."

I want you to know, brothers and sisters, that what has
happened to me has actually served to advance the gospel.
As a result, it has become clear throughout the whole
palace guard and to everyone else that I am in chains for
Christ. And because of my chains, most of the brothers
and sisters have become confident in the Lord and dare
all the more to proclaim the gospel without fear.

—PHILIPPIANS 1:12–14, NIV

When the apostle Paul wrote these words to the church at
Philippi, he was in prison, unfairly persecuted for preaching the gospel. Yet in his wrongful imprisonment, many heard the truth of salvation in Christ and began to speak boldly about Jesus. And your pain, too, is primed for kingdom purpose! When you suffer faithfully, trusting and praising God along the way, He works through you to bring others into the family of faith.

You don't have to be an apostle or a writer like Paul. You don't need a queue of Bible verses to offer people. All you need is the courage to genuinely express thanks for how the Lord is comforting you and leading you in this valley. When people see hope in you where the situation looks hopeless and gratitude where you have every right to complain, they'll want to know why. I know this doesn't mitigate or justify your pain, but cling to what was true of Paul and is true of all God's children who worship Him in hardship: His light shines the brightest in dark places. You may just be the light that someone around you needs to see.

*Lord, thank You that even my pain has purpose in You. Let my
life be a light to someone lost in darkness.*

A voice came from heaven, "You are my beloved Son;
with you I am well pleased."

—MARK 1:11

These are Father God's words, spoken over His Son, Jesus, at the start of His earthly ministry. When the Father spoke them, Jesus was already perfectly holy, the only One with whom He had always been perfectly pleased. If you're in Christ, do you believe these are also the words that God speaks over you? Can you find relief knowing that, on days you do well and days of gargantuan failure, God is not merely tolerating you but grinning ear to ear as He gazes on the perfection and beauty that Jesus purchased on your behalf?

As you're learning to manage your pain, the reentry into daily life often feels like a crapshoot. Put your feet on the floor, roll the dice, and see if today will be marked by tears or triumph, resilience or setback. Grief is so often one step forward, many steps back. Please, oh please, have grace for yourself. Be proud that you put your feet on the floor and attempted a "normal" day. Remember on the ugly days, God's response to you remains an unequivocal "You are My beloved child; with you I am well pleased." Every day, you are cherished by Him.

For what parts of this past week do you need to offer yourself more grace? Once you identify those, speak this aloud to yourself: "I am God's beloved child, with whom He is *always* well pleased."

Do not be afraid of sudden terror
    or of the ruin of the wicked, when it comes,
for the LORD will be your confidence
    and will keep your foot from being caught.

—PROVERBS 3:25–26

No matter what your default disposition—optimistic or pessimistic, glass half full or glass half empty—suffering has a way of stealing your hope. When unforeseen nightmares become reality, it's easy to start seeing the world from an alarmist perspective. But please, friend, don't start living waiting for the other shoe to drop. Expecting hardship is realistic, and Scripture warns us that "in this world you will have trouble" (John 16:33, NIV). But obsessively anticipating the worst is irrational and detrimental to your mental wellness and flourishing.

If you are walking with God in the Spirit, hope should always have the final word. Don't give fear the power to write your story. There will be painful chapters, but the way your story ends is without question pure joy, glory, healing, and ecstasy in God's presence. Difficulties will continue to be part of your reality on this earth, but remember as the fear creeps in, this earth isn't your ultimate reality. Your Living Hope for the present and future is Jesus.

Lord, when I start to expect and ruminate on endless bad possibilities, pour Your supernatural hope into me. Turn my eyes back to the present, where You are always with me.

Among the mature we do impart wisdom, although it is not a wisdom of this age or of the rulers of this age, who are doomed to pass away. But we impart a secret and hidden wisdom of God, which God decreed before the ages for our glory.

—1 CORINTHIANS 2:6–7

When things go wrong in your life, it's important to seek wise counsel. You can obviously turn to Scripture, but there is also value to be found in friends, family, professional counselors, and even social media. Though you must be careful in taking online directives to heart, I appreciate how much weight our culture gives to self-care. God calls our bodies temples of the Holy Spirit (1 Corinthians 6:19) and tells us to guard our hearts (Proverbs 4:23). It's wise to care for all parts of our being.

But be cautious about whose advice you listen to. Even some with good intentions call fruitless escapes self-care. So, what does wise self-care look like? Rather than adopting an arbitrary list of little luxuries and distractions, pause and consider what you deeply need today. Is it physical relaxation? Is it mental stillness? Is it stimulation or engagement to get you out of a funk? Little distractions aren't inherently bad practices when you are hurting, but be careful that self-care doesn't spiral into self-indulgence. Think honestly about what you are lacking today, and seek wisdom from God and others as to how best to fill that lack.

Lord, make it clear to me today where I'm truly depleted so I can take wise steps to fill that area back up.

For everything there is a season, and a time for every
matter under heaven:

> a time to be born, and a time to die;
> a time to plant, and a time to pluck up what is planted . . .
> a time to weep, and a time to laugh;
> a time to mourn, and a time to dance.

—ECCLESIASTES 3:1–2, 4

Don't you wish our lives read like a romantic comedy—quick, playful, and mostly without heartbreak? Like a stress-free montage of adventures with joy and laughter at every turn? Don't you wish Adam and Eve hadn't eaten the fruit and we could live in blissful, perfect union with God right here, right now and not just in eternity? Me too.

But death follows birth, weeping mingles with laughter, and every person experiences times to mourn as well as times to dance. We all wish we could avoid the darker parts of our stories. But Scripture reminds us: There is an important time for everything under the sun. Part of the beauty of this dynamic is that the sad and the happy enrich each other. Birth is more wondrous when we've brushed against death; joy is greater when we've seen the depths of sorrow; dancing is a freer celebration when we've known the stillness of despair. These seasons of suffering aren't what you want, but they can enrich your entire human experience—helping you revel in the good even more because you've survived the bad—if you let them.

Reflect on the last few weeks, the highs and lows you've lived. Thank God that in Him is the fullness of life.

> The Lord upholds all who are falling
>   and raises up all who are bowed down.
> The eyes of all look to you,
>   and you give them their food in due season.
>
> —PSALM 145:14–15

I know that you so desperately want reprieve and resolution; relief from the sorrow, the waiting, and the confusion; a fast pass through this valley that feels like it may never end. I understand so well.

Where you long for reprieve, God is sowing resilience. As you wait for answers, He is fostering a deeper trust in you despite the unknowns ahead. It makes me think of the Israelites in the desert after God rescued them from Egypt. As they waited there, the Lord sent them manna, a type of bread. It wasn't a delicacy. It got boring and tasteless after a while. They grumbled and complained about it. But the manna sustained them. It was their unwelcome, simple relief in the desert. As the Lord heals and refines you, He will send you small, unremarkable bits of manna, mundane daily reminders that He's with you and He won't let this desert be the end of your story.

Can you identify any bits of manna or gifts of relief from God in your life right now? Ask for the grace to notice and appreciate the manna as you continue to endure your desert.

O LORD, I call upon you; hasten to me!
  Give ear to my voice when I call to you!
Let my prayer be counted as incense before you,
  and the lifting up of my hands as the evening sacrifice!

—PSALM 141:1–2

Under the law of the old covenant (before Jesus), the ancient Isra-elites offered God a variety of sacrifices. The fundamental purpose of each offering was simply to give up something valuable as an offering to God. It was an outward expression that God is worthy, above all other good things, to be honored. He is the King of kings and should be the number one priority of His people.

Thankfully, because of Jesus' atoning work on the cross, we no longer need to make physical sacrifices to be right with God. But we may have to bring Him countless other offerings as we learn to pri-oritize Him above all. We may need to give over our pride that believes we deserve better, our self-righteousness that assumes we could do a better job at managing our lives than He does. We may need to surrender the fight against depression and anxiety that we can't seem to win. Or as the psalmist wrote, we may need to lift our hands in humble praise for God's goodness, even when we can't mus-ter the emotions. Sometimes the sweetest sacrifice we can offer is our honest worship in the valley.

What is God prompting you to bring Him as an offering? Imagine placing it before His throne.

Do not be anxious about tomorrow, for tomorrow will be
anxious for itself. Sufficient for the day is its own trouble.

—MATTHEW 6:34

Sometimes the hardest place to stay is in the present—to commit
to sitting still right in the middle of the storm you wish to outrun, or
to release the desperate grip you have on a past that feels more secure
than where you are right now. Focusing on yesterday feels like a comforting escape, and looking forward offers you a false sense of control
over things that ultimately aren't in your hands. But if you truly
believe God is "the Alpha and the Omega, the beginning and the
end" (Revelation 21:6), choose to trust Him with the yesterday and
the tomorrow that you can't control.

I believe God intentionally designed time to be the way it is
because He knew we could bear the weight of only one day at a time.
Most every day on this earth brings trial, both minor speed bumps
and debilitating blows. Don't let the anxiety of anticipation steal the
joy and goodness available to you today as you walk with the Lord.
His mercies are new every morning (Lamentations 3:22–23). He is
always faithful to supply the comfort, guidance, and strength you
need today, so stop fretting over tomorrow. Today is the day the Lord
has made for you. Walk in it with peace.

What would it look like for you to be fully present today—to
your friends, your family, yourself? To the promptings and
direction of the Lord? Pray for the focus to be right where you
are today.

Behold, I go forward, but he is not there,
    and backward, but I do not perceive him;
on the left hand when he is working, I do not behold him;
    he turns to the right hand, but I do not see him.
But he knows the way that I take;
    when he has tried me, I shall come out as gold.

—JOB 23:8–10

Job, who spoke these anguished words, knew undue suffering better than most. An ardently faithful man, he was robbed of his health, his work, his possessions, and every one of his children without explanation. And though he never strayed from his faith in God, he felt hurt and abandoned by God as he grappled with his horrific losses. No matter where he went, he couldn't seem to find God's goodness among the debris that was left of his life.

But even when Job struggled to see God, he found hope in knowing that God always saw him. Job reminded himself that his Lord was always present even if his weary human heart couldn't sense Him. Even in his devastation, he saw his inconceivable hardships as a way for God to refine him, just as one puts gold through fire to increase its quality. Even when you don't feel close to God or understand the fire you're walking through, remember that He knows your every thought, move, and breath. The Lord is with you, and after a little while, you, too, will come out of this as gold.

Meditate on this truth today: *God sees me. He knows the way that I take.*

Day 261

> The vessel he was making of clay was spoiled in the
> potter's hand, and he reworked it into another vessel,
> as it seemed good to the potter to do.
>
> Then the word of the LORD came to me: "O house
> of Israel, can I not do with you as this potter has done?
> declares the LORD. Behold, like the clay in the potter's
> hand, so are you in my hand, O house of Israel."
>
> —JEREMIAH 18:4–6

Jeremiah, the weeping prophet we've looked at before, lived during the tumultuous years when ancient Israel continued to sin against God by worshipping idols. He committed his whole sorrow-filled life to try to bring God's people into right relationship with Him. During a visit to a potter's house, God gave this word to Israel through Jeremiah, assuring them of His merciful plan to redeem them. God spoke to Israel what I hope you will speak to yourself: Nothing and no one is too spoiled to be reshaped and restored by God's powerful, creative hands.

No individual's sorrow or bitterness has left them too hardened for Him to soften and build back into something lovelier than before. No situation is so broken that He can't mend it. The Lord can make a brand-new, beautiful vessel out of your damaged clay, beloved. You are safe in the Potter's hands.

> What in your life or in your heart right now feels too broken, too ugly to be repaired? Speak it aloud, and surrender it to the good Potter today.

Many times he delivered them,
> but they were rebellious in their purposes
> and were brought low through their iniquity.
Nevertheless, he looked upon their distress,
> when he heard their cry.
For their sake he remembered his covenant,
> and relented according to the abundance of his steadfast love.
>
> —PSALM 106:43–45

We can turn away from God or turn toward Him. Once you are in Christ, you can no longer live in indifference to His lordship over your life. You can turn and hide from Him, whether in guilt and shame or disappointment and distrust, or you can turn and run to Him with abandon because you know nothing in all of creation can separate you from the love He has for you (Romans 8:39).

I've heard it taught many times that the word *repent* in Scripture means "to turn and move in the opposite direction"—to intentionally pause and do a 180 back toward the love, direction, and mercy of God. In hardship we often feel desperate for comfort and guidance, so it's easy to fall into relationships, habits, or ways of thinking that aren't good and healthy. If you find yourself at any point in an unsafe place or with people leading you away from the Lord, all you must do is repent. Turn the other direction, and sprint to safety in His abundantly merciful arms.

Have you felt uneasy or unsure about places you're going or people you're spending time with lately? If so, repent, call out for God's wisdom and grace, and praise Him that He will never turn away from you.

> God, being rich in mercy, because of the great love with which he loved us, even when we were dead in our trespasses, made us alive together with Christ—by grace you have been saved—and raised us up with him and seated us with him in the heavenly places in Christ Jesus.
>
> —EPHESIANS 2:4–6

Have you heard this before? "Nowhere else in the Bible is God described as rich in anything. The only thing he is called *rich* in is: mercy."[21] His abundant mercy for us is unfathomable. It never dwindles. It never runs out. He never rolls His eyes when we require another dose of divine grace and forgiveness. No matter how despondent or doubtful we are, He won't withhold it. His DNA is mercy, and His heart for us can't help but pour it out lovingly over us again and again and again.

When we are helpless, emotionally and spiritually flatlining with no means of reinvigorating ourselves, God is rich in mercy. When we doubt His goodness or presence in our suffering, He is rich in mercy. When we weaponize our heartbreak to hurt others, He is rich in mercy. When we refuse to forgive ourselves for our participation or our absence in this tragedy, He is rich in mercy. The list of things He covers with His outlandish grace is endless.

For what specific things do you need assurance of God's mercy today? Speak them to Him, and rejoice that His mercy never runs out.

> Little children, you are from God and have overcome them, for he who is in you is greater than he who is in the world.
>
> —1 JOHN 4:4

Have you ever considered that the reality you touch, see, and hear around you is *not* the ultimate reality for which you were made? Yes, earth is a real, tangible place made by God and sustained in a tiny part of the universe by His sovereign hand. What and who you experience here is one reality, but the spiritual world—already conquered and ruled by Jesus—is the final glorious reality for which you were made.

What does that mean for you right now, here on earth? It means the suffering you're facing, the losses you can't get back this side of heaven, is a temporary reality. It means the evil that exists in the world, created by the devil, Jesus has overcome and will eventually eliminate completely. It means the struggles and hardships you're facing now will scar you but they won't destroy you. They aren't your final end. You can endure today with boldness and confidence because the Spirit inside you is greater than the evil in the world. Stand strong. This painful reality is a temporary one, preparing you for eternity with Christ, completely free of sorrow and suffering.

Ask God today for the wisdom and faith to label your current hardship as temporary and freely anticipate the glorious reality you're heading toward.

Day 265

How long, O Lord? Will you forget me forever?
  How long will you hide your face from me?
How long must I take counsel in my soul
  and have sorrow in my heart all the day?
How long shall my enemy be exalted over me?

—PSALM 13:1–2

You may have heard or subscribed to the adage "Time heals all wounds." But is that really true? To an extent, yes. Faith, trust, courage, surrender, resilience—these things aren't installed with a quick software update. Patience isn't a natural virtue. We all have a chronic case of "Are we there yet?" And most everyone experiences the pangs of waiting for something they're not certain will come: *When will I finally be financially stable? How long will my marriage be broken? How long until these gaping emotional wounds start to heal?*

As much as I wish there were, there is no big revelation, no instant fix-it moment, in grief. No turning a single page from hurt to healed. But as time passes, God will build back your strength and your capacity for joy. Time will never take your pain away, but it can teach you how to face the pain better. Be patient with Him. You may not be where you want to be yet, but you're well on your way.

What specific thing are you feeling frustrated about? Talk about it honestly with God; share how difficult it is and why it's bothering you—then surrender it to Him as best you can.

Day 266

> Perceiving then that they were about to come and take him by force to make him king, Jesus withdrew again to the mountain by himself.
>
> —JOHN 6:15

We tend to react to pain in one of two ways—fight or flight. Some try to combat or fend off their pain by staying busy or constantly keeping people around. These distractions aren't inherently bad, but when we never allow time to acknowledge our pain and to rest, we actually prolong the grief. Others pull away and isolate themselves, hoping to somehow insulate themselves and avoid reality. Both extremes will keep you stuck.

Jesus knew and modeled for His disciples the importance of both community and rest. In this passage, He had just preached to more than five thousand people and miraculously fed them with five loaves of bread and two fish. He had spent time communing with people who needed Him but then made it a priority to withdraw—to take time to rest and refuel. The key to enduring suffering well is to know when to push through and when to pull back. Pay attention to how your body prompts you—maybe crippling worry or worst-case-scenario thinking, physical exhaustion or an unusually reactive temper—and seek out both places of supportive community and places of quiet restoration.

Lord, show me the ways I'm unhealthily isolating or overextending myself to cope with my grief. Help me learn the healthy rhythms of community and of rest.

> Your word is a lamp to my feet
>   and a light to my path. . . .
> I am severely afflicted;
>   give me life, O Lord, according to your word!
>
> —PSALM 119:105, 107

God's Word is called a lamp, a light, a tool to give us life when we're afflicted. It's *the* primary tool we need for clearer vision in any season of life. But I know well how weary your mind may feel, how impossible it is to focus. I also understand how daunting approaching the Bible can be. It can be hard to get your footing.

I suggest picking up the Gospels—Matthew, Mark, Luke, and John. These four books read most like a story and exclusively cover the events and teachings of Jesus' life. If Jesus is the living Word (John 1:1), then why not start in the books that record His time on earth? If reading feels overwhelming, listen to Scripture on an app while you walk, drive, or cook. Ask someone who knows the Bible to read with you, help you navigate it, and give you insights.

Staying in God's Word is *the* first step out of the darkness. Reprioritize some things so you can allocate time to make it a regular practice. You need wisdom and direction from outside yourself. Reach for the Lord. Cling to His Word so that, even in the darkness, He can lead you back to life.

Can you commit to spending five minutes each day in Scripture this week? Schedule it in, and ask a loved one to hold you accountable or read with you.

> The Lord answered her, "Martha, Martha, you are anxious and troubled about many things, but one thing is necessary. Mary has chosen the good portion, which will not be taken away from her."
>
> —LUKE 10:41–42

One of the most alluring escapes from grief is busyness. As a culture, we often value productivity more than rest, even more than relationship. We see this glamorizing of activity show up in many ways: workaholism, performance, people-pleasing, hustle culture, overloaded schedules—you name it.

These two sisters, both of whom followed Jesus and loved Him sincerely, show the difference in someone who chooses productivity and someone who prioritizes presence. When Jesus went to their home for a meal, Martha was frantically scrambling around, trying to clean up messes and ready the meal for the Messiah and His followers. Her intention was honorable and good, and she was certainly working with a servant's heart. But in her frenzy to complete her work, she missed out on the intimate time Mary spent simply sitting at Jesus' feet. The Lord didn't reprimand her for hard work but rather reminded her that sometimes our doing for God needs to come second to our being with God. He knows that where you are right now is messy. He's not asking you to clean it up. He's asking you to slow down. He wants to sit with you. Trust me—being messy and present with Jesus is far better than striving to have it all together.

What are some areas where you're using busyness as an escape? Confess them, surrender them, and ask the Lord to grant you peace to slow down and be present today.

He has told you, O man, what is good;
    and what does the LORD require of you
but to do justice, and to love kindness,
    and to walk humbly with your God?

—MICAH 6:8

Do you ever feel like everyone is asking too much of you? If it's not the weight of trying to do what He says is right, then it's the heavy expectations and advice of people around us. Trying to be perfect is exhausting. But because of Jesus, who lived a perfect, sinless life on your behalf, the Lord's commands don't have to overwhelm you. To Him, you are already perfect in Christ.

I love how Micah so succinctly articulated God's expectations of us. He said essentially, "What is God asking of you besides to be the best you can, to be kind and receive kindness, and to honor Him above all else?" He doesn't expect you to be perfectly patient, forgiving, or gracious when you face tragic and difficult things. He expects you to be human and to fail even as you attempt to live faithfully. So, take heart from this reminder! Be gentle with others involved in your situation, prioritize kindness as best you can, and surrender whatever afflicts you to the God who loves to redeem broken things. Take a breath, my friend. You're doing great.

I praise You, Lord, that You don't expect perfection but rather shower us with grace as we attempt to live justly, kindly, and humbly.

Even though I walk through the valley
    of the shadow of death,
  I will fear no evil,
for you are with me;
    your rod and your staff,
    they comfort me.

—PSALM 23:4

Scripture often describes us as sheep—with good reason. Just like sheep, we, too, need a good and guiding Shepherd. Sheep left to themselves will wander off. They have very little natural aptitude for defense and will eat things that may hurt or kill them. They desperately need a wise and powerful protector, especially in dark, dangerous valleys.

But what's going on with the rod and the staff? Shepherds would use a rod (a short, club-like wooden baton) to protect the sheep from predators and would use a staff (a longer, cane-like shaft with a hook on the end) to direct the sheep by gently poking and prodding them. While the means might have felt jarring to the sheep, the purpose was not to harm but to lovingly protect and direct. Some of God's pokes and prods in this hard season will feel uncomfortable or unexpected. Remember, as the Good Shepherd, He is here to guide and protect you—your mind, body, and spirit. You are safe with Him. He will never ever lead you astray. Give way to God's prods; allow Him to guide you to greener pastures.

Pray for the discernment to recognize God's nudges and the courage and humility to respond to His leading quickly.

Day 271

> You have heard that it was said, "You shall love your
> neighbor and hate your enemy." But I say to you, Love
> your enemies and pray for those who persecute you.
>
> —MATTHEW 5:43–44

Accidents happen in a broken world; we all have to come to terms with this fact in one way or another. I don't believe God causes these unexpected calamities, but He is also not surprised by them. But what about all the heartbreaks where there is a legitimate, clear cause—someone to hold responsible?

It's then that your obedience to God will be tested. When someone truly is at fault, isn't it your right to hold them accountable? The world will give you an emphatic, even outraged "Yes!" to that question. However, Scripture tells us that God alone can judge sin (Romans 12:17–21). Jesus went one step further and said to love and pray for those who harm you. How cruel this command can seem in the wake of tragedy. Remember, this passage is *not* a call to overlook, affirm, or accept intentional harm from anyone. Christ is the ultimate warrior against the abuse of His children. But this command to love and forgive those who hurt you isn't about the perpetrator so much as it's about protecting your own heart from bitterness and hatred, both poisonous emotions that, in the end, will only harm you. Loving our enemies is a hard word. But it's what Christ lovingly asks of us.

Lord, You know how hard it is to forgive those who've caused me pain. You've forgiven all my wrongs. Please help me grow in willingness to forgive others also.

273

It is he who made the earth by his power,
who established the world by his wisdom,
and by his understanding stretched out the heavens.

—JEREMIAH 10:12

Do you have a certain place where you love to watch sunsets? Or sunrises, if you're a morning person? Even before I was widowed, watching the sun rise or set felt like one of the most palpable ways to experience the presence of God. Obviously, the tranquil beauty of those times of day creates a uniquely peaceful atmosphere. But there was more to it than that. It puzzled me that a fiery star so gargantuan, so far away, could consistently produce something that appeared so delicate, so ethereal. I guess it felt like a picture of God to me in a way—mysterious but reliable, grand and far beyond comprehension but revealing itself as gentle and generously near.

There was an element of trust in the Lord that regularly sitting with sunsets or sunrises built back in me in my grief. If He has the power to keep the sun rising and falling every morning and evening *and* the wisdom to know how much we need to see it, shouldn't I trust His power and wisdom at work in my life? I experience an awe of and intimacy with the Lord in these moments. My hope is that they become a sweet reminder to you, too, of God's glory and His faithfulness to you, especially on days it doesn't feel like He's near.

Set aside time to watch and enjoy a sunrise or sunset this week. Ask the Lord to reveal something new about His character as you do.

> Blessed be the God and Father of our Lord Jesus Christ, the Father of mercies and God of all comfort, who comforts us in all our affliction, so that we may be able to comfort those who are in any affliction, with the comfort with which we ourselves are comforted by God.
>
> —2 CORINTHIANS 1:3–4

These words, written by the apostle Paul, kick off a thirteen-chapter letter that speaks boldly from start to finish about the relationship between suffering and God's great faithfulness to us in it. These words, sent to me by a dear friend not long after Ben's death, reminded me how crucial a perspective of thanksgiving is in hardship. For more than a decade, this friend has lived with chronic stress and anxiety related to her husband's frequent several monthslong deployments. Rather than withdrawing from or questioning God, her constant disposition toward Him is thanks for His love, provision, and comfort even in her husband's absence. Like Paul, she first and foremost calls the Lord blessed!

What a beautiful reminder it was to my freshly broken heart that we are constantly being built up by the Holy Spirit in our anguish. That as my friend's email did for me, I, too, would have the chance to comfort fellow sufferers as God comforted me. That was the whole purpose of Paul's letter! When we suffer, we, too, can become conduits of compassion and hope to others. As God mercifully comforts you, He equips you to do the same for others. Let our kind Father pour into you in your pain so that you can pour into another in their pain down the road.

Lord, open my heart to perceive and receive Your merciful comfort today. Equip me with the opportunities and courage to then comfort and connect with someone in need.

> You are the light of the world. A city set on a hill cannot
> be hidden. Nor do people light a lamp and put it under
> a basket, but on a stand, and it gives light to all in the
> house.
>
> —MATTHEW 5:14–15

Have you ever slowed down on the highway to gawk at a bad wreck? Are you drawn to stories where the underdog overcomes great adversity? Something about human nature makes it difficult for us to turn our eyes away from pain. And though we certainly bond with one another through positive shared experiences, shared suffering forges some of our tightest connections with others. This is in no way to glorify suffering but to remind you of the immense potential for inspiration and hope that lies within it.

When you are struggling, those around you may be more attuned to how you respond to difficulties. And though some will look from the outside with sinful, self-righteous judgment, many will watch hoping to see a little strength, a little hope in your story because they need a boost of hope in their own. During hard times, you often have a larger audience, more eyes on you, than you would when life is going well. You have a chance to be a witness, to walk out what trust in God looks like, and to exhibit to others the power that comes when you abide in Him during difficult times.

> Ask God today to help you remember the immense potential
> you have to inspire hope in someone's life today simply by
> sacrificially worshipping Him in your struggle.

I have said these things to you, that in me you may have
peace. In the world you will have tribulation. But take
heart; I have overcome the world.

—JOHN 16:33

The entire Bible, start to finish, is an honest, painful, yet totally
hopeful story about broken people enduring broken situations, who
hold tight to a good and redeeming God. Nowhere does Scripture
promise us easy, breezy lives. In fact, Jesus assures us that we will face
trial and tribulation. But how do tribulation and peace coexist? What
does peace look like for us in the middle of a raging storm?

Peace can mean many things to many people. But for me the
divine peace Jesus talked about feels like rootedness, more like stability than safety. It feels like standing with trembling knees while the
walls are ripped off but knowing the foundation you're on can't be
moved. For all intents and purposes, we're not safe. We may get hurt.
Our hearts are broken, and we've lost someone precious. But when
we remind ourselves of what we can never lose—the love we shared,
the times we cherished, the way our lives are better because of that
person, and the certainty that, in Christ, we will ultimately be
reunited—we arrive at stable ground. You can find a solid foundation of gratitude, reflection, and hope while, all around you, the
storm continues to rage.

Take time to reflect today on the love and memories that no
amount of loss or grief can steal away from you. Ask the Lord
for supernatural peace as you thank Him for these things.

Precious in the sight of the LORD
is the death of his saints.

—PSALM 116:15

Every single one of God's children is precious to Him. Even human parents can comprehend only a fraction of the love and adoration He has for His kids. So, it may seem odd that Scripture calls the death of God's children precious to Him. Death wasn't in God's design in the Garden of Eden and is strictly a result of sin entering the world. God hates death. Jesus got angry and wept at death during His time on earth (John 11:33–35). Why would the death of His saints be precious to Him?

The word *precious* here reveals two key elements of the Father's character and His heart for you. First and foremost, He does hate death, which is why Jesus came to suffer the final, retributive death for the sins of the world. Your eternal life is precious to God—it cost His Son His life. Second, all deaths are precious to the Lord because all lives are precious to Him. He knit us in our mothers' wombs (Psalm 139:13) and has our names engraved on the palms of His hands (Isaiah 49:16). But even as He grieves our deaths, He also gloriously redeems them. Death is the moment that ushers us from life on earth into perfect, eternal glory. In that way, the deaths of God's saints are precious—cherished—because they bring His children home to heaven forever.

Take a moment to express to God any fear or anger you hold about death, yours one day or that of a loved one. Then praise Him that, because of His mercy, the worst experience we can endure is actually precious for the one going home to Christ.

Day 277

> I know that you can do all things
> and that no purpose of yours can be thwarted.
>
> —JOB 42:2

I know you think you know what's best for your life. Particularly when things go wrong, do you start to question God, resent Him, or distrust Him? Of all people in Scripture, Esther certainly had reason to. An orphan and essentially a kidnap victim, she was taken as a young virgin to marry the king of Persia. Once made queen, while hiding her ethnicity and faith as a Jew, she learned of an edict made by the king to exterminate all Jews. How isolated and afraid she must have felt! Yet she trusted the Lord and boldly pleaded with the king to spare the Jews, a request she knew well could have cost her life.

Esther stood firm in her belief in God's wisdom and plan. We see in her story that nothing God orchestrates, no good He is working through His people, can be thwarted. Part of trusting in the Lord's sovereignty is continuing to ask for guidance when you don't understand. Part of persevering is accepting that hardship sometimes comes without explanation. Part of faith is taking your eyes off what feels unfair and fixing your eyes on the One who can use absolutely anything for kingdom purpose. Trusting God means surrendering your fears and your desire to understand. Get out of your head, lay your questions down at His feet, beloved, and let Him lead you toward trust, healing, and purpose.

Write down anything producing anxiety, fear, or angst in you today. Read your list aloud, and then claim this truth: "But God's good purpose in this can't be thwarted."

> This light momentary affliction is preparing for us an
> eternal weight of glory beyond all comparison, as we look
> not to the things that are seen but to the things that are
> unseen. For the things that are seen are transient, but the
> things that are unseen are eternal.
>
> —2 CORINTHIANS 4:17–18

Why do we resist the work of spiritual strengthening more than we do physical or relational strengthening? If we need to get in better shape or take medicine regularly to improve our health, we adjust our lifestyles to do so. If we have conflict in a relationship, we understand that difficult conversations or professional counseling is needed.

What if you had the same attitude toward suffering? What if the moments of sobbing on the floor led to playing hymns of worship and hope? What if you countered the onslaught of worry and fear with truths from the Word of God? What if you picked up the phone instead of the remote in moments of loneliness? Just as you must strain physical muscles for them to grow, so, too, does pushing yourself spiritually into God's and others' loving presence make you stronger and more resilient in faith. And in case you haven't noticed, you're getting stronger, friend.

*Lord, even though I hate this, don't let me miss the spiritual
strengthening and the treasure You have for me in this season.
Sustain my hope in the good that's to come like only You can.*

He said to them, "Because of your little faith. For truly, I
say to you, if you have faith like a grain of mustard seed,
you will say to this mountain, 'Move from here to there,'
and it will move, and nothing will be impossible for you."

—MATTHEW 17:20

Nowhere in Scripture does God ask you to be the hero of your
own story. Our inherent human insufficiency and weakness is the
reason Jesus came to rescue us. And what's more—He came not out
of pity but out of infinite, unconditional love for us! He couldn't
stand the idea of you struggling on your own, striving to no avail to
make yourself righteous, to handle everything perfectly, to be your
own hero.

When Jesus spoke of the disciples' "little faith" here, He was in no
way rebuking them for not having a big enough or resolute enough
faith. No! He encouraged them that all they needed was the tiniest
amount of trust in Him, who is the only hero truly powerful to save.
The mustard seed is one of the smallest known types of seed. Even
faith of that miniscule amount, in Christ, has the power to move
whole mountains. He doesn't expect you to move your own mountains, nor does He expect you to be your own hero. Come to Christ,
all who are weary, and let Him carry you through whatever impossible thing you're facing.

What burdens are you silently shouldering that you need to
release to Christ today? Picture yourself handing them over to
Him and saying, "Jesus, I trust You with _____."

Joseph called the name of the firstborn Manasseh. "For," he said, "God has made me forget all my hardship and all my father's house."

—GENESIS 41:51

I remember the first time I forgot a monthly anniversary of my husband's death. The twelfth came and went, and I hadn't noticed. On one hand, I was so grateful, finally hopeful that that day might not haunt me every month for the rest of my life. But on the other hand, I felt such guilt, or maybe fear, that I was starting to forget him. Even though I undoubtedly longed for days that felt, in any way at all, lighter or joyful or even just normal, when those better or lighter moments came, they also brought with them an unexpected sense of guilt. *If I'm feeling happy, does that mean I'm loving him less? Am I leaving the past behind? Will others think I'm moving on too quickly?*

These are natural feelings as you tow the taxing line between loss and healing, grief and restoration. But don't let the Enemy steal the divine moments of joy that do come. They are few at first, and they are miraculous mercies from God. Cherish them. Thank Him for them. You're not forgetting; you're healing. Joy and lament can exist in the same moment, in the same heart, when you're walking with Christ. Don't dismiss the good days or shame yourself for the lighter moments. Hold tight to joy whenever and however it comes.

In what ways do you feel lighter today than you have in days past? Praise God for this small sign of restoration.

If anyone does sin, we have an advocate with the Father,
Jesus Christ the righteous.

—I JOHN 2:1

An advocate is someone who pleads or supports the cause of
another. Don't you want the one representing you to have personally
felt the weight of your experience? This is exactly what we have in
Jesus.

As a man who lived the full human experience, Jesus is the perfect
advocate for humankind before God. He can perfectly represent you
to the Father because He is holy. He can tearfully plead to the Father
on your behalf because He has wept the same tears.

For a long time, I feared that I wouldn't be able to love Ben and
fully love another again. I couldn't comprehend what that might look
like. The Lord reminded me that His love is infinite, for all people
across all time, and that I was made in His image. I prayed from that
day forward for Jesus to expand my capacity for romantic love, to
advocate for that specific type of healing and growth in my heart. He
can lead and comfort you because He has been where you are and
sees perfectly what you need and where you're going.

Take a minute to connect with Jesus today by journaling or
praying. Know that He is advocating for you to the Father
and working on your behalf for your good.

Satisfy us in the morning with your steadfast love,
    that we may rejoice and be glad all our days.
Make us glad for as many days as you have afflicted us,
    and for as many years as we have seen evil. . . .
Let the favor of the Lord our God be upon us.

—PSALM 90:14–15, 17

Just as we learn to hurt honestly with God, I also wish that we will hope honestly by praying big and not pare down our dreams for fear of disappointment. Tremendous power comes from the words you speak, both to God in prayer and to yourself. Proverbs wisely advises that "death and life are in the power of the tongue" (18:21). Do you actually have the power to speak into being a specific outcome in your life? Of course not. But why not continually bring your dreams of a better, redeemed future to God, the One who can make them happen?

Since God is with you, always dwelling in your heart and spirit, why would you not fully believe that Jesus is making all things new in your life? Why would you not call on Him to make you glad for as many days as you have suffered and pour favor onto you in the days and years to come? Don't withhold your prayers for fear that God may not answer them exactly how and when you'd like. Call out to Him, your Living Hope, for the beautiful, restored life you dream of. Just the act of communicating this dream to Him will bring you peace, even as you wait.

What prayers are you holding back from God right now for fear He won't answer? Share your dreams with God and make your requests to Him.

Day 283

Every branch in me that does not bear fruit he takes
away, and every branch that does bear fruit he prunes,
that it may bear more fruit.

—JOHN 15:2

As grapevines start to flower and fruit, the winegrower assesses the
healthy branches to see which leaves and bunches should stay and
which are inhibiting grape growth. He will then prune the vines, or
cut off parts of them, to eliminate weak fruit and excessive foliage
that is blocking necessary sunlight. He doesn't cut the vine off completely; he merely trims away the parts keeping the fruit from reaching its full potential.

Jesus used this analogy to depict the very work He does in the lives
and hearts of those who follow Him. Like the winegrower, God sees
with divine wisdom the habits or misguided beliefs that are hinder-
ing your spiritual growth, blocking the rays of truth from the Light
of Life that you so desperately need. And He isn't afraid to prune
back the things that cause you to sin or that skew your understanding of His heart and His purposes. Pruning may feel painful, but the
Lord's intent is to cultivate health and growth. His purpose is always
to shape you into the richest, most beautiful, most fruitful version of
yourself.

Ask God honestly what in your life needs pruning right now.
Though this process can be painful, thank Him that this
refining work is always to promote growth and healing.

All this took place to fulfill what the Lord had spoken by the prophet:

> "Behold, the virgin shall conceive and bear a son,
>   and they shall call his name Immanuel"

(which means, God with us).

—MATTHEW 1:22–23

What do you think of when you consider this name Immanuel—God with us? Do you think only of the incarnate Jesus, born of the virgin and crucified on the cross? Certainly, that is who the prophet in this passage was speaking of when he foretold the coming Messiah. Jesus was and is the most comprehensible way for us to grasp that God is a God who is always, fully with us.

But Immanuel goes beyond just the name of the physical man Jesus and is, in and of itself, a promise that the Lord will never leave us or forsake us. A covenant that when we repent and surrender our lives to Christ, His Holy Spirit unites with ours and supernaturally begins to dwell inside each of us. God isn't just an occasional visitor or a 911 hotline when things go wrong. He is the every-moment, all-powerful, all-loving, permanent resident of your soul. He is Immanuel, God with you. In your best moments He is cheering you on, and in your worst He is spiritually and emotionally sustaining you, nourishing you, and pouring into you all that you need.

Write down on a sticky note, "Immanuel—God with me." Put it in your car, in your bathroom, or on your bedside table today.

Day 285

> He looked, and behold, the bush was burning, yet it was not consumed. And Moses said, "I will turn aside to see this great sight, why the bush is not burned." . . . God called to him out of the bush, "Moses, Moses!" And he said, "Here I am."
>
> —EXODUS 3:2–4

How disruptive do you think a talking, burning bush was to Moses's to-do list that day? How resistant do you think he felt to this crazy encounter with God? I love what Dietrich Bonhoeffer said: "We must be ready to allow ourselves to be interrupted by God."[22] Do you think Moses felt interrupted? Do you feel like God has totally, radically interrupted the plan you had for your life?

You're made in God's likeness and image (Genesis 1:26). Your love for plans and craving for control are hints at the connection between you and God as the ultimate planner and controller of the universe. You're made in the likeness of the ultimate planner, so it makes sense that you'll feel resistant when He interrupts the narrative you're working so hard to write for your life. Yet only God is "the Alpha and the Omega, the beginning and the end" (Revelation 21:6). He is the one whose plans are perfect, without a single flaw. Surrender the future you're grasping so tightly, and allow God's divine interruptions to lead you toward an even better way.

What in your life do you feel God has interrupted or disrupted? Grieve those things today. And then call on the One who is writing your beautiful narrative.

If any of you lacks wisdom, let him ask God, who gives generously to all without reproach, and it will be given him.

—JAMES 1:5

There's no way around it: Wisdom can be costly to gain. And it's often on the broken roads, in the painful seasons, that the treasure of wisdom lies. That's why Scripture repeatedly encourages us to rejoice in our suffering. Not because we should be grateful for hardship, but because hardship is such a powerful tool to transform us in wisdom, in compassion, in deeper trust in and relationship with God. Hebrews says even Jesus "learned obedience through what he suffered" (5:8).

There is grounding wisdom on the other side of pain, teaching you which things and people matter and which don't. Isak Dinesen put it this way: "I think these difficult times have helped me to understand better than ever before how infinitely rich and beautiful life is in every way and that so many things that one goes around worrying about are of no importance whatsoever."[23] Suffering is often the catalyst to true wisdom, which in turn frees you to live fully, to love abundantly, to prioritize rightly, and to start every day in a posture of gratitude for what you have, because you know how precious life is.

Pray specifically that God draw out and make clear to you every bit of biblical wisdom buried for you in this hard season.

> Having said these things, he spit on the ground and made
> mud with the saliva. Then he anointed the man's eyes
> with the mud and said to him, "Go, wash in the pool of
> Siloam" (which means Sent). So he went and washed and
> came back seeing.
>
> —JOHN 9:6–7

Nothing is too broken, too flawed, or too far gone for Jesus' healing hand. But just as with the blind man, the ways in which He heals you may not be quite what you expect. Why use saliva and mud to restore this man's sight? I'm sure Jesus' process here puzzled the man and any onlookers.

Many times in your life, the way God brings about restoration will surprise you. Sometimes He'll let you get even messier before He cleans you up. Sometimes His healing balm feels less like a soothing ointment and more like gritty mud and spit. But wouldn't you rather have divine sovereignty over human logic? God's comprehensive plan for your life is so beyond your understanding that often His ways and His timing won't make sense to you. Sometimes the most powerful and profound work He does in you feels like mud on your eyes. But trust Him, friend. He is sovereign and gracious, and He can restore your losses.

What in your life feels like spit and mud right now? Surrender it to the Lord today, and pray that you can trust in His unfathomable ability to heal in just the right way.

> After you have suffered a little while, the God of all grace, who has called you to his eternal glory in Christ, will himself restore, confirm, strengthen, and establish you.
>
> —I PETER 5:10

Take heart in the apostle Peter's tender words here. He clung tightly to the truth that, in Christ, all suffering is only for "a little while," never dismissing its difficulty but also not succumbing to despair in hard times.

You aren't alone in this. As He was with Peter, Christ is with you always. But also, you aren't suffering in solitude. The Lord has prepared brothers and sisters who have hurt like you are hurting now. Ask Him to connect you with these people. Once I sought help from God and from those in my community, I found many widow mentors to shepherd me in the early years. Learning their healing stories helped restore my hope for love in the future. They confirmed my struggles and fears were normal. They prayed for strength for me and supported me when I was weak. They challenged me to reestablish all identity in Christ and Christ alone. He is constantly working in you through others as you move toward healing.

Ask the Lord for mentors to help restore, confirm, strengthen, and establish you as you move forward.

The righteous will never be moved;
  he will be remembered forever.
He is not afraid of bad news;
  his heart is firm, trusting in the LORD.
His heart is steady; he will not be afraid,
  until he looks in triumph on his adversaries.

—PSALM 112:6–8

Every so often, we cross paths with people who have endured the worst things we can imagine and yet continually bring out the best in everyone they're around. These people are tender toward the atrocities of this world but maintain an unwavering peace and inexplicable joy. They do so as a result of experiencing the world through the lens of God's merciful, redeeming gospel.

Endless ideas shape how you perceive and respond to the world. And while most worldviews do have some moral, wise tidbits to offer, none will ever anchor you in immovable hope like the true gospel worldview does. Those who are actively anchored in God's Word and God's presence truly can't be moved. And though pain and worry afflict them just like everyone else, their hearts are firm and rooted in the Living Hope. Learn from these people. Listen to what they say, and read what they've written. Allow them to be your mentors, up close or from afar, as you find your firm footing. You, too, can be immovable.

Identify one or two people, in the past or present, who live and believe the way you hope to. What is one thing you can learn from them today?

> "I the LORD do not change; therefore you, O children
> of Jacob, are not consumed. . . . Return to me, and I
> will return to you," says the LORD of hosts.
>
> —MALACHI 3:6–7

It's okay to be disappointed with God. He knows your every thought, dream, and desire and is aware how defeated you feel when your expectations go unmet. Because you're made intentionally in God's image, you're a dreamer with wonderful expectations. Your heart is wired for the bliss, glory, and perfection of eternity. So, when situations and relationships keep breaking, disappointment is the appropriate reaction. Lysa TerKeurst said, "Disappointment isn't proof that God is withholding good things from us. Sometimes it's His way of leading us Home."[24]

Though God doesn't afflict us in cruelty, in His kindness He does call us back through our pain. It's in the disappointment that you remember all the glory you're made for and turn your heart and eyes back home. God designed you for heaven, for the Garden-of-Eden life, for a perfect existence in glory with Him. When your expectations aren't met, take time to grieve. But also let disappointment reawaken you to the reality of the eternal kingdom that you're ultimately made for and that Christ has secured for you.

Air all your disappointments, large and small, to the Lord today. Whenever you feel resentful toward Him, remind yourself of His infallible goodness and love toward you in all things.

Day 291

When he drew near and saw the city, he wept over it,
saying, "Would that you, even you, had known on this
day the things that make for peace!"

—LUKE 19:41–42

Jesus wept. So the Jews said, "See how he loved him!"

—JOHN 11:35–36

All who suffer devastating loss wonder at some point, *Since God is
sovereign over all—even tragedies—does He endorse all?* Nothing could
be further from the truth. Consider these two instances in the Gospels. The first is when Jesus stood on a hilltop overlooking Jerusalem.
He knew well this was where He would be brutally beaten and
unjustly crucified. He was fully aware of the betrayal and hatred He
would experience at the hands of His own people, yet He wept *for
them* because they were missing out on the redeeming peace that can
come only through belief in Him, the Messiah.

The second is when Jesus stood at the tomb of His dear friend
Lazarus, who had died. Even though Jesus knew He would soon raise
Lazarus from the dead, He so hates death and how it afflicts His
people that He stood in anguish and wept. God doesn't approve of
tragedy, sin, or death any more today than Jesus did as He wept over
the brokenness of humanity. His bleeding heart for His children
breaks every time they hurt. He is grieving this pain with you, beloved.

How does it change your perspective today to consider not
only that God didn't approve of what's happened to you but
also that He is crying with you?

Still the vision awaits its appointed time;
  it hastens to the end—it will not lie.
If it seems slow, wait for it;
  it will surely come; it will not delay.

—HABAKKUK 2:3

In grief, a strange sense of time settles over us. Sorrow makes us long for the future but also feel inextricably chained to the present. C. S. Lewis wrote, "Grief still feels like fear. Perhaps, more strictly, like suspense. Or like waiting; just hanging about waiting for something to happen. It gives life a permanently provisional feeling. . . . Up till this I always had too little time. Now there is nothing but time. Almost pure time, empty successiveness."[25] How long will we feel stuck here, waiting for life and time to get back to some semblance of normalcy?

Grief can force you into an uncomfortable empty space. Try to take advantage of a little slower pace in this season to prioritize rest and connection in a way that may not be possible in busier, happier times. Find out what activities or places fill up your soul; then do those things and go those places. Allow yourself to exhale, even hope, for a moment. Explore different ways of connecting with God and with others who love you. Sit with Him and with those people. I know you long for life to go back to a more familiar pace. I know you don't want to take time to sit in the worst of your pain and your fear. But it's in these slow seasons that the Holy Spirit does His most restorative work in you. Be still, child, and know that God is with you.

What are one or two things you can do today to create a moment of energy, connection, and joy?

Children were brought to him that he might lay his hands on them and pray. The disciples rebuked the people, but Jesus said, "Let the little children come to me and do not hinder them, for to such belongs the kingdom of heaven."

—MATTHEW 19:13–14

Take a moment to consider what was unfolding in this moment. Close your eyes, and step into this scene, where Jesus delightedly welcomed a group of young children. These innocent kids were drawn toward Jesus, not because they understood theology or were convinced He was the Messiah but simply because He exuded love and kindness and treated them with as much dignity as He would a crowd of kings. They felt safe and worthy in His presence even though they had nothing at all to offer Him.

This is how Jesus wants you to come to Him, beloved: fearless, shameless, and empty-handed. There can be misguided expectations in the church that spiritual maturity means emotional resignation or staunch mental strength. But when you lose the vulnerable, childlike impulse to draw near to God, relying on your own feeble strength and knowledge rather than His, you're missing the tender mercies and big spiritual bear hugs He has to give you. Don't get seduced by the lie that grown-upness is spiritual maturity. Come to Jesus, fearless, shameless, and empty-handed, for it's the little children to whom His kingdom belongs.

Drop all pretenses, and approach Jesus with your messy, unpolished, unfiltered, childlike prayer today.

I know the plans I have for you, declares the LORD, plans for welfare and not for evil, to give you a future and a hope. Then you will call upon me and come and pray to me, and I will hear you. You will seek me and find me, when you seek me with all your heart.

—JEREMIAH 29:11–13

This promise is often pulled from its context and used to falsely reassure someone suffering that everything will be okay. On one hand, this is true. All will be made right, redeemed, and renewed on the last day. But on the other hand, evil does happen and some situations can't be fixed. I remember wondering what welfare and hope could possibly look like when my loss and its ripple effects on my life were so final. What did this promise mean for me when everything most certainly wouldn't be okay?

Six years later, I see God's plan for my welfare and hope. I've lived and celebrated those things! But all through the valley, I simply had to choose to believe the parts of this promise I couldn't yet see. Because when you come to the Lord and seek Him with all your heart, you always find Him. He is always faithful to comfort you and embolden you as you wait for your hope, for your better future. God's ultimate plan for your future is an eternal life of connection and holy revelry with Himself, and He's using everything you face here on earth to ready you for it.

Lord, I pray that You restore _____ for me right now. And also, I praise You that Your greatest plan for me is closeness to and trust in You.

Day 295

> Do not lie to each other, since you have taken off your
> old self with its practices and have put on the new self,
> which is being renewed in knowledge in the image of its
> Creator.
>
> —COLOSSIANS 3:9–10, NIV

What a freeing reminder that, in Christ, we're living in new, redeemed, righteous skin! We have the power of God to live with wise discipline and holy joy. But often as we struggle to manage the wear and tear of grief, parts of ourselves that we don't love become exposed, parts of that old self we thought we'd shed. You may be making great progress, feeling more hopeful, patient, and positive much of the time. And then *that* thing pops back up. Don't feel discouraged or like you've failed when old habits or coping mechanisms resurface. You're human. It happens. Healing isn't linear.

Everyone makes mistakes, and no one can manage grief perfectly, but you've been made new by the Holy Spirit in you. He is the power you need to reset the bad practices of your old self. And when you do react sinfully, don't shame yourself or dwell on it. Focus less on your mistakes and more on your true identity: a perfectly redeemed and holy child of God. Look more at Jesus and His adoration for you than at your regret because "as we look to Him, the glory of His image gets imprinted upon us. When our self-image gets so wrapped up in God that we lose ourselves in the process, we're free."[26]

Confess any sinful actions to God today. Receive His radical forgiveness, and then stop dwelling on your sin. Keep your eyes on Jesus, and remember how He sees you: righteous.

By this is love perfected with us, so that we may have
confidence for the day of judgment, because as he is so
also are we in this world. There is no fear in love, but
perfect love casts out fear.

—1 JOHN 4:17–18

Fear is one of the most innate human emotions. In a world so evidently full of evil, you can't help but feel afraid, because most of the things that happen to you and around you are ultimately out of your control. That's why "Do not fear" is the most repeated command in Scripture.

So, what is the remedy to fear? More planning, resources, productivity, and distraction? All these things may help shield your heart from hurt or contribute to its healing when it breaks, but the only true antidote to fear is love. Perfect love—*God's love* for you—is the antidote to fear. If you're in Christ, you can do nothing that will make Him love you any more or any less than He does at this moment. Every hurt you fear here on earth, you can trust the Lord will heal in eternity. Anyone you fear losing here on earth, you can trust you'll see again in heaven if they're following Christ. Every heartbreak you endure will be restored. Nothing in this life that you fear is permanent. Everything is in God's perfectly loving, redeeming hands.

Ask the Holy Spirit to engulf you with love today so that any
fears that come against you will wither in light of how safe
and adored you are in Christ.

> The LORD went before them by day in a pillar of cloud to lead them along the way, and by night in a pillar of fire to give them light, that they might travel by day and by night. The pillar of cloud by day and the pillar of fire by night did not depart from before the people.
>
> —EXODUS 13:21–22

Here God is making two important promises to His people. First, that His perfect, guiding presence won't depart from us. Second, that even as we follow Him, the path will likely not be clear. As Moses led the Israelites through the wilderness, God shepherded them day by day, step by step, toward the promised land. But He didn't send Moses detailed instructions or a start-to-finish map. He sent him a pillar of cloud and a pillar of fire. With these two signs, the Israelites were given just enough information to make it through the day and night. God's guidance required constant trust.

Just as God never left the Israelites, He will never leave you. Like the Israelites, who got frustrated with and grumbled at Him throughout their journey, you will struggle to trust at times too. God understands this. You don't have to like the unknowns that following Him brings, but you will find supernatural peace as you learn to trust Him day and night.

Have you noticed any specific "pillars" God has been using to guide you? Stay close to these pillars; keep following Him.

> Peter answered him, "Lord, if it is you, command me to come to you on the water." He said, "Come." So Peter got out of the boat and walked on the water and came to Jesus.
>
> —MATTHEW 14:28–29

You may recall this story from Scripture, but do you remember that this miracle took place while the disciples were navigating some very rough seas (John 6:18)? Jesus had gone up on a mountain to pray, and the disciples' boat had been swept "a long way from the land, beaten by the waves, for the wind was against them" (Matthew 14: 24). Then after fighting all night to maneuver their way back to safety (verse 25), Jesus stepped into the storm and bade Peter walk on water. And as long as Peter's eyes stayed on Christ, he stayed afloat. As soon as he looked back at the wind and waves, he started to sink.

Though Peter's faith walk here was physical, defying gravity by way of Jesus' divine power in him, what Jesus asks of you requires no less faith. Your humanness and your fear in suffering push you into fight-or-flight mode. Will you bow up and try to overcome the obstacle in your own way? Maybe turn and run? Or will you step out onto the water, into the chaos, and keep your eyes locked on Jesus and His power? He is the only refuge from the wind and waves, the only true north through the storm. Trust Him with total abandon, and you'll be amazed at the miracles He begins to work in you.

Cry out to Jesus for His presence, and ask Him to help you walk on the water without being overcome by fear.

Day 299

Whoever walks with the wise becomes wise,
   but the companion of fools will suffer harm.

—PROVERBS 13:20

God designed His people to function collectively, as a united community of believers. We need direction and support from one another, in good times and in bad. And as we spend time with others, we inevitably tend to take on attributes, habits, and perspectives of those with whom we spend the most time. You may have been warned as a child to be careful of the company you keep. This is wise advice.

So especially in tough seasons, when you feel run-down and discouraged, be cautious about the people from whom you seek comfort; carefully consider the ones you allow real access to your heart, which Scripture warns you to guard above all else (Proverbs 4:23). Surround yourself with people who bring both gentle grace and convicting truth to your situation. But more than anything, remember the power you have access to when you spend time near God. It's revitalizing for you to be in His presence. There is no safer place. There is no sounder counsel. There is no greater refuge as you endure difficult times.

As you draw near to God today, ask Him to make clear who is safe company for you and who is not.

301

Deep calls to deep
    at the roar of your waterfalls;
all your breakers and your waves
    have gone over me.
By day the LORD commands his steadfast love,
    and at night his song is with me,
    a prayer to the God of my life.

—PSALM 42:7–8

Does this psalm feel erratic, even contradictory to you? Drowning at one moment, then serenaded with divine lullabies in the next? This is what honest, faithful suffering looks like, friend, and God Himself is right there at rock bottom with you. He feels the pang of your loneliness and the overwhelming frustration of feeling like a victim of your own life. Deep calls to deep. Jesus knows how low you feel.

But also remind yourself, as the psalmist did: The Lord will sustain you and comfort you at every turn. He is faithful in your most hopeful and hopeless hours. He is fighting for you, working in you, and singing over you even when you can't hear it. He pours out His limitless love to fill you all day and all night. Let Him in! It's in your most broken moments that God reveals the deepest parts of Himself to you.

Meditate on these verses: "Deep calls to deep at the roar of your waterfalls. . . . By day the LORD commands his steadfast love, and at night his song is with me."

This is the day that the LORD has made;
    let us rejoice and be glad in it.

—PSALM 118:24

You may have seen this wonderful psalm of praise sewn on a pillow or heard it sung as part of a children's church song. It's certainly an easy one to memorize and excitedly claim when life is going well. After all, it offers you a biblical invitation to celebrate life!

But certainly for me there were days when rejoicing felt forced at best and deeply painful at worst. It was hard to see things to be glad about. It was even harder to sing songs of worship. When life was a mess with very little, if anything, to celebrate, I found the first step to rejoicing was focus—intentional focus on God's faithfulness. Every day that passes is a day that He has made. And even when the contents of your day are distressing, each sunrise and sunset can be a tangible reminder of God's faithfulness—to the universe and to all His children in it. Consider the millennia of new days that have come and gone and come again as evidence of His sovereignty and tender attention to creation. If God is that faithful to the earth, sun, and moon, how much more faithful can you trust Him to be to you, the absolute jewel of His creation?

Ask the Holy Spirit to illuminate your vision and direct your focus to God's faithfulness in the world around you.

Day 302

> I am the vine; you are the branches. Whoever abides in
> me and I in him, he it is that bears much fruit, for apart
> from me you can do nothing.
>
> —JOHN 15:5

Healing from any type of loss is a slow journey. But as the initial shock and devastation wear off, as you take feeble strides back into "normal" routines, you're reaching what can be called the *middle miles:* "These are the most exhausting, challenging miles on the path, when the exhilaration of beginning the journey has evaporated into drudgery and the promise of the path's end has not yet given new energy for the stepping."[27]

As you start to take steps into more stable rhythms, into the middle miles, you may feel more capable than you did weeks or months ago. You may be tempted to rely less on God and more on yourself as the recovery gets underway. But don't loosen your grip on God! Seek discernment and direction, and keep your eyes attentive to God's leading. Don't lose connection with Him as you slowly begin to heal. The intimacy you're building through your suffering will be invaluable for all the days and miles ahead.

Reflect on the last several weeks. Have your time and communication with the Lord declined in any way? If so, commit some extra time today to stay connected to the Vine.

Day 303

Hear my cry, O God,
    listen to my prayer;
from the end of the earth I call to you
    when my heart is faint.
Lead me to the rock
    that is higher than I.

—PSALM 61:1–2

Most creatures, including humans, have a practical instinct to seek higher ground when they're lost or in danger. If you're stranded in a forest or floodwaters start to rise, the only way to reestablish your bearings and find a way to safety is to climb to a higher place. It's not that getting to a more elevated spot necessarily gets you to safety, but it does expand your perspective and enable you to see beyond the immediate peril in front of you.

Life with God doesn't keep you from getting lost in the forest or keep floods from coming. Hard things still happen, and faithful people still lose their way. But when you seek the Lord in your confusion and fear, He always carries you to higher ground. He offers you a greater perspective of hope and security because you know He knows the way out. The Lord can lead you to a promised land that you can't yet see. He will never abandon you where you are. He is your high ground. Let your Savior direct you to safety as you navigate out of this place together.

Lord, bring me to higher ground. I need Your Holy Spirit to clarify my perspective and align my gaze with Your divine hope.

Blessed are those who hunger and thirst for righteousness, for they shall be satisfied.

—MATTHEW 5:6

The crowd to whom Jesus spoke these words were mostly people in financial and social poverty. Yet His invitation to kingdom life extended far beyond monetary resources. Jesus always acknowledged, welcomed, and blessed anyone who knew they needed mercy, knew they needed forgiveness, knew they needed a Messiah to save them. It was not the self-righteous religious leaders He came to bless but the afflicted, the abandoned, and the guilty. Christ came for everyone who knew they couldn't lead a self-sufficient, holy life.

Food and water are necessities—fundamental needs—not luxuries. Those who hunger and thirst for righteousness are desperate to be close to Jesus. They know that, on their own, they're spiritually poor. They don't consider Jesus a nice addition to their lives; they grasp for Him because they know that He is their sole sustenance. The Living Water. The Bread of Life. Don't treat Christ like a sugary after-dinner dessert. Savor Him as the whole feast because only when you realize your desperate need for Him and go to Him will you be filled by the goodness of the kingdom of heaven.

Jesus, without You, I am spiritually homeless, hungry, and helpless. With You, I am filled with every gift and the power and joy of Your kingdom. Fill me with Yourself today, Lord!

Day 305

My thoughts are not your thoughts,
> neither are your ways my ways, declares the LORD.
For as the heavens are higher than the earth,
> so are my ways higher than your ways
> and my thoughts than your thoughts.

—ISAIAH 55:8–9

If you're really honest, do you sometimes wonder if God has made a mistake? Do you wish you could be in the driver's seat? I feel a lot of relief when reading Lysa TerKeurst's candid words: "When His timing seems questionable, His lack of intervention seems hurtful, and His promises seem doubtful, I get afraid. I get confused. And left alone with those feelings, I can't help but feel disappointed that God isn't doing what I assume a good God should do."[28]

I know, in seasons of hurt and confusion, you may be tempted to think you could manage your life better than God can. We often expect comfort, ease, and success. But only God—in His infinite, holy understanding—knows what is truly good. Don't risk losing your trust in Him. It's impossible for you to see all He sees and know all He knows, so as blunt as it sounds, your options are quite simply resentment or trust. The choice is up to you.

What makes you disappointed, doubtful, or even resentful that you need to talk about with Him and ask for the humility to trust Him with?

Is anyone among you suffering? Let him pray. Is anyone cheerful? Let him sing praise. Is anyone among you sick? Let him call for the elders of the church, and let them pray over him, anointing him with oil in the name of the Lord.

—JAMES 5:13–14

Do you think of the Bible more as prescriptive or descriptive? Is it a literal list of rules to follow, or is it full of examples to emulate? The whole of Scripture should absolutely be embraced as both. There is a reason it's filled with both laws and stories, commandments and real-life characters. Take God's instructions on how to live a flourishing life at face value. Obey His commands. But also, empathize with those whose stories compose Scripture. You can always glean something about what they did right, what they did wrong, and how they communed with God in both instances. Live by God's rules as best you can, and pursue the kind of relationship with Him that those in Scripture display.

The more you dive into biblical stories, the more you'll find that just what James prescribed is how many of Scripture's heroes endured and overcame—pray, praise, and pray again. This should be your mode of operation no matter what your circumstances: Invite God and invite faithful others into your blessings and your brokenness. Celebrate and grieve together, and surrender all the happenings of your life to God's sovereign care.

Let this be your guiding strategy of communicating this week, with God and with others—pray, praise, and pray again.

Day 307

Do not be deceived, my beloved brothers. Every good gift and every perfect gift is from above, coming down from the Father of lights, with whom there is no variation or shadow due to change.

—JAMES 1:16–17

When we walk through trials, we tend to look at our surroundings in one of two ways. Some let their pain shadow every corner of their lives, becoming despondent and rejecting any notion of joy or goodness. And others become so desperate for a little joy that they look for signs of hope and reassurance at every turn. I beg you, friend—be the second person. Don't dismiss hope. Don't let the darkness of your current situation keep you from seeing the merciful beams of light shining through to you.

And when you do experience a good gift—a kind text from a friend, a warm breeze, a long nap, a favorite old song that makes you smile—pause, thank God for how personal and tender He is with you, and celebrate it! Every good and perfect gift is from your Father, and right now, He knows you need unexpected bursts of joy as you worry and weep. Don't chalk miraculous moments up to silly coincidences. Lean into these joyful incidents. You need some sweet, good gifts right now, and the Lord loves giving them to you!

What three good gifts can you thank God for today? Praise Him, and ask Him to train your eyes to always be on the lookout for His favor.

Give ear to my words, O LORD;
   consider my groaning.
Give attention to the sound of my cry,
   my King and my God,
   for to you do I pray.
O LORD, in the morning you hear my voice.

—PSALM 5:1–3

Do you feel frustrated that God isn't answering your prayers in the way or time frame you feel you need? Are you angry with or bitter toward Him because He didn't give you the outcome you begged for? I get it! You're not crazy. It's difficult to be in the middle of a story and have no idea what the ending will be. To exist in the unknowns and the unresolved is stressful.

But like the psalmist, I want you to take comfort simply in God's merciful presence. He will always give ear to your words; He's constantly aware of and grieving with you at the sound of your cries. Your voice—even as it wails at God—is a beautiful sound to His ears because He loves that you continue to come to Him in prayer. One of the names of God that we've mentioned before is Wonderful Counselor (Isaiah 9:6). Just as you would with an earthly counselor, go to the Lord to vent all your sorrows and frustrations. And even when He doesn't fix what's broken in your life, remember that you have His merciful, undivided attention. The Counselor is here. He's listening. He's working in and around you more than you know.

What counsel do you need from God today? Lay your requests before Him, and spend some time listening for a word or resting in His stillness.

> He took a cup, and when he had given thanks he gave it
> to them, saying, "Drink of it, all of you, for this is my
> blood of the covenant, which is poured out for many for
> the forgiveness of sins."
>
> —MATTHEW 26:27–28

We talked earlier about God's covenant with us. It's an unbreakable promise to all who believe, a holy commitment that is *unconditional*. No amount of anger or doubt can ever break His forever covenant of love for you. That's why the practice of communion is not just a call to honor Christ's sacrifice but also a call to remember. In the taking of bread and wine, we remember the sacrifice Jesus chose to make on our behalf. God knew we, as worry-prone humans, would distrust and forget His divine devotion. He knew we needed a ritual to remind ourselves of His radical, life-giving love, which can never be lost.

I've made mention of this, but one of the most precious moments in those first days following Ben's death was when I stood on our back deck and took communion with fifteen or so of his best friends. We used white sandwich bread and a cheap pinot noir, and we remembered. I had never taken communion outside church before, but I knew I needed a tangible reminder that I could trust God. As we took communion, we remembered that the cross meant Ben was in heaven. But more than that, it was a tremendously powerful reminder of the Lord's faithfulness to me at a time when my faith in Him felt so shaky.

When a peaceful moment presents itself, find some bread or crackers, a little wine or juice, and read these verses aloud. Take communion, and pause to remember Jesus' divine devotion to you, which never wavers.

> Jesus came and said to them, "All authority in heaven
> and on earth has been given to me. . . . And behold,
> I am with you always, to the end of the age."
>
> —MATTHEW 28:18, 20

Most of us realized quickly after our heartbreak happened that much of our lives isn't actually in our control. And even now, as hard as you've been working to grieve, heal, and prepare for what's ahead, you may find yourself feeling helpless all over again. Like you're back at square one. Don't worry, dear friend. Don't fall into thinking you'll be stuck here forever. As we know well now, God is with us always.

Take heart that Jesus' words here are still true for you as you tenderly move into new seasons. By way of faith in Christ, you have constant and complete access to *all authority* in heaven and on earth. And of course, this means access to all the fruit of the Spirit we've talked about. But this also offers me a needed reminder that even as I heal, Jesus remains the final authority. He is with us always and is generous to give us the spiritual provisions we need, but He is still the leader, and we are still to trustingly follow. Ask for the ability to yield to His ways and His timing as you continue forward. Because as much as we resist it, the days ahead lie mostly out of our control.

Even though I wish I had more control over my situation, thank You, Jesus, that what I need more than control, You abundantly give me: peace for the days ahead as I follow You.

"He has redeemed my soul from going down into the pit,
   and my life shall look upon the light."
Behold, God does all these things,
   twice, three times, with a man,
to bring back his soul from the pit,
   that he may be lighted with the light of life.

                      —JOB 33:28–30

It's perhaps the most universal protest against God: *If God is good, why does He let bad things happen?* If you've felt this—perhaps more than once—don't shame yourself. That grief reflects the image of God in you, designed with a fighting spirit of mercy that craves justice for all. But because God's ways are unfathomably greater than we can comprehend, we will likely not get our answer in the form we want. However, Elihu, this passage's writer, understood just what quadriplegic Joni Eareckson Tada knows well: "Sometimes, God permits what He hates to accomplish what He loves."[29]

We won't fully know why God allows tragedy, but we do see that, through heartbreak, we learn to cling more tightly to—and anticipate with greater joy—the kingdom of heaven. Sometimes it takes being broken by the brokenness of this life for you to remember you were made for a better one. Your Father cherishes and values you so deeply beyond your comprehension that He holds your long-term flourishing above your temporary happiness. Though we hate it, it's at rock bottom that we finally find God our softest, surest place to land.

Lord, though I hate this pit that I'm in right now, I thank You that You use the worst to accomplish the best. Help me go deeper and deeper in love and dependence on You this week.

He was despised and rejected by men,
　　a man of sorrows and acquainted with grief;
and as one from whom men hide their faces
　　he was despised, and we esteemed him not.

—ISAIAH 53:3

When you're terrified or in pain, don't you long to talk to someone who's been where you are and made it through? How comforting is the companionship of one who's felt what you feel, struggled as you're struggling, and yet overcome. We are fragile, worrisome beings, and we need others to break the isolation of our suffering and empower us through hard times.

The One who's known the burdens you're bearing, cried the tears you've cried, and felt the pain of your heartbreak, betrayal, or loss is the Savior of the universe. You may know that Jesus is the Son of God, but do you forget that He lived with the same flesh, blood, stress, and heartbreak that you do? He was a man "despised and rejected by men." He was misunderstood and hated and had His words constantly twisted by those who wanted to eliminate Him. He can sympathize with your every weakness and worry, and because of that, He calls you to draw on His powerful grace with unrestrained confidence (Hebrews 4:15–16)! Christ gets it. Run to the sympathetic, all-powerful Lord. He is closer in your pain than anyone else could ever be.

Jesus Himself has felt the same worries and pains. Talk to Him about everything in your day today, and see how it changes your mindset.

You who have made me see many
        troubles and calamities
    will revive me again;
from the depths of the earth
    you will bring me up again.
You will increase my greatness
    and comfort me again.

—PSALM 71:20–21

Notice the repetition of the word *again.* This simple psalm describes in two sentences the cycle of God's mercy throughout all human history. If you look at the arc of the Old Testament—the history of the Jewish nation—you repeatedly see their disobedience, the consequences of their disobedience (usually in the form of suffering), their cry to God for help, and His merciful forgiveness and restoration. Does your life tend to operate like Israel's?

Maybe you know the one you've lost is at peace but you continue wrestling with your own internal turmoil. Maybe you've courageously tied up loose ends or been able to let some things go but you're anxious about a whole new list of must-dos. Maybe you can even celebrate the beauty of the past but you feel like a stranger in your new present. The Lord will revive you; He will pull you out of your depths faithfully again and again! He will deliver you and comfort you without ever tiring of rescuing you. He will restore you again and again because of His outlandish love for you.

Praise God today that His mercy and rescue are infinite, that no matter what you face or how many times, He is your Savior again and again.

Truly, truly, I say to you, unless a grain of wheat falls into the earth and dies, it remains alone; but if it dies, it bears much fruit.

—JOHN 12:24

As painful as it may seem, God is always working through death to bring life. Not because He approves of death—He hates death and never intended His children or His creation to be subjected to it. But when sin infected the universe, death became the consequence. It's inevitable for every person, animal, and plant. All that lives will eventually die. And in addition to your one physical death, you will suffer countless emotional deaths over the course of your lifetime.

When you lose dreams, lay down plans, or grieve the loss of someone you love, it feels like you lose a part of yourself that you'll never get back. But when you hand these painful losses to God, He does what He always does: He brings life from death. He may not replace the person or plans you've lost, but He will restore you to a fuller version of who you've always been. There is richer life on the other side of experiencing death. Don't be afraid to lay down things that have passed. He is making you—and all things—new (Revelation 21:5)!

What is a spiritual, relational, or physical death that you need to release to the Lord in order to move toward new life?

The law came in to increase the trespass, but where sin increased, grace abounded all the more.

—ROMANS 5:20

This is the universal, unbreakable blanket promise for all who know Christ. This is the bottom line, the cornerstone, the heart of the gospel: Where sin increases, grace abounds all the more. Hard seasons put pressure on everyone involved, and without fail, the ugly parts of people come out at some point. Discord festers everywhere in hurtful words, mean misunderstandings, harsh judgments, and both intentional and unintentional betrayals.

No one handles grief or hardship perfectly. But remember, the secret to grieving well is grace. Remind yourself regularly of God's abounding grace as you navigate tough situations. His grace constantly washes over your sins and the sins of others against you. Rest in the fact that nothing you do or don't do is too big for God's grace and forgiveness to cover. And as you find peace in God's radical mercy, ask for the courage to offer grace to others as you all learn how to struggle well together.

Lord, thank You that Your grace for me is radical and endless. Give me the desire and the strength to extend grace to those navigating this tough season with me.

He arose and came to his father. But while he was still a
long way off, his father saw him and felt compassion, and
ran and embraced him and kissed him.

—LUKE 15:20

I know you've heard the story of the prodigal son. It's perhaps one
of the most widely known biblical stories in our culture. But I would
argue that the star of the show is not actually the rebellious son but
rather the welcoming, forgiving father.

This young man deserved not only to be dismissed by his father
for brazenly and recklessly squandering his whole inheritance but
also certainly to be held accountable for his actions. The son expected
to have to work off his debt as a slave. But the wildly compassionate
father rejoiced and ran with abandon to welcome his lost, ashamed
son home.

I hope now, every time you think of the prodigal son, you remember what this merciful father reveals about God, about His character
and how ridiculous His love is for us. The Lord can't resist celebrating
every time you, His child, turn back to Him. Nothing you can do—
no mistakes, doubts, or wrong turns—will ever cause God's uninhibited love for you to cease. In fact, He is overwhelmed with joy at your
spiritual homecoming each time you stray and then return home to
Him.

Call to mind your lowest lows from this past week. In Jesus'
name, tell the guilt and shame to go, and then picture God
rejoicing, grinning, and welcoming you home.

Create in me a clean heart, O God,
    and renew a right spirit within me.
Cast me not away from your presence,
    and take not your Holy Spirit from me.
Restore to me the joy of your salvation,
    and uphold me with a willing spirit.

—PSALM 51:10–12

This is a brave and bold prayer to pray, for sure, but there is no better time for a heart assessment than in seasons of hardship. When you're in fight-for-survival mode, your flaws can be more difficult to hide. Your weak spots often surface. And though this doesn't feel good by any means, don't be afraid of God's tender exposure. Ask the Holy Spirit to use these tough times to refine you, challenge you, and build back a cleaner, more resilient heart in you. All it takes is a willing spirit.

Often the heart work God does in you in hard times is painful at the start, revealing its beautiful progress only later down the road. You may try over and over to patch up broken windows or the damaged roof on a house, when the Builder knows it's even more important to repair the foundation. Don't be afraid to let God complete the work of reconstructing your life. Surrender your heart to Him, and let Him build back something stronger and more beautiful than surface-level patches could ever make.

Though it may require some bravery, write down Psalm 51:10–12 where you'll see it often, and pray it throughout the day.

> We do not want you to be uninformed, brothers, about those who are asleep, that you may not grieve as others do who have no hope.
>
> —I THESSALONIANS 4:13

This truth about death for believers became a lifeline for me. Believers alone can grieve with hope. Why? Because in Christ, death for us isn't the end. Of course, it's a physical ending, one that devastates those of us left here rather than those who have gone ahead. But Paul used the word *asleep* instead of *dead* to remind us that our separation is temporary.

C. S. Lewis referred to this verse after the loss of his wife, saying, "What St. Paul says can comfort only those who love God better than the dead, and the dead better than themselves."[30] Does Lewis's call here feel impossible to you? It did to me. But quickly I realized how radically this perspective could change me. For months and months, the only thought that gave me any relief was the truth that Ben "had won the lottery," as I often told myself. When I focused on all Ben had gained in being with the Lord, I was able to honestly, though tearfully, feel glad for him. Every pain and fear I had, he was free from! What was a devastating ending for me was a glorious beginning for him. It may sound churchy and trite, but if you believe the gospel and you love someone deeply, remembering everything they've gained can be a source of hope as you seek to accept all you've lost.

Lord, I don't know how it's possible, but let me be glad and rejoice for _____. Let the understanding of their joy bring supernatural hope into my grief.

Day 319

> The man from whom the demons had gone begged that he might be with him, but Jesus sent him away, saying, "Return to your home, and declare how much God has done for you." And he went away, proclaiming throughout the whole city how much Jesus had done for him.
>
> —LUKE 8:38–39

I think this story of the possessed man's healing offers such a lovely model for us as we seek to share our stories with others. We've talked much about how suffering primes us for powerful kingdom testimony. There's weight and authority to the faith you share with others, because it has been so strenuously tested. Embrace the opportunities at work, in your community, even on social media, to witness to God's goodness in your grief.

But what I love about Jesus' instruction to this man is that He didn't tell him to go to the whole city. He told him to first go *home*. My grief journey was very public, but my strength to share it—and, more importantly, my ability to daily perceive God's hand in my life—came from regular conversations and prayers in my home with my closest people. If you don't have this, please make time to meet regularly with a handful of trusted friends, to share the best and most difficult moments of your week or month. Recall and record these things so you first will be a regular witness to your own testimony. Let a few close people help you remember and write down God-nods and little miracles as you go so that you will have the bandwidth and joy to share with others outside your home.

Who could you meet with regularly to share your ups and downs? What friend will help keep your eyes on God's faithfulness in this journey?

Day 320

> I heard a loud voice in heaven, saying, "Now the salvation and the power and the kingdom of our God and the authority of his Christ have come, for the accuser of our brothers has been thrown down, who accuses them day and night before our God. And they have conquered him by the blood of the Lamb and by the word of their testimony."
>
> —REVELATION 12:10–11

The accuser, the enemy of your soul, knows well that times of grief and trial open doors for him to slither into your mind. He has no authority over you but is cunning in the lies he feeds you, always working to make you second-guess God and His promises. When you are disappointed in how God has answered or held off on answering your prayers, Satan will work to have you doubt His goodness. When you feel alone in your struggle, he will say that God has abandoned you and that no one else can understand.

Remember, when doubts, worries, or ideas that directly contradict God's Word creep in, that Jesus' work on the cross has forever thrown the Enemy down! He has been crushed under Christ's heel and has no power over you (Genesis 3:15); his only ammunition is lies, which you can choose to either listen to or renounce in Jesus' name. How do you overcome his attacks? By trusting Jesus and remembering how God is and has been faithful. Speak truths about God to yourself, and have faithful friends speak them over you as well. The Enemy has no power against the truth.

Praise You, Jesus, that You have defeated Satan for good! In Your powerful name, I reject his lies of _____.

Day 321

> If Christ is in you, although the body is dead because of
> sin, the Spirit is life because of righteousness. If the Spirit
> of him who raised Jesus from the dead dwells in you, he
> who raised Christ Jesus from the dead will also give life to
> your mortal bodies through his Spirit who dwells in you.
>
> —ROMANS 8:10–11

As a Christian you live with a redeemed spirit at the same time
that you live in a not-yet-redeemed body. This tension between death
of body and life of spirit is your reality until Jesus' second coming
when all bodies will be resurrected as His is.

Especially in suffering, we feel the weakness of our embodied selves.
We struggle to maintain physical, mental, and emotional strength.
But remember the magnificent power source to which you are forever connected. As you feel depleted in all parts of your being, the
same God who will physically redeem your body at the end of time is
currently dwelling and working in you through His Holy Spirit. You
have access, through Christ, to supernatural physical, mental, and
emotional strength. You can be spiritually joyful and hopeful on your
weariest days. Remember the remarkable power that is in you, who
is interceding with the Father on your behalf (Romans 8:26), and
remember how *alive* you are, even when your body and mind are
worn down!

Ask the Holy Spirit today for specific physical, spiritual,
mental, and emotional needs, and thank God that He is the
source of power so great, it raised Christ's lifeless body from
the dead.

> Truly, I say to you, there is no one who has left house or
> wife or brothers or parents or children, for the sake of the
> kingdom of God, who will not receive many times more
> in this time, and in the age to come eternal life.
>
> —LUKE 18:29–30

Suffering may be our greatest teacher when it comes to surrender.
Surrender is unnatural for us and painful, to be sure. This world is
full of good things we wish would never fade or fall away. James
reminds us that "every good and perfect gift is from above" (1:17,
NIV). We serve an adoring God who revels in blessing His children
with things and people we rightfully cherish.

But we must remember, every gift we're given was God's before it
was ours. When we lose someone dear to us, a vital part of moving
toward acceptance is entrusting that person back to their Creator.
This is so hard. I tried to hold on as tightly as I could to Ben's things
and my memories of him for fear of forgetting or losing my love for
him. But holding on too tightly didn't help my love for him flourish;
it just left me feeling trapped, my mind locked up by grief. This is
why we must learn the sacrifice of surrender. We must confess to
God that this person, this gift, is ultimately His. This doesn't mean
we love, cherish, or miss them any less! But when we change our
perspective to surrender, it helps free us from feeling paralyzed in our
grief.

*Lord, reveal to me anything I need to surrender to You. Grant me
the grace to entrust my memories to You and peace in the discomfort of letting go.*

> That the God of our Lord Jesus Christ, the Father of glory, may give you the Spirit of wisdom and of revelation in the knowledge of him, having the eyes of your hearts enlightened, that you may know what is the hope to which he has called you, what are the riches of his glorious inheritance in the saints, and what is the immeasurable greatness of his power toward us who believe.
>
> —EPHESIANS 1:17–19

This is the fruit of seeking God with hungry faith—wisdom, revelation, enlightenment, hope, riches, power. This is an outlandish prayer, yet all this fruit is available to you if you're walking in relationship with Christ. And the beauty of these revelations is not necessarily greater head knowledge of God but rather the receiving of His glorious hope and divine gifts. Time with the Lord, His power in you, yields valuable treasures and takeaways to help you start living differently as you heal.

One of these new ways of living for me was learning to slow down. The Lord's revelation to me was not "Here's how we get there faster" but "Here's why it matters that you do this at My pace." And then with slowing came the ability to be present. Because the more you trust Him and the more willing you become to surrender tomorrow, the greater capacity you have to experience today. And when you learn to live in today, you start to have access to biblical contentment. Contentment doesn't mean you're happy with your situation, but it does help you focus on the love, hope, or gratitude you feel today even as you wait for a happier season ahead.

As you spend time with the Lord today, ask Him to show you the invaluable treasures of slowness, presence, and contentment.

My days are swifter than a runner;
  they flee away; they see no good.
They go by like skiffs of reed,
  like an eagle swooping on the prey.

—JOB 9:25–26

When you are grieving or in pain, some days seem impossibly long, yet some pass so quickly you wonder where they went. You feel the tension of wishing this uncomfortable season to pass as quickly as possible but also trying to be intentional and present in the moment. I understand you may not be where you want to be. Today is overwhelming and draining, and it hurts. But rather than letting another day, week, or month slink away as you go through the motions of your suffering, look for an anchor.

The function of an anchor is simply to keep a boat tethered safely in place while the elements push and pull. Grief is chaotic. Loss leaves you feeling victim to emotions and fears bombarding you from every direction. This is why you need an anchor. Lean into the activities, practices, and people that will bring a touch of lightness to your days. Anchor the days.

Who or what would bring you a few moments of respite and lightness today? Commit to doing that thing, going to that place, or talking with that person today.

> He said, "Abba, Father, all things are possible for you.
> Remove this cup from me. Yet not what I will, but what
> you will."
>
> —MARK 14:36

In a few words, Jesus modeled for us what perfect surrendered prayer looks like. When He uttered this desperate plea to the Father, He was just hours from His arrest, beating, and torturous death. He knew exactly what was coming, because He had made this redemption plan before the creation of the world. And as a man He was in distress because of the unfathomable pain He was about to endure. As God He was faithful to carry out the plan of saving His people.

"Abba, Father, all things are possible for you." Jesus was praising both God's gentleness as a kind Father and His sovereignty as almighty God. "Remove this cup from me." As a man He called on God for an easier way out, a less painful resolution to what lay ahead. "Yet not what I will, but what you will." As the perfectly obedient Lamb of God, He followed His cry for rescue with a humble statement of submission to God's greater plan. Could you follow Jesus' lead? Could you pray this way in your suffering, with your fear?

Pray Jesus' own prayer over your life today: "Abba, Father, all things are possible for you. Remove this cup from me. Yet not what I will, but what you will."

> If anyone else thinks he has reason for confidence in the flesh, I have more. . . . Indeed, I count everything as loss because of the surpassing worth of knowing Christ Jesus my Lord.
>
> —PHILIPPIANS 3:4, 8

The reason for confidence Paul referred to here was his impressive résumé of accolades as a former leader of the Jewish religion. But he counted it loss because religion doesn't save us; only Jesus can save. Randy Alcorn said, "The grace of Jesus isn't an add-on or makeover that enhances our lives. It causes a radical transformation of our lives. Religions can alter behavior. Only Jesus has the power to transform the heart. Only the work of Jesus is the foundation on which we can build a new life."[31]

Jesus isn't here to make sure you're doing religion right. He's not here to give you a checklist for suffering well. He's here to transform you from the inside out, at soul level, and make you more full of life than you've ever been before. Religious, or liturgical, practices absolutely help create a structure of regular time with the Lord. Prayer, church, worship—all these things keep gospel truths fresh on our minds. But without Jesus, there is no gospel. Without Jesus, those truths stay on paper and fail to take root in our hearts. As you engage in any of these practices this week, be sure to pray and invite the person of Jesus into them with you, asking Him to illuminate exactly what your heart needs to hear from them that day.

Thank You, Jesus, for the ways religion helps us stay connected to Your promises. Help me remember that nothing I do can save me from this but that everything I do is intended to draw me closer to You.

Day 327

> His disciples asked him, "Rabbi, who sinned, this man or
> his parents, that he was born blind?" Jesus answered, "It
> was not that this man sinned, or his parents, but that the
> works of God might be displayed in him."
>
> —JOHN 9:2–3

In Jesus' tender meeting with a blind man, we see so clearly a fundamental difference between our nature and God's. The disciples here jumped to one conclusion about the man's affliction: Someone had sinned. There had to be some justification for this man's difficulty. We have a punitive mindset. We want retribution, payback; we want life to be fair, although it simply isn't.

God is perfectly holy, yet His heart for His children is not one of punishment but one of mercy. Just as this man's lifelong blindness wasn't a result of God's wrath, neither are your losses, struggles, or afflictions. In fact, when God does allow hardship in your life, He always repurposes it as a display of His love and power through you—through your trust, endurance, and healing. Don't for a second think God is punishing you because you're not good enough, child. He's using you for glorious kingdom work because you're more than enough for Him in Christ.

If you have believed—or heard it said—that your suffering is punishment from God, deny it as the lie it is and say out loud, "God loves me and is merciful to me."

I wait for the LORD, my soul waits,
    and in his word I hope;
my soul waits for the Lord
      more than watchmen for the morning,
      more than watchmen for the morning.

—PSALM 130:5–6

Waiting on the Lord is mentioned repeatedly in Scripture, by different people in all sorts of circumstances. I think the repetition is intentional because God knows waiting is one of the hardest things for us to do. Waiting feels stressful and frustrating to us because we crave resolution. We want control. We want a detailed map of where God is taking us. But God doesn't work this way. He's a Good Shepherd leading you with love, not a GPS detailing directions.

But, friend, you don't have to flounder and worry in the waiting. God is not asking you to sit on your hands and fret while He works. Waiting is an action, not a state of being. When Scripture calls you to wait for the Lord as watchmen do for morning, it means to eagerly expect Him to unveil what's next. Fight for clarity in prayer, ask Him for peace in the unknown, and look forward with hope to what He has in store for you. Open your eyes as the watchmen do! Open your heart with excitement for what's to come.

Ask God where He is moving in your life right now. Pray for patience and discernment to see His work.

Day 329

Blessed are the meek, for they shall inherit the earth.

—MATTHEW 5:5

People often mistake meekness for weakness. This isn't at all what Jesus meant when He spoke of meekness in His Sermon on the Mount. By definition, meekness is quietness and gentleness. Don't misconstrue these attributes as weakness. It takes tremendous strength to be quiet in life's chaos. It takes great control to stay gentle in a culture that craves power and humble in one that celebrates dominance. Jesus is the ultimate example of one laying aside power in order to meet and love people gently.

When you suffer, you have an opportunity to learn how beautiful meekness can be. When all falls out of your control and you're faced with the futility of your own efforts to fix what's broken, you learn humility. You learn that joy and healing come not from strength but from surrender to Christ's mighty power. This act of getting quiet, living gently, and submitting to God's plans and purposes for your pain is glorious meekness. It's a worshipful act of obedience.

Consider the wondrous salvation that Jesus worked through His great humility. How is God inviting you to be quiet or gentle today?

> You shall have no other gods before me.
>
> —EXODUS 20:3

When life seems to go more smoothly after a troubling season, we might stockpile all the good things—all the people, stuff, and other blessings we cherish—and hold them hostage in our hearts because we don't want to lose anything else. And we might not even realize we're doing it. But when you cling too tightly to the blessings in life, what start as good things can slowly become ultimate things. When what you've come to idolize is inevitably lost, the safety locks of your heart are broken open. What you've built your happiness on crumbles.

Richard Baxter said, "Suffering so unbolts the door of the heart, that the word hath easier entrance."[32] We may hate that this is true, but don't miss the fruit of the fallout! Hold the good in your life gently; keep your hands open. God may use your hard losses to lead you to put Him and His Word back in their rightful place as the only ultimate things in your life. Let the Holy Spirit help you reset your priorities and reshape your vision to put God above all else again.

Ask the Holy Spirit to reveal anything or anyone that you've idolized. Then ask for His help, clinging to Him even as you hold gently the good gifts in your life.

> Jesus said to him, "Again it is written, 'You shall not put
> the Lord your God to the test.'"
>
> —MATTHEW 4:7

The *him* to whom Jesus boldly spoke here is Satan. After Jesus had fasted forty days in the desert, Satan was trying to stir up cynicism and doubt in His heart toward the Father because Jesus was physically and mentally worn down. I bet you've felt him do the same to you these past months. But you've seen evidence of God's goodness in your grief that you can now use to deflect the lies, and better yet, you have all Scripture to speak back to the Enemy as well.

As you move forward in hope and strength, you have more tools to fight doubts and lies that surge in, but it certainly doesn't mean that Satan will give up. It doesn't mean that all of a sudden your anxieties and fears are done with. When you feel new pangs of loneliness or dread over new seasons, don't let the Enemy twist those things into reasons to pull back from God. You know what to do. You know how to fight. God has a track record of faithfulness through this valley. You can trust Him. Don't get discouraged when new mental battles arise. Speak truth in response to everything that Satan tells you isn't true of God.

Have any new doubts or condemning thoughts started to come up lately? Run quickly to Scripture, and arm yourself with the truth to defeat the Enemy's schemes of deceit.

There's an opportune time to do things, a right time for
everything on the earth . . .

> A right time to search and another to count your losses,
> A right time to hold on and another to let go.
> —ECCLESIASTES 3:1, 6, MSG

This verse touches on one of grief's most haunting questions:
When is the right time to _____? Fill in the blank. We'll
ask this question hundreds of times. The hardest part is there's no
universal right time to do anything. In fact, your personal right time
to do hard things will likely sneak up and surprise you. Grief doesn't
plan well. With time I started to recognize what the tension between
courage and fear felt like—a quickened heartbeat, cramping in my
hands, but a unique loosening of my shoulders and clarity of mind.

When I felt these sensations as I prayed about (and worried about!)
a task or action, I knew it was my right time—to box up his things,
to move from our home, to start writing, to start dating. These gigan-
tic steps forward rip at your heart because you want to keep holding
on. They feel like, *If I let go, I may never get this feeling, these memories,
this connection back.* But please trust me when I tell you, letting go at
your right time doesn't mean losing. It's opening your hands to better
receive whatever new is coming. You won't forget them. You won't
love them any less. In fact, as you free up mental energy by releasing
the things you're scared to let go, you might actually find a new
capacity to love them even deeper.

Is there a next big thing you're worried about? Ask God to
make clear your right time to act and to give you the courage
to let go even in the fear.

> Indeed our fellowship is with the Father and with his Son Jesus Christ. And we are writing these things so that our joy may be complete.
>
> — I JOHN 1:3–4

Every year on Ben's birthday, I have two things I know I must do to be able to rejoice over the life he did live, the years I did get with him. First thing in the morning, I set aside extended time, always in nature, with God. It's where I break down, look at old pictures, and play songs of praise to remind myself of all God has carried me through. Then I enjoy Ben's favorite meal with close friends who loved him. This rhythm of lament and celebration has become life-changing for me. We really can feel deep pain and true joy in the same moments.

This is what I challenge you to on the hardest days. Though all around you is wrong and in pieces, part of what enables moments of joy and pain to coexist is *remembering*. Remembering what was and remembering you're not alone. Your circumstances may not change, at least not in all the ways you desire them to. But as you simply reflect, reminisce, and honor what was, God will begin to change your heart and your perspective. You may not be smiling or laughing yet, but intentional celebration with community is a sacred place to find peace when all around you is falling apart.

Think of an event coming up. What plans can you make to both grieve and celebrate with God and close friends and family?

You did not receive the spirit of bondage again to fear,
but you received the Spirit of adoption by whom we cry
out, "Abba, Father."

—ROMANS 8:15, NKJV

Fear is a powerful, powerful force. It can blur your thinking, your judgment, your actions. It can cause unnecessary rifts in relationships and hold you back from chasing beautiful dreams. And in seasons of pain and grief, fear has a way of keeping you wounded, keeping you bound. Don't let fear dictate your decisions. Don't let fear be the primary voice you hear in your head.

You are not responsible for managing your own fate. You aren't expected to carry the weight of your burdens on your own. Because Christ died for you and made you a cherished son or daughter of God, you can now call out "Abba, Father!" and release your fears to Him. God knows the plans He has for your future, and He won't leave you here in this pain. There is goodness in your future. He will continue to empower you through the worry and despair. Your fears are legitimate. The place you're in is hard. But don't let fear drive your life; walk in the peace and strength of your Father.

How is fear holding you back or sending you into unhealthy, unhelpful patterns? Speak it all out to the Lord today, and ask Him for full mercy, faith, and power to overcome this fear-based mindset.

Day 335

The LORD your God is in your midst,
    a mighty one who will save;
he will rejoice over you with gladness;
    he will quiet you by his love;
he will exult over you with loud singing.

—ZEPHANIAH 3:17

Hear this encouragement, friend: You can't save yourself from this. Just as you have no power to save yourself from sin and death without Christ, so you can't pull yourself up by your bootstraps every time life knocks you down. God is the mighty one who saves both your eternal soul and your right-now broken heart. Whether the hardship you're walking through unjustly happened to you or was an accident or even a consequence of your sinful actions, it isn't beyond redemption and restoration in the Lord's hands.

God is in the midst of your every question, fear, and regret. He will rejoice over you with gladness as you surrender your suffering and shame to Him. He is always glad when you come to Him to bind your wounds or wash you clean from sin. He will quiet your worries with His supernatural peace and love. He will sing songs of celebration over you even as you mourn because He knows the beautiful end of your story. He is tender with you in your current pain, and He is ecstatic because He knows the redemption that is coming for you. God is saving you as we speak.

Ask the Lord to pour into you supernatural hope for the future today, knowing He is already rejoicing over the goodness ahead that you can't yet see.

> They feast on the abundance of your house,
>   and you give them drink from the river of your delights.
> For with you is the fountain of life;
>   in your light do we see light.
>
> —PSALM 36:8–9

Imagine climbing Mount Everest, trekking across the Sahara, or swimming the Atlantic Ocean—but you brought no food, no fuel, with you. How far do you think you'd get? Olympians and triathletes know that efforts of extreme endurance require triple or more the amount of nutrition than the average person takes in. What's true of feeding your physical body when it's doing extreme work is true of feeding your soul.

There is no more crucial time to be feasting on God's Word than when you are suffering. In my first year of grief, I felt ravenous for His truths, His promises, and His presence. If you don't feel that way, don't worry. You can still be diligent to feed yourself! You can choose it even if you don't feel it. Pray for a craving for spiritual fuel. Ask the Holy Spirit specifically to pour so much life, hope, and supernatural peace into you that you overflow. Closeness to God and constant refueling with His Word will give you the energy and capacity to reach the other side of this challenge. Fill yourself up. Drink deeply of the fountain of life. And then keep going.

Lord, I praise You that Your Word is the greatest sustenance available to me in my suffering. From Your abundance continue to pour strength, endurance, and life into me today.

Day *337*

Love bears all things, believes all things, hopes all things, endures all things.

Love never ends.

—I CORINTHIANS 13:7–8

The perfect way Jesus loves you is utterly inconceivable. The love that you feel for and share with others—even your most beloved family members—pales in comparison with Christ's unconditional, eternal covenant love for you. He is the only source of perfect love, a love that can truly sustain you through anything.

As you spend time with the Lord this week, remember that it's His joy to help bear your burdens with endless compassion. Ask Him for the faith to keep trusting Him when theologically you believe but, in the moment, you need help in your unbelief (Mark 9:24). When your thoughts start to veer into dark places, call out to Jesus, who is able to fill you with His Living Hope. When looking forward to another day or another week feels crushing, praise Him that with His Spirit you can endure all things. When you bring every thought and struggle to the Lord, you *can* do this. His love for you never ever ends.

Praise God today for His matchless, endless love for you.

The LORD is near to the brokenhearted
    and saves the crushed in spirit.
Many are the afflictions of the righteous,
    but the LORD delivers him out of them all.

—PSALM 34:18–19

I hope by now you know this passage to be true in profound, personal ways. That in your suffering, your struggle, and your stress Christ draws palpably close to you and speaks the most clearly to you. At the deepest core of His being, Jesus is consumed with love for the brokenhearted. In all things—big and small—seek His presence and guidance.

And if your days are starting to feel a bit lighter, even joyful, praise God for that! But consider, Are you starting to hear His voice less? Are your prayers getting slightly less frequent and more rushed? Do you feel any less close to God? I assure you, He's not less close to you. But as the Lord delivers you into new weeks and months of healing, you may not feel as desperate for His presence as you did at the beginning. You may feel a new sense of confidence, which, again, you should praise God for! But don't stop your daily communion and communication with Him. Just because He may not be shouting to you today is no reason to feel He has resigned and wished you good luck. Keep your relationship rich with the Lord as you continue to heal. He is no less close on a good day than a bad.

If you haven't spent still time with God recently, remedy that. Thank Him that He's just as near on tearful days as He is on ones of progress.

When the sixth hour had come, there was darkness over
the whole land until the ninth hour. And at the ninth
hour Jesus cried with a loud voice, "Eloi, Eloi, lema
sabachthani?" which means, "My God, my God, why
have you forsaken me?"

—MARK 15:33–34

This moment of Jesus' final breaths on earth is one many people—
both of faith and not of faith—are familiar with. From the cross,
Jesus cried out because, for His sacrifice to be complete, He had to
bear the full penalty of sin: not just physical death but also spiritual
separation from God. Jesus Christ, the physical manifestation of
God, had been coexisting and cooperating with the Father and the
Holy Spirit since before the foundation of the world, and for the first
time, He was cut off from the other two persons of the Trinity (and,
thus, all love, goodness, joy, hope, and every other good thing that
comes from God). He chose to be expelled from Their perfect, supernaturally connected presence so that you will never have to be.

Until now you may have been leaning on the Lord for mere survival, to combat hopelessness, sorrow, and despondency. But as some
of the initial wounds start to scab over, you may need new divine
tools that come from walking in God's presence. Because you are
forever bound to God through Jesus, holy hopefulness, contentment,
and anticipation are yours for the taking as you move into new seasons! The Lord can provide you with those gifts. He is so, so near.

Take a moment to consider every goodness that comes from
being united with God. Ask Him for just what you need
today, and know you are secure!

The LORD gave, and the LORD has taken away; blessed be
the name of the LORD.

—JOB 1:21

After a devastating loss, praise certainly doesn't feel like our default
mode of operation. Lament is still an imperative part of your healing,
but there is a point we reach where praise is essential. Not just obedient praise for who God is, but praise for the person or thing He gave
us even though He's since taken it away. Why? Because it's one of the
few ways we can move forward in love.

C. S. Lewis knew the pains and joys of this well. He reminds us
that praise is rooted in love: "Praise is the mode of love which always
has some element of joy in it. Praise in due order; of Him as the giver,
of her as the gift. Don't we in praise somehow enjoy what we praise,
however far we are from it?"[33]

When you praise God for the years you had with your loved one
even after they're gone, you reexperience some of the joy you felt
being with them. When you thank Him for specific memories or
gifts, they become more concrete in your mind. It's nothing short of
miraculous. It may feel unnatural, but this practice honors God as
well as keeps the love you feel for your person all the nearer.

*Lord, give me the courage to reflect on past years and moments
I'm most thankful for and to praise You that the love I feel for
the person I've lost can be sustained in the future.*

Me he caught—reached all the way
   from sky to sea; he pulled me out
Of that ocean of hate, that enemy chaos,
   the void in which I was drowning.

—PSALM 18:16–17, MSG

Horatio Spafford lost all four of his daughters in a shipwreck en route to Europe in the 1870s. He wasn't on the ship but had sent them ahead, planning to follow later. As a devout believer, Horatio continued to cling tightly to God's Word, knowing well that peace in the aftermath of absolute devastation can come only from the Lord. In reflection of his loss, he wrote these words:

> When peace like a river, attendeth my way,
> When sorrows like sea billows roll—
> Whatever my lot, Thou hast taught me to know
> It is well, it is well with my soul.[34]

These glorious lyrics became the classic hymn "It Is Well with My Soul." In them we see the perfect picture of surrender. Horatio testified that even in the worst storms, when sorrows are so overwhelming they wash over you like crashing waves, there is unwavering peace with God. He shows us what honest grief and defiant hope look like. When all was completely unwell, he turned to the source of transcendent peace: the only One who could make it well with his soul.

Lord, You are my peace. Work in me so I, too, can say, "It is well with my soul." Comfort me as I go through another dark day.

Mary said,

> "My soul magnifies the Lord,
>   and my spirit rejoices in God my Savior,
> for he has looked on the humble estate of his servant.
>   For behold, from now on all generations will call me
>   blessed;
> for he who is mighty has done great things for me,
>   and holy is his name."

—LUKE 1:46–49

This beautiful song of praise from Mary, the mother of Jesus, is called the Magnificat, meaning "magnifies" in Latin.[35] Readers might assume that Mary was rejoicing after Jesus' birth. *Of course she was praising God for this beautiful baby, who had come to save His people!* However, Mary's outburst of worship didn't come after Jesus' birth but following her visit from the angel Gabriel. She'd just been told that she, as a virgin teenager, would be pregnant with the Son of God.

I think my reaction would have been one of fear or doubt, even refusal of this overwhelming call. Mary knew she'd be scorned, possibly outcast, by a community that wouldn't believe her divine conception story. Yet she trusted. She worshipped. In the face of a call that would upend her whole life, she praised the God who she believed would carry her through. It's scary to go all in when we stand at an unprecedented starting line with the Lord. You may not know what He has for you in this next chapter. But like Mary, you can praise Him. You can look back on the mighty things He's done for you and trust He'll do it again.

Lord, I don't know what the month or year ahead holds, but I know how faithful You've been to me thus far. Thank You that I know You'll deliver and protect me again.

Blessed are the poor in spirit, for theirs is the kingdom of heaven.

Blessed are those who mourn, for they shall be comforted.

—MATTHEW 5:3−4

When Jesus spoke here of the poor, He didn't just mean those who lacked financial resources. Anyone can be poor in spirit, regardless of their economic status. Being poor in spirit doesn't mean being depressed or downtrodden; it means having the humble conviction that you can contribute nothing to secure God's mercy. It means admitting that you can't earn God's love and celebrating that everything you need for eternal life has been given to you through the grace of the cross. You have nothing to give; therefore, Jesus gives you everything.

It's often those who are mourning or in pain whose hearts are most humbled and open to receive Christ's help. They know they need it. It's the victims, the grieving, and the ashamed that cry out for rescue and comfort because they know their suffering is more than they can handle. Don't reject the notion of spiritual poverty or scorn your seasons of mourning. Let your need draw you nearer to Jesus and remind you to celebrate the miraculous gift of grace that secures your place in His kingdom. Blessed are you, Jesus says.

Ask the Holy Spirit to enable you to embrace the poverty of your spirit right now. And praise Jesus that He has already gifted you all the grace you need in order to endure this valley and flourish on the other side.

> If a man has a hundred sheep, and one of them has gone astray, does he not leave the ninety-nine on the mountains and go in search of the one that went astray? And if he finds it, truly, I say to you, he rejoices over it more than over the ninety-nine that never went astray.
>
> —MATTHEW 18:12–13

At our wedding, Ben and I took communion while the hymn "Come, Thou Fount" played. It starts with these lines: "Come, Thou Fount of every blessing, tune my heart to sing Thy grace."[36] For us it was a reminder that all blessings, our marriage included, came from God alone. But the song also speaks to a much harder truth I realized only in my grief:

> Prone to wander, Lord, I feel it;
> Prone to leave the God I love.
> Here's my heart; O, take and seal it,
> Seal it for Thy courts above.[37]

Humans are a wandering people, and God is constantly bringing us home again. He is faithful to find the one that's gone astray. Whatever wilderness you find yourself in—whether the grip of depression or a toxic method of escaping reality—you are never too far gone for the Good Shepherd to find. However intentionally or unintentionally you've wandered, however far you've strayed, God is quick to lead you back to Himself. You may feel alone, but He is with you. You may feel overlooked and forgotten, but Jesus carries you back to safety. You may feel deserted and too broken to fix, but He is Messiah, who rescues broken people. Let the Lord lead you back home.

Meditate on this truth: *Lord, You are my perfect rescuer.*

You will be sorrowful, but your sorrow will turn into joy.
—JOHN 16:20

I love the boldness of Jesus' statement here. He didn't say, after your sorrow, you'll feel joy. Or even because of your sorrow, you'll feel greater joy. (Both of which I've experienced to be true!) But He said, your sorrow will *become* joy. The days that have haunted you year after year will be transformed into days of joyful remembrance. This may still sound crazy impossible to you. But it's true. It's miraculously possible if you continue to surrender and entrust your healing to our mighty God.

Ben's birthday, the anniversary of his death, and our wedding anniversary all fall within seven weeks of one another. The first several years, I dreaded them. I was anxious, distracted, and exhausted leading up to those monumental dates. Then, after years of both mourning him and celebrating him on those days, the tide seemed to turn. They're always tender, of course; I always reflect on and grieve the ways I wish he were still present in my life. But there was a supernatural shift one year, where the days felt a tiny bit more sweet than sorrowful. I smiled at memories even as I cried. I felt a little more thankful for those days than resentful they were gone. I can't explain it, but it happens. Stick with your Redeemer. He truly can turn your sorrow into joy.

Lord, I can't imagine sorrowful days bringing joy. Help me believe that it's true, that those days are coming for me too.

> Everyone then who hears these words of mine and does them will be like a wise man who built his house on the rock. And the rain fell, and the floods came, and the winds blew and beat on that house, but it did not fall, because it had been founded on the rock.
>
> —MATTHEW 7:24–25

There is no logic in seasons of grief. Nothing about grief is linear. It often feels as emotionally tumultuous as the storm described in this passage. Julian of Norwich explained it this way: "I felt there was no ease or comfort for me except faith, hope and love, and truly I felt very little of this. And then presently God gave me again comfort and rest for my soul . . . And then again I felt the pain, and then afterwards the delight and the joy, now the one and now the other, again and again, I suppose about twenty times."[38] So, how on earth can we find solid ground?

Exactly as Jesus instructs us: Solid ground is *His* words. Solid ground is Scripture. Solid ground is the Bible sitting open on your bedside table, not stuffed in your drawer. Never underestimate the grounding power of staying in the Word when you're hurting. Don't believe the lie that it's outdated and out of touch with modern reality. In the torrents of suffering, there is no more secure place to spend your time and plant your feet than God's Word. Begin and build each day on the rock of God.

Spend ten minutes today reading Jesus' words in the Gospels (Matthew, Mark, Luke, and John) or revisiting favorite, anchoring passages.

He will wipe away every tear from their eyes, and death shall be no more, neither shall there be mourning, nor crying, nor pain anymore, for the former things have passed away.

—REVELATION 21:4

Today's verse describes the final chapter of the story of your life. It's the final line in a divinely written script before the credits roll. You are home, and every broken part of your life is now redeemed into something beautiful. This is a literal promise from the risen Jesus to you and me as a glimpse of the happy ending that will be true for every one of God's children. It may seem impossible or sound like a fairy tale, but it's true. It's the promise of God.

Having confidence in the happy ending waiting for you is powerful. It gives you a healthy perspective on what really matters. It helps you endure the hard right-now parts of your story because you know without a shadow of a doubt where you're headed. Remember that the sufferings of your present can't even compare with the glory that will be revealed to you (Romans 8:18). Fix your mind on the glory of eternity. Your future in Christ is the only fairy tale certain to come true.

Meditate on this today: *Death will be no more; neither will there be mourning, crying, or pain. The Lord redeems all.*

> Since we have such a hope, we are very bold. . . . Now
> the Lord is the Spirit, and where the Spirit of the Lord
> is, there is freedom.
>
> —2 CORINTHIANS 3:12, 17

You may still be feeling quite uncertain about your future or even your present. That's understandable—confidence comes with time. But now isn't the time to shrink back from God or the future He has for you. Now isn't the time to retreat in despair and give up on fighting for the blessings and provisions He's prepared. Now is the time to be bold in prayer and courageous in hope.

But how? How can you possibly be bold or brave when so much around you has fallen apart? It can feel scary to hope. You might be waiting for the other shoe to drop. But you have two choices as you start to settle into your "new normal." Either you can stand idly by, fearful of any more difficulties or setbacks, or you can start to dream again with God. You can entrust your best-case scenarios to Him in prayer. You can boldly ask Him to open doors for better financial opportunities or new relationships. You can pray for the confidence to learn new skills or pursue some life-giving hobbies or activities. The Lord is always creating new life, always restoring His people. You are free to come to Him with every need and dream.

What is a deep desire or need that you've been afraid to ask God for? Boldly ask Him for it in detail today, knowing that Jesus is delighted when you dream big with Him.

> She went down to the threshing floor and did just as her mother-in-law had commanded her. . . . He said, "Who are you?" And she answered, "I am Ruth, your servant. Spread your wings over your servant, for you are a redeemer."
>
> —RUTH 3:6, 9

Do you remember the story of Ruth? The young Moabite widow who, in great loyalty, returned to a foreign land with her mother-in-law, Naomi? Ruth was a stranger, a non-Jew, in the town of Bethlehem. As Ruth worked, harvesting grain for their food, she and Naomi sought God to provide for them and also to bring forth a new husband to redeem and restore Ruth's life. In the fields, she met a man named Boaz who offered to protect her. And as Ruth began to trust Boaz, she boldly went to his workplace and stayed there until he woke. She pursued him.

This might sound too bold, even pushy, to us. But Ruth knew that, along with our prayers, we must also take responsibility for moving toward the things we desire. The Lord had shown Ruth and Naomi that Boaz was a good man, and Ruth pursued him. Progress certainly should start with bold prayer. But I love that Ruth shows us the importance of acting on our prayers as well. You can't control or guarantee the outcome, but you can put yourself in a position to better recognize and receive what God may have for you.

Is there something you've been covering in prayer but haven't taken any steps to pursue? Ask God for boldness to take one step forward with His leading.

The waters closed in over me to take my life;
    the deep surrounded me;
weeds were wrapped about my head
    at the roots of the mountains.
I went down to the land
    whose bars closed upon me forever;
yet you brought up my life from the pit,
    O LORD my God.

—JONAH 2:5–6

Jonah's situation here sounds pretty hopeless, doesn't it? Deep waters overhead, weeds wrapped around, bars closed. Well, Jonah said all this while sitting in the stomach of a fish! Consider the darkness, the motions, the noises, the smells, even the physical process of being swallowed up and pushed down the throat of a giant sea creature. It must have felt like wet, fishy hell to him!

Yet Jonah knew God was his only rescuer. What is beautiful about his prayer is that he prayed in past tense what hadn't yet happened. Jonah praised God for hearing his prayer and saving him from death not after the fish spit him up but while he was still terrified, stuck in the belly of an enormous animal. Claim the victory and deliverance you need as if God has already done it, knowing and believing even in the darkest, most hopeless places that there is nothing too disastrous for Him to save you from.

Where in your life are you feeling trapped and hopeless right now? Start praying God's deliverance over that situation as if it's already happened.

The LORD is near to all who call on him,
    to all who call on him in truth.
He fulfills the desire of those who fear him;
    he also hears their cry and saves them.
The LORD preserves all who love him.

—PSALM 145:18–20

Think about what these verbs really mean: He will *fulfill* your desire—maybe not in every detail, but He will fulfill your desire for peace, refuge, and freedom from the burdens you're bearing. He will *hear* your cry and *save* you—maybe not from the temporal situation you're in, but from feeling victim to a situation that is only temporary, from the lie that where you are now is where your story ends. And He will *preserve* you because you love Him—He will take care of you and safeguard you from the threats of the world and attacks of the Enemy, who seeks to destroy your faith. Your heart, mind, and soul are safe in the loving Father's hands.

Even as I grieved my husband, the Lord filled the gaping hole left by the love I'd lost with endless outpourings of love from others in my life. It didn't replace Ben's love, of course, but it fulfilled my need to be embraced and cared for. As I mourned no longer being a wife, God saved me from rooting my worth in anything but my identity as His child. When I thought the passing of time would separate me from Ben, the Lord showed me tender ways to preserve and honor his legacy. When you call to the Lord in truth, He shows up big. He moves to fulfill, save, and preserve you, His beloved.

What do you need the Lord to fulfill, save you from, or preserve as you move forward? Know He is near to you as you call on Him.

> The word of God is living and active, sharper than any
> two-edged sword, piercing to the division of soul and
> of spirit, of joints and of marrow, and discerning the
> thoughts and intentions of the heart.
>
> —HEBREWS 4:12

Does the long and tedious process of grief feel exhausting, even aggravating? Sometimes I felt like God insisted on holding me in uncomfortable places during the healing process when I wanted to move on. But what if the tool being used to cut isn't a sword so much as a scalpel? This is how C. S. Lewis understood God's hand in his own pain: "Suppose that what you are up against is a surgeon whose intentions are wholly good. The kinder and more conscientious he is, the more inexorably he will go on cutting. If he yielded to your entreaties, if he stopped before the operation was complete, all the pain up to that point would have been useless."[39]

The Lord, our surgeon, won't give up on the process. And yes, the process is painful and scary and demands much recovery. But as God works kindly and meticulously with His spiritual scalpel, I promise, you will be stronger, healthier, and more resilient in your faith on the other side. If you resist the work God's doing in your heart as you suffer, your pain may be in vain. Let Him finish the hard heart work He's doing in you. You can trust that every cut is absolutely for your good.

*God, I hate this pain You're putting me through. But above all, I
don't want it to be wasted. Use it to divinely refine, strengthen,
and bless me.*

Day 353

> The Word became flesh and dwelt among us, and we have
> seen his glory, glory as of the only Son from the Father,
> full of grace and truth. . . . For from his fullness we have
> all received, grace upon grace.
>
> —JOHN 1:14, 16

Sometimes Scripture is hard to connect with—whether because of our inability to focus or the reality of the demands on our time. When the Bible is hard to get into, reach out to connect with the Word that became flesh. Jesus is "the radiance of the glory of God and the exact imprint of his nature" (Hebrews 1:3). Jesus is the heart of God, the Word of God, and the glory, grace, and truth of God all wrapped into a comprehensive package *for you*. Not that Jesus is separate from the Father or the Holy Spirit (they are all incredibly one!), but He expresses God's divine nature in human form; we can know God because we know Jesus. What's more—Jesus suffered alongside real people and exists alongside you right here, right now.

And Jesus—fully God, the Word made flesh—pours grace upon grace over you. For the days of anguish and tears, grace. For the days of unbelief and anger, grace. For the days of sinful escapes and unforgiveness, grace. For the days of desperate, dwindling hope, grace. For the days of dreams and desires, grace. For the days of joy and laughter, grace. For the days of discovering new life ahead, grace, grace, grace.

Thank Jesus that, in His perfect love and holiness, He never runs out of grace for you.

> Put on then, as God's chosen ones, holy and beloved,
> compassionate hearts, kindness, humility, meekness,
> and patience, bearing with one another and, if one has
> a complaint against another, forgiving each other; as
> the Lord has forgiven you, so you also must forgive.
>
> —COLOSSIANS 3:12–13

In suffering, our focus on our spiritual health is often renewed. But as the intensity of our pain ebbs and we start to feel more energy, the pressures of life also start pushing back in and our focus can slip. Compassion for others turns to indifference; kindness to a calloused heart; humility and meekness to self-righteousness or harsh judgment; patience to a short temper; forgiveness to self-preservation. Don't shame yourself. God no longer holds your fleshly reactions against you. All He sees is Christ's perfect robe of righteousness over every part of you.

You don't need to tear yourself down for operating out of your default sinful setting. But do be aware of these tendencies. Be prayerful. Ask the Lord for the desire and strength to actively cultivate the fruit of the Spirit. Put safe people in place to gently hold you accountable for your actions when you're under stress. Keep your focus, friend.

Empower me, God, to keep cultivating the fruit of the Spirit with each action and interaction today.

Day 355

The Spirit of the LORD GOD is upon me,
    because the LORD has anointed me
to bring good news to the poor;
    he has sent me to bind up the brokenhearted, . . .
    to give them a beautiful headdress instead of ashes,
the oil of gladness instead of mourning,
    the garment of praise instead of a faint spirit;
that they may be called oaks of righteousness,
    the planting of the LORD, that he may be glorified.

—ISAIAH 61:1,3

This is the passage we read on September 17, 2018, at Ben's burial. Every time I hear it, I can see his casket, with his white, felt cowboy hat on top, being lowered into the ground. I'd heard this scripture, a prophecy about Jesus coming to free His people, months before, and something about the idea of "oaks of righteousness" stuck with me. And in those five days after Ben's death, the Lord brought it to my clouded, grieving mind, the only message with a shred of hope I could think of.

Since that day, Ben's body has been "planted," with his life and legacy continuing to glorify the Lord. Since that day, much of who I am has been planted . . . buried too. Your future and mine, friend, *is* beauty, is gladness, is a legacy of praise and glory to the One who brings good news and binds up the brokenhearted. This promise is for every one of God's children. I've seen the Lord redeem the details of my life time and time again since Ben's death, and you can trust it for yours as you continue to walk through this valley with Him.

With all you've lost, all the days of ashes, mourning, and a faint spirit that you've endured, praise God that your future and your legacy is beauty, gladness, and glory. Thank Him that that is His eternal promise to you.

The LORD is gracious and merciful,
  slow to anger and abounding in steadfast love.
The LORD is good to all,
  and his mercy is over all that he has made.

—PSALM 145:8–9

Like the comfort of a warm towel when you're wet and cold or a soft pillow when your body aches, I want you to lean into Jesus and relax. Try to take small, intentional moments today to pause, exhale, and imagine being wrapped up in Christ's strong, gentle arms. Like children do with their parent, find safety in the tender, loving presence of "the Father of mercies and God of all comfort" (2 Corinthians 1:3), who longs to hold you in your hurt. I assure you, He is the softest place for you to land.

When you find yourself at rock bottom—or still at rock bottom—I want you to picture Jesus right there holding you. When you have nothing left mentally, emotionally, or physically, I want to remind yourself that the love and comfort God has for you aren't just enough; they're abounding and endless. When you hold yourself to unrealistic expectations of how to grieve, how long it should take, or how to navigate the difficulties in front of you, take a breath. Remember, God's gracious and merciful love holds no shortcomings against you. You're doing just fine, friend.

Close your eyes, and imagine the comfort of Jesus as tangibly as you can. Try to feel His arms around you. Let His presence calm your mind.

> Behold, a woman who had suffered from a discharge of blood for twelve years came up behind him and touched the fringe of his garment, for she said to herself, "If I only touch his garment, I will be made well." Jesus turned, and seeing her he said, "Take heart, daughter; your faith has made you well." And instantly the woman was made well.
>
> —MATTHEW 9:20–22

This kind of miraculous healing is just as possible for you as it was for the woman who grabbed Jesus' robe. Do you believe that? Do you believe that your own faith truly can make you well? I can relate to how this woman surely felt—afraid that her situation was beyond repair yet in desperation wondering if maybe, maybe there was still hope. We must cling to hope! Grasp for any type of contact with Jesus, our Savior, knowing that even the smallest encounters with Him bring supernatural healing.

Through the Holy Spirit, you and I have more opportunities to access His presence—His touch—than those who knew Jesus only in the flesh. Cling to His Word. Hear His reassurance in hymns and songs and His guidance through prayer. Hold hands with others who love God as they pray over you. Whatever grabbing the fringe of Jesus' garment looks like for you in this season, friend, continue doing it. There is healing for you in His presence. Just keep reaching.

What is one way you can connect with Jesus that isn't a part of your regular routine? Practice that today.

> [Jesus] said to Thomas, "Put your finger here; see my
> hands. Reach out your hand and put it into my side.
> Stop doubting and believe."
>   Thomas said to him, "My Lord and my God!"
>
> —JOHN 20:27–28, NIV

Have you ever wondered why, after Jesus' resurrection, His scars weren't healed? If His body had been fully restored and made whole, why preserve evidence of His torturous death? I can't help but believe He chose to keep them for us—for all the Thomases out there. Though he loved the Lord, Thomas was skeptical, a logical guy. He needed undeniable proof that Jesus was who He said He was, evidence that it was safe to keep trusting Him in the future.

I think our scars can be gifts to help us hope in the same way. It would be foolish and unhelpful to try to forget or file away what we've gone through. Your experience, your loss, is permanent, but the gaping wounds won't always be open. They *will* eventually become scar tissue. Let those scars buoy your trust that the Lord can carry you through whatever you face in the future. They are evidence of your ability to persevere and grow. You've experienced something devastating, yet you still stand. Let your scarring wounds be a reminder to yourself and others of the ways God has been good to you. You, too, have been broken and raised again to life. Never forget that.

If you feel inclined to dismiss the gravity of the suffering you've endured, remember Jesus' scars. Remember the power your own scars have to bring you back to hope in the future.

> As for God, his way is perfect:
>   The LORD's word is flawless;
>   he shields all who take refuge in him.
>
> —PSALM 18:30, NIV

If we believe these descriptors of God's way and His words—that they are perfect and flawless—what happens when His way doesn't align with ours? When His words confront a long-held desire or dream that is no longer possible? If His way is immovable, then it's we who must adjust. A. W. Tozer said it this way: "Much of our difficulty as seeking Christians stems from our unwillingness to take God as He is and adjust our lives accordingly."[40]

See, our nature is to take our reality and adjust our view of God. This is where distrust and disappointment rush in. So, how do we take His way and words as perfect and immovable and adjust our lives accordingly? For me, it meant surrendering my future and being openhanded with my expectations. I surrendered to God, over and over, the family I'd pictured with Ben. I had to relinquish my plan to have my first child at thirty like I'd hoped. You, too, in a hundred ways are going to have to surrender the life you imagined before loss. But as you do, remember, the Lord sees the complete picture. No pivots or adjustments are news to Him but are simply another means of loving you and leading you into whatever goodness He has for you next.

Lord, it's impossible for me to see how what You're doing right now is good. Help me surrender and adjust my expectations of _____ so I can continue forward in full trust of Your way.

He drew me up from the pit of destruction,
  out of the miry bog,
and set my feet upon a rock,
  making my steps secure.
He put a new song in my mouth,
  a song of praise to our God.
Many will see and fear,
  and put their trust in the LORD.

—PSALM 40:2–3

As much as we wish it weren't so, it often takes falling into the pit and the miry bog for us to remember how good and how powerful God is as our Redeemer. We cling to Him more fiercely in struggle than when life is going well. His glory shines exponentially brighter in the darkness. We know this well now!

You've had a year of wrestling with God and walking with Him through this valley. As you move forward, you may encounter others who need to glean hope from your story. When those earlier in their journey see you trusting God, seeking God, and—craziest of all—praising God as you struggle, you can ignite their desire to draw near to the Lord in their hardship. You become the new song of praise that those around you can't help but hear and sing for themselves. Though your healing is far from finished, you can find great purpose and joy in sharing God's faithfulness to you with those fresh in their grief.

Thank You, Lord, that Your glory shines through every part of my suffering and healing. Put someone in my path who needs to witness Your faithfulness in my story.

Day 361

> Father, I desire that they also, whom you have given me, may be with me where I am, to see my glory that you have given me because you loved me before the foundation of the world.
>
> —JOHN 17:24

When Jesus uttered this prayer for us to the Father, He was speaking directly to God's divine plan for eternal salvation for all who believe. He was reaffirming that His atoning death and resurrection would secure our place in heaven forever—that we might be with Him where He is. We'll experience His glory in full when we go home. But don't miss the invitation to chase after God's glory right here, right now. Scripture says, "He is the image of the invisible God, the firstborn of all creation. For by him all things were created, in heaven and on earth, visible and invisible" (Colossians 1:15–16).

I hope, over this year and in practicing these spiritual rhythms, your senses have become better tuned to perceiving God's glory in your everyday life—in people and in creation, in beauty and even in the connectivity of sorrow. Paul Tripp calls this "sign glory" because "every glorious thing in creation was designed to be a sign that points us to the inestimable glory of the one who made it."[41] We don't have to miss out on the experience of God's glory today. One of the greatest ways you'll sustain hope all throughout life is to keep your eyes peeled daily for sign glory.

Jesus, thank You that Your glory is gloriously inescapable. Keep training me to search for and cherish signs of Your glory in my daily life.

Be gracious to me, O Lord,
　　for to you do I cry all the day.
Gladden the soul of your servant,
　　for to you, O Lord, do I lift up my soul.
For you, O Lord, are good and forgiving,
　　abounding in steadfast love to all who call upon you.

—PSALM 86:3–5

The Lord cherishes all the prayers His children offer to Him. Nothing gladdens a father's heart more than his kids trusting him and sharing their hearts with him. The sound of your voice always delights your Father. But all too often when you pray, you ask only for God to change what's happening to you.

But what if you started to pray for your soul more than for your situation? As you settle in on a bit more solid ground, ask the Lord to gladden your heart and refine your character, your soul, as you continue to heal. The prayers God will always answer yes to are prayers for sanctification—to cultivate even more of the fruit of the Spirit in you. Prayers for faith, hope, and love are always answered yes! So, when you pray, ask honestly for what changes you need in your circumstances moving forward. *All* prayer is a divine conversation to be cherished. But also ask with boldness and confidence for the Lord to complete the work He knows you need in your soul.

Consider your soul today—how it's strong and how it's weak. Invite Jesus to complete His refining work in you.

> Since therefore the children share in flesh and blood, he himself likewise partook of the same things, that through death he might destroy the one who has the power of death, that is, the devil, and deliver all those who through fear of death were subject to lifelong slavery.
>
> —HEBREWS 2:14–15

It's the most repeated command in all of Scripture: "Do not fear." And if we're honest, there are few things most of us fear more than death—the physical nature of it but also the mystery of it. Even for believers, death brings with it an onslaught of questions: *Did my loved one feel pain? How immediate upon their last breath was their welcoming into God's presence? Can they see or hear us at any point after their spirit leaves their body?*

Most of our questions about death and Christian afterlife won't get answered until we're there ourselves. But what this passage assures us of is that there's no reason for believers to fear it. Jesus experienced physical death, and His Word tells us not to worry. As Christians, we know that death ushers us into glory. You truly can be free from anxiety about this life's end when you're in Christ. And even as you grieve those you miss so much here, you can truly be glad for those who pass knowing Jesus, because their reality is now constant, unimaginable pleasure and joy. You can still hate death without fearing it. It no longer has any hold on you. Live freely and rejoice!

Really consider the truth that your death and the death of anyone you love who knows Christ is not an ending but a glorious beginning. Let that reality free you from fear and help you praise God today.

He heals the brokenhearted
    and binds up their wounds.
He determines the number of the stars;
    he gives to all of them their names.
Great is our Lord, and abundant in power;
    his understanding is beyond measure.

—PSALM 147:3–5

Our God is a God who heals. He is the Great Physician. Reliance on Christ's healing presence is how you'll continue to endure this season and emerge a richer version of yourself. But even more than tender comfort, the Lord offers you an unshakable identity.

When you're in seasons of struggle and loss, they can leave you grappling with identity and diminish how you perceive your own worth. You've gone from a spouse to a widow or widower, a parent to a bereaved parent, married to single, a son or daughter to an orphan. These roles are so painful to let go of, and as you do so, it becomes easy to forget who you are. But God knows you. He has chosen you, and you are His family. He has given you your identity—a beloved child of God, a brother or sister of Christ, the apple of God's eye, part of a chosen people and a royal priesthood (1 Peter 2:9). Remind yourself that, since the foundation of the world, God has willingly and joyfully claimed you. You are His to shepherd and care for. He will comfort you. You will be victorious because you're claimed in Jesus' name.

Praise You, Lord, that You not only comfort me in my brokenness but also remind me who I am: Your beloved, protected, adored child. Help me see myself this week as You say I am.

We are afflicted in every way, but not crushed; perplexed, but not driven to despair; persecuted, but not forsaken; struck down, but not destroyed; always carrying in the body the death of Jesus, so that the life of Jesus may also be manifested in our bodies.

—2 CORINTHIANS 4:8–10

There is no clearer picture of a Christian's experience than Paul's words here—of simultaneously living in the world and living in God's kingdom. Nearly all of Paul's ministry as an apostle was marked with affliction, confusion, and persecution. Yet the reality of his pain always came second to the reality of the power of Christ in him. He never downplayed the hardship that plagued him. It's not valiant to dismiss your pain. This world is broken, and life will hurt you again and again. Part of living with kingdom hope is facing the brokenness with honesty.

But as in Paul's life, the reality of the gospel must always trump the reality of your pain. Anything can hurt you; nothing can destroy you. Anyone can betray you; no one can pluck you from the Father's loving hand (John 10:29). You will face more suffering than you can handle on your own, but you have constant, inextinguishable access to the same power that raised Jesus' lifeless body from the grave (Romans 8:11). God's Holy Spirit in you is what sets the reality of His kingdom and His power above the reality of how painful this life can be. Nothing is too big or too broken for you to survive if you're facing it with Christ. This isn't the end for you, beloved. There is nothing you can't overcome with God's magnificent Spirit working in you.

Meditate on this truth today: *I am afflicted, but not crushed; perplexed, but not driven to despair; persecuted, but not forsaken; struck down, but not destroyed—because the power of Christ's Spirit lives in me.*

Acknowledgments

This book wouldn't exist without the faithful community who loved me through the worst of my valley, who, in simply being who they are, helped love me back to life.

To Connor: You came into my life at a time when most men would have walked away. When all my work and my time was committed to sharing Ben and my story with the world, you became my biggest cheerleader. You listened when I worried and reassured me that you loved me not in spite of my story but because of it—because, without it, I wouldn't be the woman you love and choose today.

To Mom and Dad: I can't imagine the crushing weight of seeing your child hurt so badly. Every day, I knew you'd give the world if you could fix my heartbreak in an instant. Thank you for loving me as you always have, being patient with me when I grieved poorly, and providing everything possible to lighten the burden of this journey for me.

To Ali and Dani: Somehow at ages far too young to endure this type of tragedy, you walked this bravely with me. As your big sister, my bent is always to take care of you, but you both rose with compassion and empathy beyond your years when I needed you.

To Mark and Brenda: You suffered the most atrocious loss any human will ever experience. Yet I watched you, month after month, year after year, praise God. For your love, for your family and its legacy, I am forever grateful.

To Ginger and Rachel, Alita and Carolyn: I wouldn't have known how to hurt and hope well without you. I wouldn't have had anyone to ask the embarrassing or not-so-church-appropriate questions to. Your lives are truly purposed to show young widows like me what beauty from ashes can look like. You cheered for me, prayed with me, laughed and cried with me. You made me believe that redemption and love were not only possible but also possible for me.

To my girls: Y'all know who you are. If it wasn't so before, through this valley you became so much more than friends to me. You are now family. What our circle of friends has as adult women is nothing short of miraculous. Y'all are my rocks, my safe places, my stand-up comedians, my prayer warriors, my sisters. Thank you for holding my grief so gently and never letting me lose sight of who I was through this valley.

To Estee and the whole WaterBrook team: Thank you for believing in this gargantuan undertaking of a project. Thank you for trusting me when I told you I could do it. Thank you for challenging me to make this book the most valuable and vulnerable resource we possibly could for those who will weep on its pages. Thank you for how fearfully and tenderly you hold the Word of God and have helped me represent it here.

And to Jesus, the sweet Savior who continues to rescue me again and again and again—there's no better way to end this than with Your blessing to those who open its pages:

Blessed are the poor in spirit, for theirs is the kingdom
of heaven.
Blessed are those who mourn, for they shall be comforted.
Blessed are the meek, for they shall inherit the earth.
Blessed are those who hunger and thirst for righteousness, for they shall be satisfied.

—Matthew 5:3–6

Notes

Introduction

1. Elisabeth Kübler-Ross, *On Death & Dying: What the Dying Have to Teach Doctors, Nurses, Clergy & Their Own Families* (New York: Scribner, 2019).

Day 28

2. C. S. Lewis, *A Grief Observed* (New York: HarperOne, 1994), 5.

Day 32

3. Joni Eareckson Tada, "The Goodness of Good Friday," Joni and Friends, March 30, 2018, https://joniandfriends.org/news/good-friday -2018.

Day 37

4. Charles Dickens, *Dombey and Son,* ed. Alan Horsman (Oxford: Oxford University Press, 2008), 256.

Day 40

5. Lysa TerKeurst, *It's Not Supposed to Be This Way: Finding Unexpected Strength When Disappointments Leave You Shattered* (Nashville, Tenn.: Nelson Books, 2018), 57.

Day 75

6. *Encyclopaedia Britannica,* s.v. "kintsugi," last modified November 23, 2023, www.britannica.com/art/kintsugi-ceramics.

Day 78

7. Adapted from Encyclopedia.com, s.v. "endurance," last modified August 13, 2018, www.encyclopedia.com/history/historians-and-chronicles/historians-ancient/endurance.

Day 102

8. "The Symbolism of the Olive Tree in the Jewish Faith," My Olive Tree, March 2, 2018, www.myolivetree.com/symbolism-olive-tree-jewish -faith.

Day 106

9. Lysa TerKeurst, *It's Not Supposed to Be This Way: Finding Unexpected Strength When Disappointments Leave You Shattered* (Nashville, Tenn.: Nelson Books, 2018), 9.

Day 107

10. *Heidelberg Catechism: Modern English Version,* 450th anniversary ed. (The Reformed Church in the United States, 2013), 19.

Day 152

11. C. S. Lewis, "The Weight of Glory," in *The Weight of Glory and Other Addresses* (New York: HarperOne, 2001), 27.

Day 171

12. Mattie Jackson, "The spirit & science of hope with Dr. Lee Warren," October 24, 2023, in *Joy Life with Mattie Jackson,* podcast, 47:00, https://podcasts.apple.com/us/podcast/the-spirit-science-of-hope-with -dr-lee-warren/id1667357187?i=1000632461215.

Day 189

13. C. H. Spurgeon, "The Trial of Your Faith" (sermon, Metropolitan Tabernacle, London, December 2, 1888), www.spurgeon.org/resource -library/sermons/the-trial-of-your-faith.

Day 190

14. C. S. Lewis, *The Problem of Pain* (New York: HarperOne, 2001), 91.

Day 192

15. J. C. Ryle, *Expository Thoughts on the Gospel of Matthew,* rev. ed. (Abbotsford, Wis.: Aneko, 2019), 158.

Day 193

16. Randy Alcorn, *Ninety Days of God's Goodness: Daily Reflections That Shine Light on Personal Darkness* (Colorado Springs, Colo.: Multnomah Books, 2011), 27.

Day 230

17. C. S. Lewis, *A Grief Observed* (New York: HarperOne, 1994), 22–23.

Day 233

18. Randy Alcorn, *Ninety Days of God's Goodness: Daily Reflections That Shine Light on Personal Darkness* (Colorado Springs, Colo.: Multnomah Books, 2011), 86.

Day 234

19. "Strong's G1018—Brabeuō," Blue Letter Bible, www.blueletterbible .org/lexicon/g1018/kjv/tr/0-1.

Day 241

20. C. H. Spurgeon, "This Thing Is from Me" (sermon, Metropolitan Tabernacle, London, July 22, 1886), www.spurgeon.org/resource -library/sermons/this-thing-is-from-me.

Day 263

21. Dane Ortlund, *Gentle and Lowly: The Heart of Christ for Sinners and Sufferers* (Wheaton, Ill.: Crossway, 2020), 172.

Day 285

22. Dietrich Bonhoeffer, *Life Together,* in *Life Together and Prayerbook of the Bible,* ed. Gerhard Ludwig Müller, Albrecht Schönherr, and Geffrey B. Kelly, trans. Daniel W. Bloesch and James H. Burtness (Minneapolis: Fortress, 2005), 99.

Day 286

23. Isak Dinesen, *Out of Africa* (New York: Vintage Books, 1972).

Day 290

24. Lysa TerKeurst, *It's Not Supposed to Be This Way: Finding Unexpected Strength When Disappointments Leave You Shattered* (Nashville, Tenn.: Nelson Books, 2018), 4.

Day 292

25. C. S. Lewis, *A Grief Observed* (New York: HarperOne, 1994), 33.

Day 295

26. Stormie Omartian, *The Power of a Praying Wife* (Eugene, Ore.: Harvest House, 2014), 183.

Day 302

27. Henry E. Woodruff, quoted in Martha Whitmore Hickman, *Healing After Loss: Daily Meditations for Working Through Grief* (New York: Avon Books, 1994), July 11.

Day 305

28. Lysa TerKeurst, *It's Not Supposed to Be This Way: Finding Unexpected Strength When Disappointments Leave You Shattered* (Nashville, Tenn.: Nelson Books, 2018), 23.

Day 311

29. Joni Eareckson Tada, "The Goodness of Good Friday," Joni and Friends, March 30, 2018, https://joniandfriends.org/news/good-friday -2018.

Day 318

30. C. S. Lewis, *A Grief Observed* (New York: HarperOne, 1994), 26.

Day 326

31. Randy Alcorn, *Ninety Days of God's Goodness: Daily Reflections That Shine Light on Personal Darkness* (Colorado Springs, Colo.: Multnomah Books, 2011), 210.

Day 330

32. Richard Baxter, *The Saint's Everlasting Rest* (Manchester, UK: Allen and Gleave, 1799), 179.

Day 340

33. C. S. Lewis, *A Grief Observed* (New York: HarperOne, 1994), 62.

Day 341

34. "The Touching Story Behind 'It Is Well with My Soul,'" The Tabernacle Choir, www.thetabernaclechoir.org/articles/it-is-well-with-my-soul.html.

Day 342

35. *ESV Study Bible* (Wheaton, Ill.: Crossway, 2008), 1945.

Day 344

36. Robert Robinson, "Come, Thou Fount of Every Blessing," 1758, Hymnsonline.org, https://hymnsonline.org/come-thou-fount-of-every -blessing.

37. Robinson, "Come, Thou Fount."

Day 346

38.   Julian of Norwich, *Revelations of Divine Love,* ed. Grace Warrack (London: Methuen, 1901), 35.

Day 352

39.   C. S. Lewis, *A Grief Observed* (New York: HarperOne, 1994), 43.

Day 359

40.   A. W. Tozer, *The Pursuit of God* (Chicago: Moody, 2015), 105.

Day 361

41.   Paul David Tripp, *Do You Believe? 12 Historic Doctrines to Change Your Everyday Life* (Wheaton, Ill.: Crossway, 2021), 428.

About the Author

MATTIE JACKSON is a bestselling author, podcaster, and speaker. She lost her husband of less than a year, Ben Selecman, in September 2018 after he suffered a traumatic brain injury while on vacation. Mattie has dedicated herself and her story to helping others in their grief. With co-founder Brooke Tometich, she manages a philanthropic foundation dubbed NaSHEville in order to help women and children in need—specifically orphans, widows, and trafficked women—and actively supports Never Alone Widows organization.

About the Type

This book was set in Garamond, a typeface originally designed by the Parisian type cutter Claude Garamond (c. 1500–61). This version of Garamond was modeled on a 1592 specimen sheet from the Egenolff-Berner foundry, which was produced from types assumed to have been brought to Frankfurt by the punch cutter Jacques Sabon (c. 1520–80).

Claude Garamond's distinguished romans and italics first appeared in *Opera Ciceronis* in 1543–44. The Garamond types are clear, open, and elegant.